HEBREW

in 10 minutes a day®

by Kristine Kershul, M. A., University of California, Santa Barbara

adapted by M. R. Jacoby

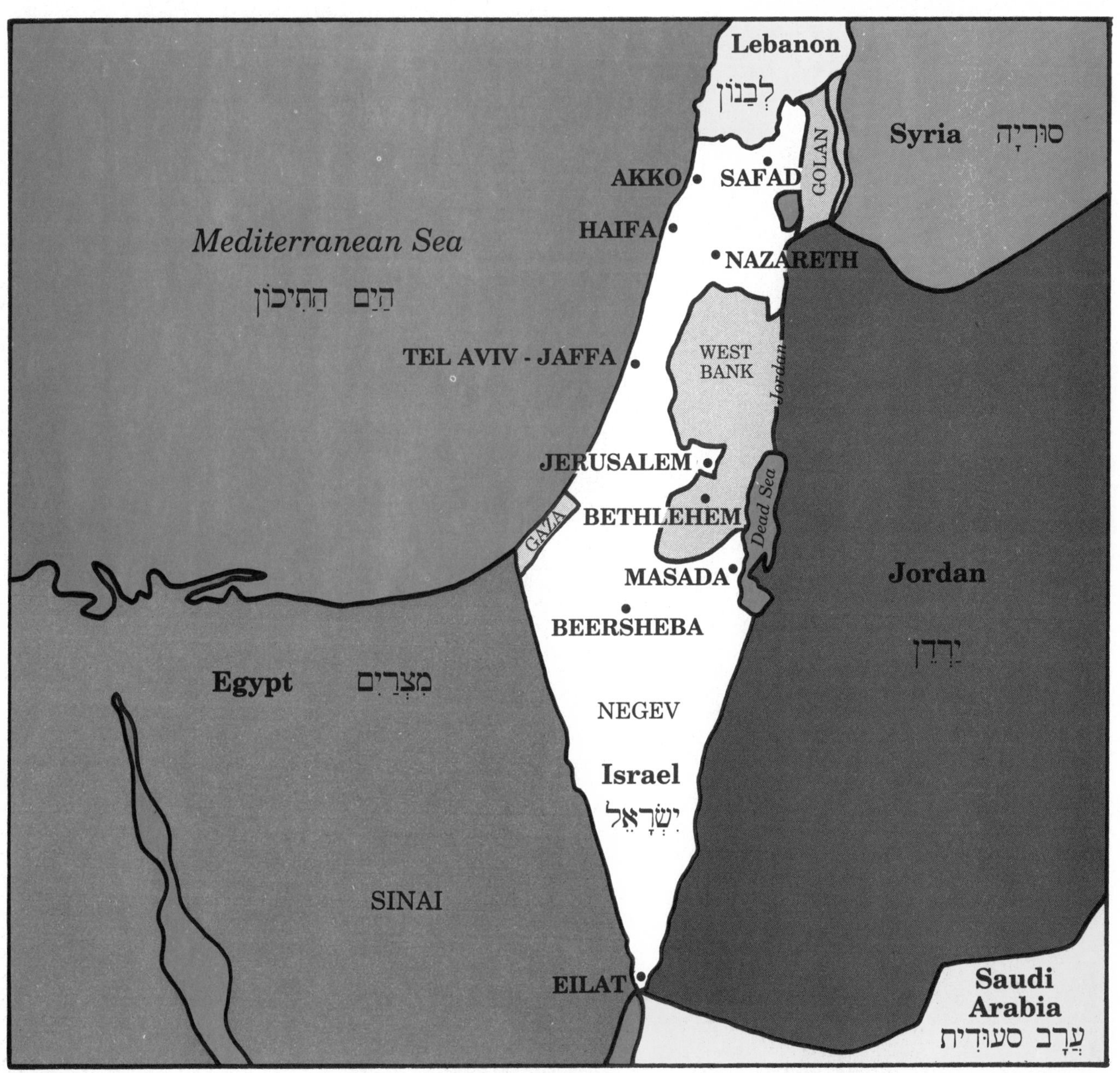

Published by
Bilingual Books, Inc.
6018 Seaview Avenue N.W.
Seattle, Washington 98107
Telephone: (206) 789-7544
Telex: 499 6629 BBKS UI

Distributed by
USA: Cliffs Notes, Box 80728, Lincoln, Nebraska 68501
UK: Ruskin Book Services, 15 Comberton Hill, Kidderminster, Worcestershire DY10 1QG
 (ISBN 0-944502-24-5) 8-7-1-1

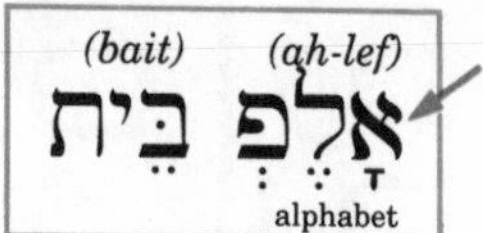

When you first see words like טַקְסִי and מָלוֹן , Hebrew can appear to be forbidding. However, it is not, when you know how to decode these new letters. To learn these new Hebrew letters, work through the examples on this page. This page is intended as a guide, so refer to it whenever you need help.
Important: Hebrew is written from right to left, but don't worry, just practice, practice, practice!

Practice here!	English sound	Hebrew letter	Practice here!	English sound	Hebrew letter
________	n	נ	________	(silent)	א
________	p	פּ	________	(silent)	ע
ר, ר, ר	r	ר	בּ, בּ, בּ	b	בּ
________	s	ס	________	d	ד
________	s	שׂ	________	f	פ
________	sh	שׁ	________	g	ג
________	t	ט	________	h	ה
________	t	ת	________	H = hk (breathe hard)	כ
________	ts	צ	________	H = hk (breathe hard)	ח
________	v	ב	________	k	כּ
________	v	ו	________	k	ק
________	y	י	________	l	ל
________	z	ז	________	m	מ

Vowels in Hebrew are dots and dashes below, above or next to the above letters. These dots and dashes are used initially to make it easier for you to learn to pronounce Hebrew. Later, when you are more comfortable with the language, you will not need them anymore.

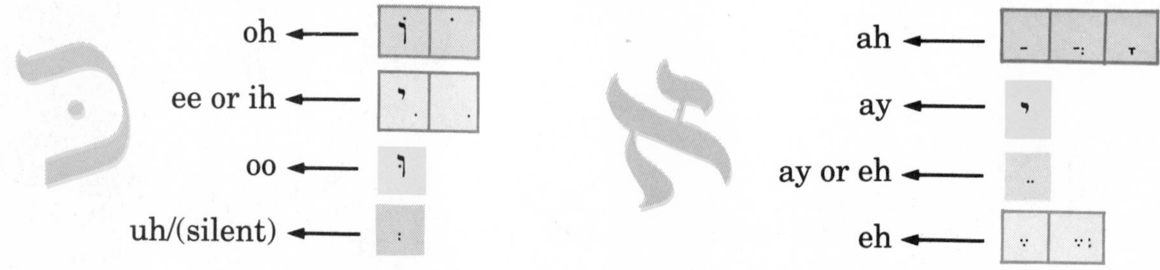

Now let's try some sample words.

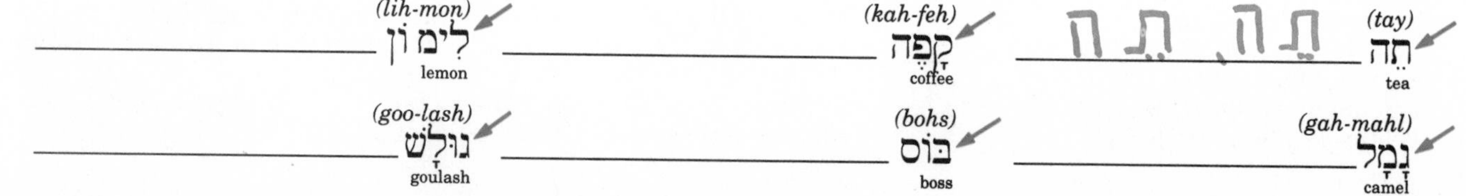

Seven Key Question Words

Step 1

When you arrive in יִשְׂרָאֵל (yiss-rah-el) Israel the very first thing you will need to do is to ask questions — "Where is the bus stop?" "Where can I exchange money?" "Where (אֵיפֹה) (ay-foh) where is the lavatory?" "אֵיפֹה (ay-foh) where is a restaurant?" "אֵיפֹה (ay-foh) where do I catch a taxi?" "אֵיפֹה (ay-foh) where is a good hotel?" "אֵיפֹה (ay-foh) where is my luggage?" — and the list will go on and on for the entire length of your visit. In Hebrew, there are SEVEN KEY QUESTION WORDS to learn. The seven key question words will help you to find out exactly what you are ordering in a restaurant before you order it — and not after the surprise (or shock!) arrives.

Take a few minutes to study and practice saying the seven basic question words listed below. Then cover the עִבְרִית (iv-rit) Hebrew words with your hand and fill in each of the blanks with the matching עִבְרִית (iv-rit) Hebrew word. Notice that the words for "what," "who," and "when" all begin with the same letter — "מ" (which is pronounced like "m").

אֵיפֹה, אֵיפֹה, אֵיפֹה, אֵיפֹה ______	WHERE	=	אֵיפֹה (ay-foh)	.1
______	WHAT	=	מָה (mah)	.2
______	WHO	=	מִי (me)	.3
______	WHEN	=	מָתַי (mah-tie)	.4
______	WHY	=	לָמָה (lah-mah)	.5
______	HOW	=	אֵיךְ (ayH)	.6
______	HOW MUCH/ HOW MANY	=	כַּמָּה (kah-mah)	.7

Now test yourself to see if you really can keep these מִלִּים (mih-lim) words straight in your mind. Draw lines between the עִבְרִית (iv-rit) Hebrew and English equivalents below.

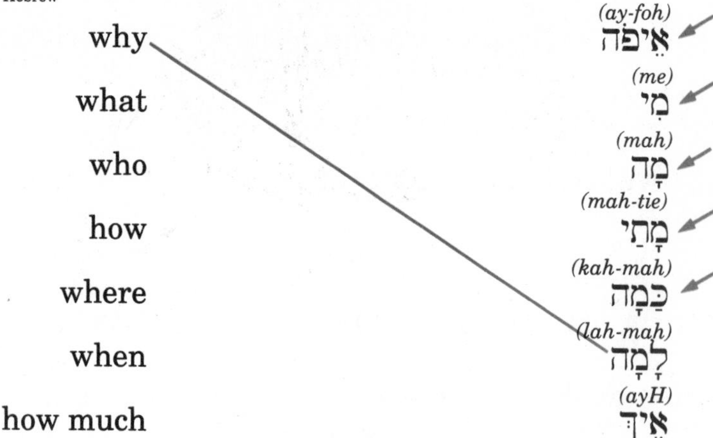

Examine the following questions containing these מִלִּים (mih-lim) words. Practice the sentences out loud וְ (vuh) and then quiz yourself by filling in the blanks below with the correct question מִלָּה (mih-lah) word.

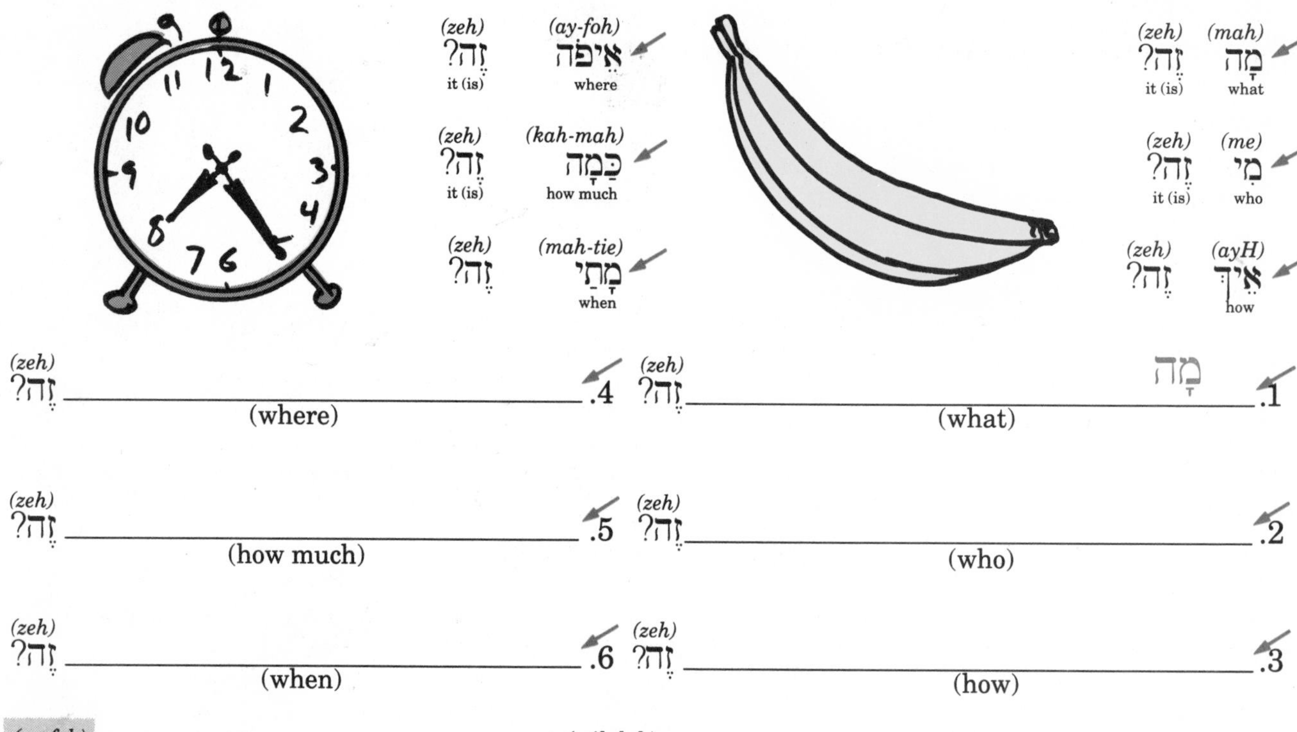

אֵיפֹה (ay-foh) where will be your most used question מִלָּה (mih-lah) word, so let's concentrate on it. Say each of the following עִבְרִית (iv-rit) Hebrew sentences aloud. Then write out each sentence without looking at the example. If you don't succeed on the first try, don't give up. Just practice each sentence until you are able to do it easily. The arrows are there to remind you to read and write from right to left!

(ken) כֵּן (yes), you can hear similarities between (iv-rit) עִבְרִית (Hebrew) and (ahn-glit) אַנְגְּלִית (English) if you listen closely. Don't let the Hebrew alphabet confuse you. The many similarities in pronunciation will surprise you and make your work here easier. Listed below are five "free" words beginning with א to help you get started. Be sure to say each (mih-lah) מִלָּה (word) aloud (vuh) וְ (and) then write out the (iv-rit) עִבְרִית (Hebrew) word in the blank to the left.

______________	א	lake	(ah-gahm)	אֲגַם
______________		autograph	(oh-toh-grahf)	אוֹטוֹגְרָאף
______________		vending machine	(oh-toh-maht)	אוֹטוֹמָאט
______________		Australia	(oh-strahl-yah)	אוֹסְטְרַלְיָה
______________		opera	(oh-peh-rah)	אוֹפֶּרָה

Free (mih-lim) מִלִּים (words) like these will appear at the bottom of the following pages in a yellow color band. They are easy — enjoy them!

Step 2 — Odds 'n Ends

(iv-rit) עִבְרִית (Hebrew) does not have words for "a" or "an," which makes things easier for you. The letter ה in front of a Hebrew word (on the right) means "the." Here are some examples.

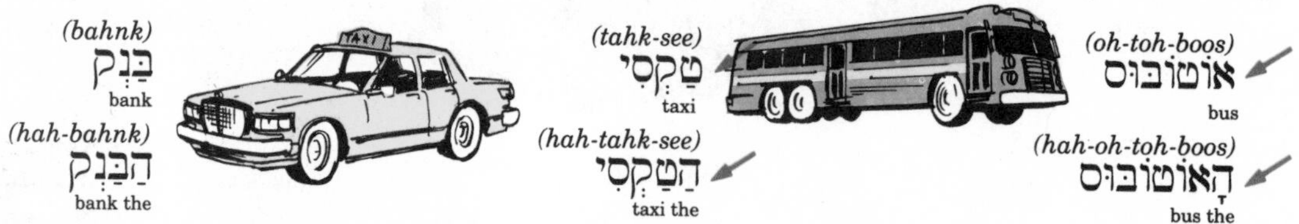

Don't forget that the "H" seen above the Hebrew letters ח and כ means you breathe hard while pronouncing a "hk" sound.

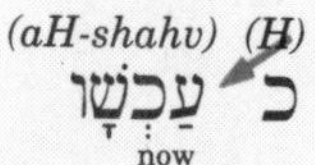

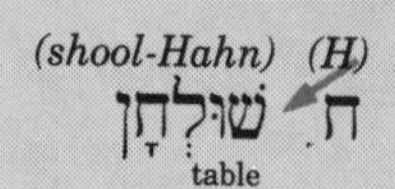

(Hoom) (H)
ח חוּם
brown

(Hah-tool) (H)
ח חָתוּל
cat

Remember to read from right to left — the red arrows are there to help you!

Step 3 — Look Around You

Before you proceed (im) עִם (with) this Step, situate yourself comfortably in your living room. Now look around you. Can you name the things that you see in this (Hed-er) חֶדֶר (room) in (iv-rit) עִבְרִית (Hebrew)? After practicing these (mih-lim) מִלִּים (words) out loud, write them in the blanks below (vuh) וְ (and) on the next page.

________________________ picture = (tmoo-nah) תְּמוּנָה

________________________ ceiling = (tik-rah) תִּקְרָה

____

____

____

____

____

א

baker . . . . (oh-feh) . . . . אוֹפֶה
nurse . . . . (ah-Hoht) . . . . אָחוֹת
Italy . . . . (ee-tahl-yah) . . . . אִיטַלְיָה
Europe . . . . (ay-roh-pah) . . . . אֵירוֹפָּה
European . . . . (ay-roh-pee) . . . . אֵירוֹפִּי

corner = (pee-nah) פִּינָה

window = (Hah-lon) חַלּוֹן

lamp = (mnoh-rah) מְנוֹרָה

light = (or) אוֹר

sofa = (sah-pah) סַפָּה

כִּסֵא, כִּסֵא, כִּסֵא, כִּסֵא

chair = (kis-eh) כִּסֵא

carpet = (shah-tee-aH) שָׁטִיחַ

table = (shool-Hahn) שׁוּלְחָן

door = (del-et) דֶלֶת

clock = (shah-on) שָׁעוֹן

curtain = (vee-lon) וִילוֹן

wall = (keer) קִיר

You know that (iv-rit) עִבְרִית (Hebrew) has no words for "a" or "an." The pronunciation of the (iv-rit) עִבְרִית (Hebrew) word for "the" ה varies. The correct form will always be given to familiarize you with the variations. Open your book to the sticky labels (between pages 48 and 49). Peel off the first 14 labels (vuh) וְ label these items in your home. This will help to increase your (iv-rit) עִבְרִית word power easily. Don't forget to say (hah-mih-lah) הַמִלָה (word the) as you attach each label.

Ask yourself, "(ay-foh) אֵיפֹה (yesh) יֵשׁ (tmoo-nah) תְמוּנָה (picture)?" and point at it while you answer, "(shahm) שָׁם (there) (yesh) יֵשׁ (tmoo-nah) תְמוּנָה (picture)". Continue down the list until you feel comfortable with these new (mih-lim) מִלִים. Say, "(ay-foh) אֵיפֹה (yesh) יֵשׁ (tik-rah) תִקְרָה (ceiling)?" Then reply, "(shahm) שָׁם (yesh) יֵשׁ (tik-rah) תִקְרָה" and so on. When you can identify the items on the list, you are ready to move on. Now, let's learn some basic parts of the house.

א

Ireland . . . . (eer-lahnd) . . . . אִירְלַנְד
farmer . . . . (ee-kahr) . . . . אִכָּר
algebra . . . . (ahl-geh-brah) . . . . אַלְגֶבְּרָה
elegant . . . . (eh-leh-gahn-tee) . . . . אֶלֶגַנְטִי
alcohol . . . . (ahl-koh-hohl) . . . . . . אַלְכּוֹהוֹל

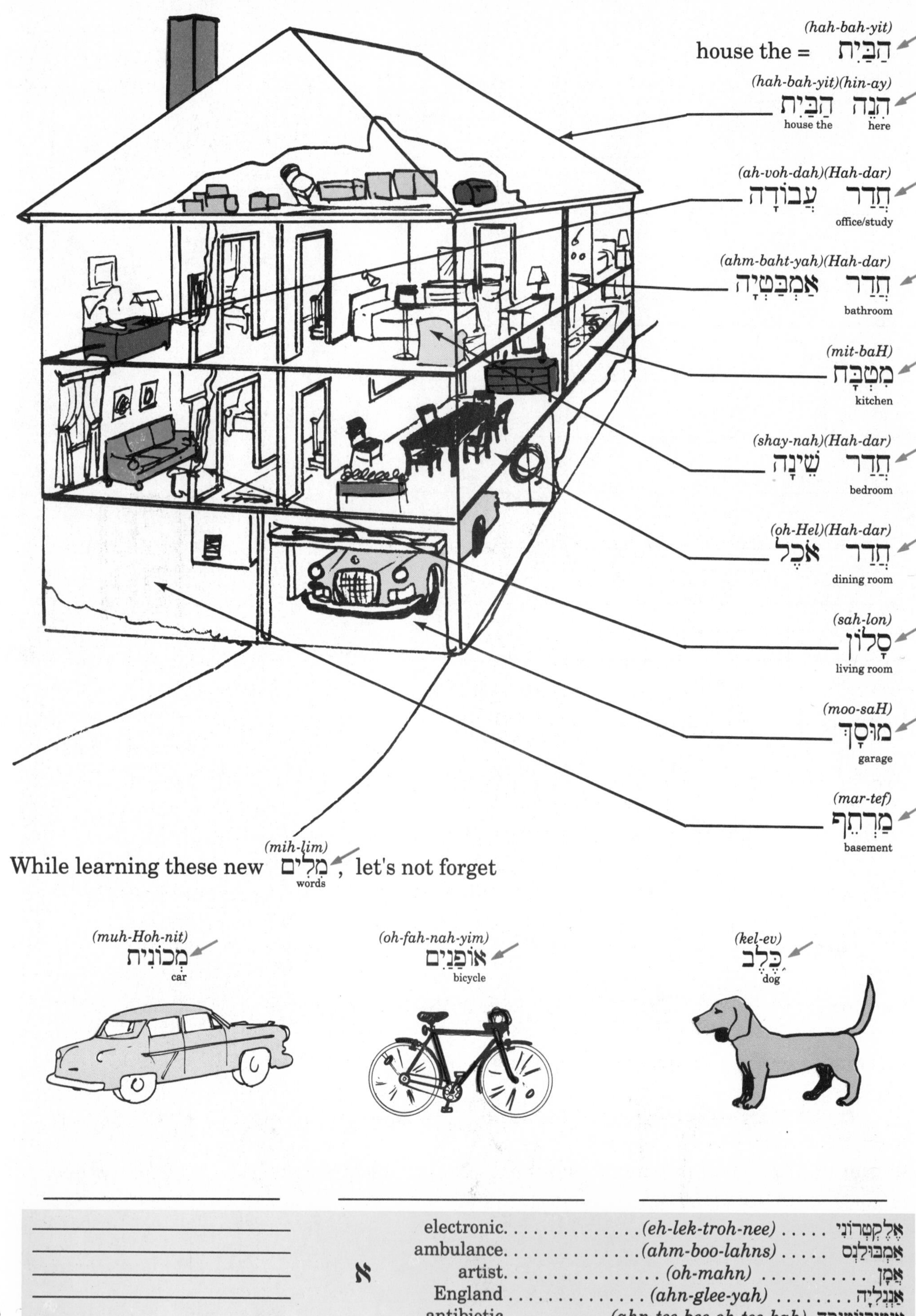

While learning these new (mih-lim) מִלִּים (words), let's not forget

א

electronic. . . . . (eh-lek-troh-nee) . . . . . אֶלֶקְטְרוֹנִי
ambulance. . . . . (ahm-boo-lahns) . . . . . אַמְבּוּלַנְס
artist. . . . . (oh-mahn) . . . . אָמָן
England . . . . (ahn-glee-yah) . . . . אַנְגְלִיָה
antibiotic . . . . (ahn-tee-bee-oh-tee-kah) אַנְטִיבִּיוֹטִיקָה

(Hah-tool) חָתוּל
cat

(gahn) גַּן
garden

(doh-ar) דוֹאַר
mail

______________ ______________ דוֹאַר, דוֹאַר, דוֹאַר

(doh-ar) (tay-vaht) תֵּיבַת דוֹאַר
mailbox

(praH-im) פְּרָחִים
flowers

(pah-ah-mon) פַּעֲמוֹן
doorbell

______________ ______________ ______________

Peel off the next set of labels וְ (vuh) wander through your בַּיִת (bah-yit, house) learning these new מִלִּים (mih-lim). Granted, it will be somewhat difficult to label your כֶּלֶב (kel-ev, dog), חָתוּל (Hah-tool, cat) or פְּרָחִים (praH-im, flowers), but use your imagination.

Again, practice by asking yourself, "אֵיפֹה יֵשׁ גַּן?" (ay-foh) (yesh) (gahn, garden) and reply "שָׁם יֵשׁ גַּן" (shahm) (yesh) (gahn, garden). Now for the following:

אֵיפֹה יֵשׁ כֶּלֶב? (ay-foh) (yesh) (kel-ev, dog) אֵיפֹה יֵשׁ חָתוּל? (Hah-tool, cat) אֵיפֹה יֵשׁ אוֹפַנַּיִם? (oh-fah-nah-yim, bicycle) . . .

א

______________	American	(ah-meh-ree-kah-ee)	אֲמֶרִיקָאִי
______________	America	(ah-meh-ree-kah)	אֲמֶרִיקָה
______________	Latin America	(ah-meh-ree-kah-hah-lah-tee-neet)	אֲמֶרִיקָה הַלָּטִינִית
______________	infection	(in-fek-tsee-yah)	אִנְפֶקְצְיָה
______________	energy	(eh-nairg-yah)	אֶנֶרְגְיָה

Step 4

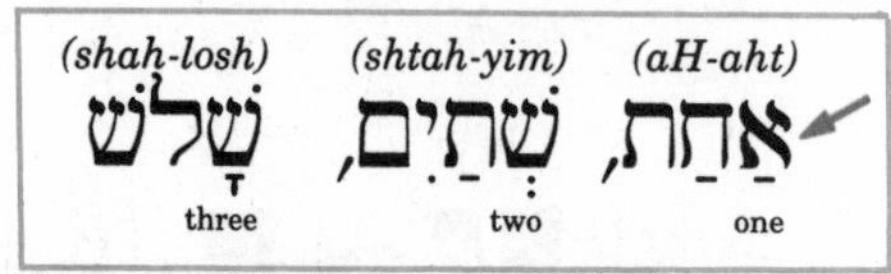

שְׁמוֹנֶה

שֶׁבַע

שֵׁשׁ

חָמֵשׁ

אַרְבַּע

שָׁלשׁ

שְׁתַּיִם

אַחַת

For some reason, numbers are not the easiest thing to learn, but just remember how important they are. How could you tell someone your phone number, your address or your hotel חֶדֶר (Hed-er) room if you had no מִסְפָּרִים (mis-pah-rim) numbers? And think of how difficult it would be if you could not understand the time, the price of an orange or the correct bus to take. When practicing הַמִּסְפָּרִים (hah-mis-pah-rim) numbers the below, notice the similarities (underlined) between אַרְבַּע (ar-bah) four and אַרְבַּע עֶשְׂרֵה (ar-bah) (es-reh) fourteen – שֵׁשׁ (shesh) six and שֵׁשׁ עֶשְׂרֵה (shesh) (es-reh) sixteen and so on. There are two sets of מִסְפָּרִים (mis-pah-rim) numbers in עִבְרִית (iv-rit). Learn this set thoroughly. When you see the second set, don't be surprised.

אֶפֶס, אֶפֶס, אֶפֶס, אֶפֶס ______	0			0 (ef-es) אֶפֶס
______	1	(es-reh) (aH-aht) אַחַת עֶשְׂרֵה	11	1 (aH-aht) אַחַת
______	2	(es-reh) (shtem) שְׁתֵּים עֶשְׂרֵה	12	2 (shtah-yim) שְׁתַּיִם
______	3	(es-reh) (shlosh) שְׁלשׁ עֶשְׂרֵה	13	3 (shah-losh) שָׁלשׁ
______	4	(es-reh) (ar-bah) אַרְבַּע עֶשְׂרֵה	14	4 (ar-bah) אַרְבַּע
______	5	(es-reh) (Hah-mesh) חֲמֵשׁ עֶשְׂרֵה	15	5 (Hah-mesh) חָמֵשׁ
______	6	(es-reh) (shesh) שֵׁשׁ עֶשְׂרֵה	16	6 (shesh) שֵׁשׁ
______	7	(es-reh) (shvah) שְׁבַע עֶשְׂרֵה	17	7 (sheh-vah) שֶׁבַע
______	8	(es-reh) (shmoh-neh) שְׁמוֹנֶה עֶשְׂרֵה	18	8 (shmoh-neh) שְׁמוֹנֶה
______	9	(es-reh) (tshah) תְּשַׁע עֶשְׂרֵה	19	9 (tay-shah) תֵּשַׁע
______	10	(es-rim) עֶשְׂרִים	20	10 (es-er) עֶשֶׂר

א

people . . . . (ah-nah-shim) . . . . אֲנָשִׁים
Asia. . . . .(ahs-yah) . . . . אַסְיָה
African . . . .(ah-free-kah-ee) . . . . אַפְרִיקָאִי
Africa . . . . (ah-free-kah) . . . . אַפְרִיקָה
academy . . . . (ah-kah-deh-mee-yah) . . . . אַקָדֶמְיָה

Use these מִסְפָּרִים (mis-pah-rim) [numbers] on a daily basis. Count to yourself בְּעִבְרִית (biv-rit) [Hebrew in] when you brush your teeth, exercise, אוֹ (oh) [or] commute to work. Now fill in the following blanks according to הַמִּסְפָּרִים (hah-mis-pah-rim) [numbers the] given in parentheses.

Note: This is a good time to start learning these two important phrases.

אֲנִי (ah-nee) [I] רוֹצֶה (roh-tseh) [want] . . . בְּבַקָּשָׁה (buh-vah-kah-shah) [please] = I want . . . please = ______________________

אֲנַחְנוּ (ah-naH-noo) [we] רוֹצִים (roh-tsim) [want] . . . בְּבַקָּשָׁה (buh-vah-kah-shah) [please] = we want . . . please = ______________________

אֲנִי (ah-nee) [I] רוֹצֶה (roh-tseh) [want] חָמֵשׁ (5) בְּבַקָּשָׁה (buh-vah-kah-shah) [please]. ______ (5) כַּמָּה (kah-mah) [how many]?

אֲנִי (ah-nee) [I] רוֹצֶה (roh-tseh) [want] ______ (9) בְּבַקָּשָׁה (buh-vah-kah-shah) [please]. ______ (9) כַּמָּה (kah-mah) [how many]?

אֲנִי (ah-nee) רוֹצֶה (roh-tseh) ______ (2) בְּבַקָּשָׁה (buh-vah-kah-shah). ______ (2) כַּמָּה (kah-mah)?

אֲנִי (ah-nee) רוֹצֶה (roh-tseh) ______ (4) בְּבַקָּשָׁה. ______ (4) כַּמָּה (kah-mah)?

אֲנִי רוֹצֶה ______ (7) בְּבַקָּשָׁה. ______ (7) כַּמָּה?

אֲנַחְנוּ (ah-naH-noo) [we] רוֹצִים (roh-tsim) [want] ______ (10) בְּבַקָּשָׁה. ______ (10) כַּמָּה (kah-mah)?

אֲנַחְנוּ (ah-naH-noo) [we] רוֹצִים (roh-tsim) [want] ______ (1) בְּבַקָּשָׁה. אַחַת (1) כַּמָּה (kah-mah)?

אֲנַחְנוּ רוֹצִים (roh-tsim) ______ (8) בְּבַקָּשָׁה. ______ (8) כַּמָּה (kah-mah)?

אֲנִי (ah-nee) רוֹצֶה (roh-tseh) ______ (16) בְּבַקָּשָׁה. ______ (16) כַּמָּה?

אֲנַחְנוּ (ah-naH-noo) רוֹצִים (roh-tsim) ______ (20) בְּבַקָּשָׁה. ______ (20) כַּמָּה?

אֲנִי (ah-nee) רוֹצֶה (roh-tseh) ______ (3) כַּרְטִיסִים (kar-tih-sim) [tickets] בְּבַקָּשָׁה. ______ (3) כַּמָּה?

אֲנַחְנוּ (ah-naH-noo) רוֹצִים (roh-tsim) ______ (6) גְּלוּיוֹת (gloo-yoht) [postcards] בְּבַקָּשָׁה. ______ (6) כַּמָּה?

אֲנַחְנוּ רוֹצִים ______ (5) בּוּלִים (boo-lim) [stamps] בְּבַקָּשָׁה. ______ (5) כַּמָּה?

בּ

______________	ballet	(bah-let)	בָּאלֶט
______________	bar	(bar)	בָּאר
______________	bedouin	(bed-oo-ee)	בֶּדוּאִי
______________	Bulgaria	(bool-gah-ree-yah)	בּוּלְגַרְיָה
______________	boss	(bohs)	בּוֹס

Now see if you can translate the following thoughts into עִבְרִית (iv-rit). הַתְּשׁוּבוֹת (hah-tshoo-voht) [answers the] are at the bottom of הָעַמּוּד (hah-ah-mood) [page the].

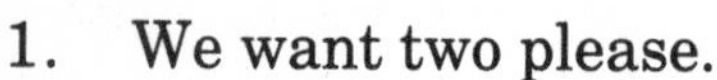

1. We want two please.

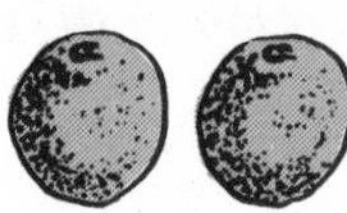

____

2. We want three please.

____

3. I want seven postcards please.

____

4. I want four stamps please.

____

Review מִסְפָּרִים (mis-pah-rim) [numbers] 1 through 20 וְ (vuh) answer the following שְׁאֵלוֹת (shuh-eh-loht) [questions] aloud, וְ then write הַתְּשׁוּבוֹת (hah-tshoo-voht) [answers the] in the blank spaces.

שָׁלֹשׁ ______________ כַּמָּה (kah-mah) [how many] יֵשׁ (yesh) פֹּה (poh) [here]?

______________ כַּמָּה (kah-mah) [how many] יֵשׁ (yesh) פֹּה (poh) [here]?

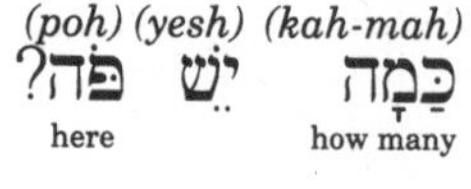

______________ כַּמָּה יֵשׁ פֹּה?

הַתְּשׁוּבוֹת

1. אֲנַחְנוּ רוֹצִים שְׁתַּיִם בְּבַקָּשָׁה.
2. אֲנַחְנוּ רוֹצִים שָׁלֹשׁ בְּבַקָּשָׁה.
3. אֲנִי רוֹצֶה שֶׁבַע גְּלוּיוֹת בְּבַקָּשָׁה.
4. אֲנִי רוֹצֶה אַרְבָּעָה בּוּלִים בְּבַקָּשָׁה.

(poh) (yesh) (kah-mah)
כַּמָה יֵשׁ פֹּה?
here — how many

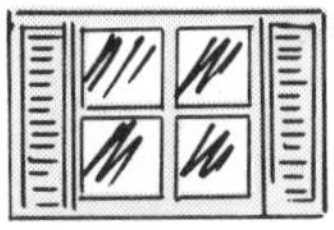

____

אַחַת ______________

(yesh) (kah-mah)
כַּמָה יֵשׁ פֹּה?

____

(kah-mah)
כַּמָה יֵשׁ פֹּה?

____

כַּמָה יֵשׁ פֹּה?

____

כַּמָה יֵשׁ פֹּה?

____

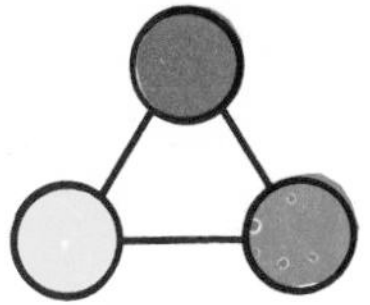

Step 5

(tsvah-im) צְבָעִים (colors) are the same in (yiss-rah-el) יִשְׂרָאֵל (Israel) as they are in (ah-meh-ree-kah) אֲמֶרִיקָה (America) – they just have different (sheh-moht) שֵׁמוֹת (names). The flag of (yiss-rah-el) יִשְׂרָאֵל (Israel) is not only blue and white but also (kah-Hohl) כָּחוֹל (blue) and (lah-vahn) לָבָן (white)! The flag was created by taking the (kah-Hohl) כָּחוֹל (blue) and (lah-vahn) לָבָן (white) background of the traditional prayer shawl ן adding the Star of David, the symbol of Judaism. Let's learn the basic (tsvah-im) צְבָעִים (colors). Once you have read through the list on the next (ah-mood) עַמוּד (page), cover the (iv-rit) עִבְרִית with your (yahd) יָד (hand), and practice writing out the (iv-rit) עִבְרִית next to the (ahn-glit) אַנְגְלִית (English). Once you've learned (hah-tsvah-im) הַצְבָעִים quiz yourself. What color are your shoes? Your eyes? Your hair? Your house?

בּ

hospital. . . . . (bait-Hoh-leem) . . . . בֵּית חוֹלִים

factory. . . . .(bait-Hah-roh-shet) . . בֵּית חֲרֹשֶׁת

synagogue. . . . .(bait-kness-et) . . . . . בֵּית כְּנֶסֶת

Bethlehem. . . . .(bait-leh-Hem) . . . . . בֵּית לֶחֶם

workshop. . . . . (bait-muh-lah-Hah). . בֵּית מְלָאכָה

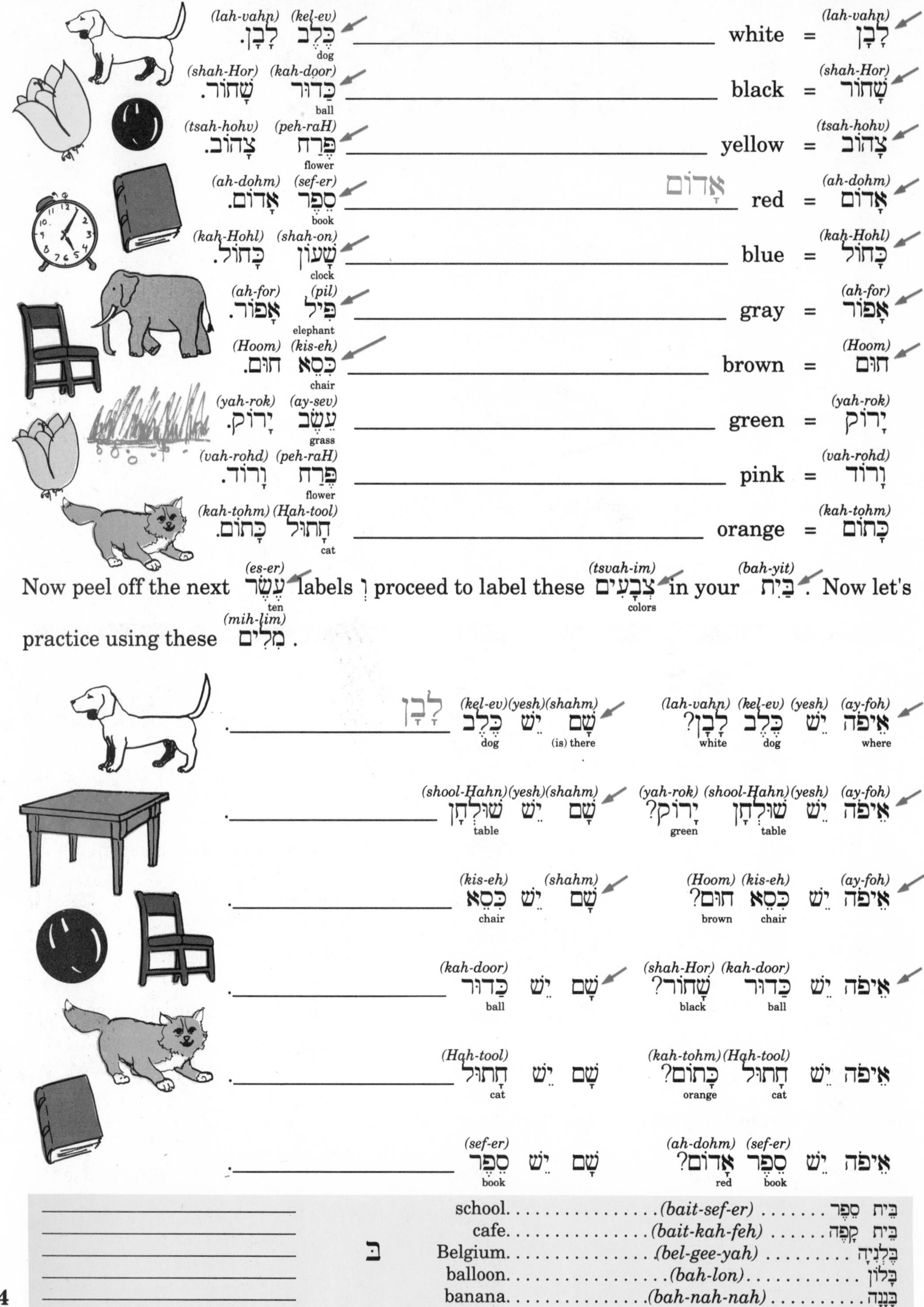

כֶּלֶב לָבָן. (kel-ev) dog (lah-vahn)	______	white	= לָבָן (lah-vahn)
כַּדּוּר שָׁחוֹר. (kah-door) ball (shah-Hor)	______	black	= שָׁחוֹר (shah-Hor)
פֶּרַח צָהוֹב. (peh-raH) flower (tsah-hohv)	______	yellow	= צָהוֹב (tsah-hohv)
סֵפֶר אָדוֹם. (sef-er) book (ah-dohm)	אָדוֹם	red	= אָדוֹם (ah-dohm)
שָׁעוֹן כָּחוֹל. (shah-on) clock (kah-Hohl)	______	blue	= כָּחוֹל (kah-Hohl)
פִּיל אָפוֹר. (pil) elephant (ah-for)	______	gray	= אָפוֹר (ah-for)
כִּסֵּא חוּם. (kis-eh) chair (Hoom)	______	brown	= חוּם (Hoom)
עֵשֶׂב יָרוֹק. (ay-sev) grass (yah-rok)	______	green	= יָרוֹק (yah-rok)
פֶּרַח וָרוֹד. (peh-raH) flower (vah-rohd)	______	pink	= וָרוֹד (vah-rohd)
חָתוּל כָּתוֹם. (Hah-tool) cat (kah-tohm)	______	orange	= כָּתוֹם (kah-tohm)

Now peel off the next עֶשֶׂר (es-er) ten labels וְ proceed to label these צְבָעִים (tsvah-im) colors in your בַּיִת (bah-yit). Now let's practice using these מִלִּים (mih-lim).

אֵיפֹה (ay-foh) where יֵשׁ (yesh) כֶּלֶב (kel-ev) dog לָבָן? (lah-vahn) white	שָׁם (shahm) יֵשׁ (yesh) (is) there כֶּלֶב (kel-ev) dog לָבָן.
אֵיפֹה (ay-foh) יֵשׁ (yesh) שׁוּלְחָן (shool-Hahn) table יָרוֹק? (yah-rok) green	שָׁם (shahm) יֵשׁ (yesh) שׁוּלְחָן (shool-Hahn) table ______.
אֵיפֹה (ay-foh) יֵשׁ כִּסֵּא (kis-eh) chair חוּם? (Hoom) brown	שָׁם (shahm) יֵשׁ כִּסֵּא (kis-eh) chair ______.
אֵיפֹה יֵשׁ כַּדּוּר (kah-door) ball שָׁחוֹר? (shah-Hor) black	שָׁם יֵשׁ כַּדּוּר (kah-door) ball ______.
אֵיפֹה יֵשׁ חָתוּל (Hah-tool) cat כָּתוֹם? (kah-tohm) orange	שָׁם יֵשׁ חָתוּל (Hah-tool) cat ______.
אֵיפֹה יֵשׁ סֵפֶר (sef-er) book אָדוֹם? (ah-dohm) red	שָׁם יֵשׁ סֵפֶר (sef-er) book ______.

בּ

school. . . . .(bait-sef-er) . . . . בֵּית סֵפֶר
cafe. . . . .(bait-kah-feh) . . . . בֵּית קָפֶה
Belgium. . . . .(bel-gee-yah) . . . . בֶּלְגְיָה
balloon. . . . .(bah-lon) . . . . בָּלוֹן
banana. . . . .(bah-nah-nah) . . . . בָּנָנָה

(peh-raH) (shahm) (tsah-hohv) (peh-raH)
איפֹה יֵשׁ פֶּרַח צָהוֹב? שָׁם יֵשׁ פֶּרַח ________________.
flower yellow flower

(shah-on) (kah-Hohl) (shah-on)
איפֹה יֵשׁ שָׁעוֹן כָּחוֹל? שָׁם יֵשׁ שָׁעוֹן ________________.
clock blue clock

(pil) (ah-for) (pil)
איפֹה יֵשׁ פִּיל אָפוֹר? שָׁם יֵשׁ פִּיל ________________.
elephant gray elephant

Note: In עִבְרִית (iv-rit) "I have" and "we have" are written as follows.

יֵשׁ לִי (yesh) (lee) have I ________________ יֵשׁ לָנוּ (yesh) (lah-noo) have we ________________

Let's review "I want . . . please" and "we want . . . please" and learn "יֵשׁ לִי" (yesh) (lee) have I and "יֵשׁ לָנוּ" (yesh) (lah-noo) have we. Repeat each sentence out loud many, many times.

(ah-nee) (roh-tseh) (buh-vah-kah-shah)
אֲנִי רוֹצֶה . . . בְּבַקָּשָׁה.

(ah-naH-noo) (roh-tsim) (shloh-shah) (kar-tih-sim)
אֲנַחְנוּ רוֹצִים שְׁלֹשָׁה כַּרְטִיסִים בְּבַקָּשָׁה.
we want three tickets

(ah-nee) (roh-tseh) (Hah-mish-ah) (boo-lim)
אֲנִי רוֹצֶה חֲמִשָּׁה בּוּלִים בְּבַקָּשָׁה.
five stamps

(ah-naH-noo) (roh-tsim) (muh-Hoh-nit)
אֲנַחְנוּ רוֹצִים מְכוֹנִית בְּבַקָּשָׁה.
car

(yesh) (lee)
יֵשׁ לִי . . .

(yesh) (lah-noo) (shloh-shah) (kar-tih-sim)
יֵשׁ לָנוּ שְׁלֹשָׁה כַּרְטִיסִים.
have we three tickets

(lee) (Hah-mish-ah) (boo-lim)
יֵשׁ לִי חֲמִשָּׁה בּוּלִים.
five stamps

(lah-noo) (muh-Hoh-nit)
יֵשׁ לָנוּ מְכוֹנִית.
car

Now fill in the following blanks with, יֵשׁ לִי, אֲנִי רוֹצֶה, יֵשׁ לָנוּ or אֲנַחְנוּ רוֹצִים.

________________ (have we) שְׁלֹשָׁה כַּרְטִיסִים. (shloh-shah) (kar-tih-sim) three

________________ (want we) מְכוֹנִית בְּבַקָּשָׁה. (muh-Hoh-nit) car

________________ (have I) חֲמִשָּׁה בּוּלִים. (Hah-mish-ah) (boo-lim) five stamps

________________ (want I) כַּרְטִיס בְּבַקָּשָׁה. (kar-tis) ticket

ג

גַּן	(gahn)	garden	________________
גַּן חַיּוֹת	(gahn-Hah-yoht)	zoo	________________
גַּן עֵדֶן	(gahn-ay-den)	Garden of Eden	________________
גֶּרְמַנְיָה	(gair-mahn-yah)	Germany	________________
גֶּרְמָנִית	(gair-mah-nit)	German	________________

(aH-shahv) עַכְשָׁו (now) a quick review of (tsvah-im) צְבָעִים (colors). Draw lines between the (iv-rih-yoht) עִבְרִיּוֹת (Hebrew) (mih-lim) מִלִּים and the correct (tsvah-im) צְבָעִים. On your mark, get set, GO!

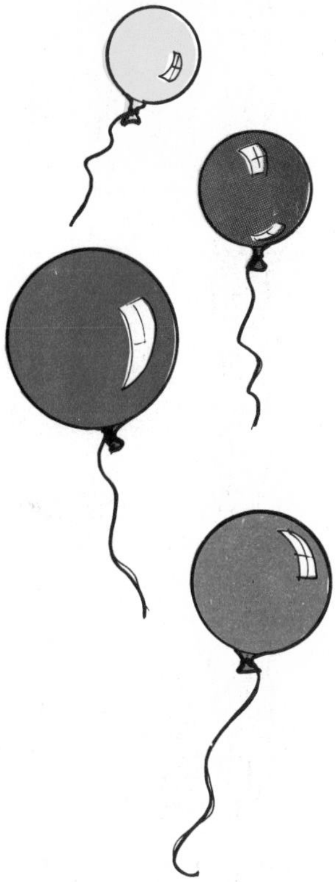

Hebrew	English
(tsah-hohv) צָהוֹב	gray
(shah-Hor) שָׁחוֹר	green
(yah-rok) יָרוֹק	pink
(lah-vahn) לָבָן	orange
(ah-dohm) אָדוֹם	brown
(kah-Hohl) כָּחוֹל	yellow
(kah-tohm) כָּתוֹם	red
(vah-rohd) וָרוֹד	black
(ah-for) אָפוֹר	blue
(Hoom) חוּם	white

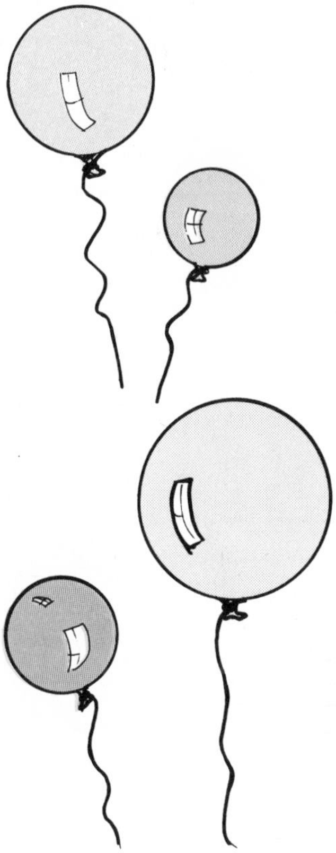

Keep a close eye on these five (iv-rit) עִבְרִית letters: צ מ נ פ כ. Notice how they change at the end of a word.

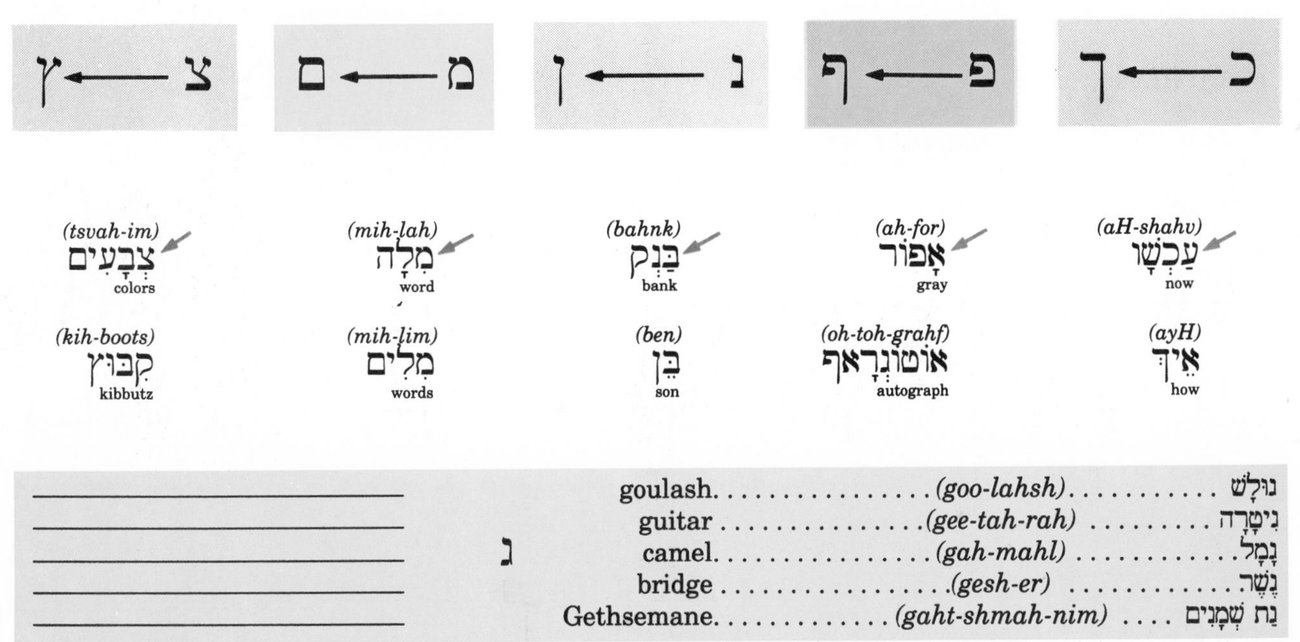

צ ← ץ　　מ ← ם　　נ ← ן　　פ ← ף　　כ ← ך

(tsvah-im) צְבָעִים colors　　(mih-lah) מִלָּה word　　(bahnk) בַּנְק bank　　(ah-for) אָפוֹר gray　　(aH-shahv) עַכְשָׁו now

(kih-boots) קִבּוּץ kibbutz　　(mih-lim) מִלִּים words　　(ben) בֵּן son　　(oh-toh-grahf) אוֹטוֹגְרָאף autograph　　(ayH) אֵיךְ how

ג

goulash. . . . . (goo-lahsh) . . . . גוּלָשׁ
guitar . . . . (gee-tah-rah) . . . . גִיטָרָה
camel. . . . . (gah-mahl) . . . . גָמָל
bridge . . . . (gesh-er) . . . . גֶשֶׁר
Gethsemane. . . . . (gaht-shmah-nim) . . . . גַת שְׁמָנִים

Step 6

Before starting this Step, go back and review Step 4. Make sure you can count to עֶשְׂרִים (es-rim, twenty) without looking at this סֵפֶר (sef-er, book). Let's learn the larger מִסְפָּרִים (mis-pah-rim, numbers) now, so if something costs more than 20 שְׁקָלִים (shkah-lim, shekels), you will know exactly כַּמָּה (kah-mah, how much) it costs. After practicing aloud the עִבְרִית numbers 10 through 1000 below, write these מִסְפָּרִים (mis-pah-rim) in the blanks provided.

Again, notice the similarities (underlined) between מִסְפָּרִים (mis-pah-rim) such as <u>אַרְבַּע</u> (ar-bah) (4), עֶשְׂרֵה <u>אַרְבַּע</u> (es-reh) (ar-bah) (14) and <u>אַרְבָּ</u>עִים (ar-bah-im) (40).

עֶשֶׂר עֶשֶׂר ________	10	(אַרְבַּע four + שֵׁשׁ six = עֶשֶׂר)	עֶשֶׂר (es-er) 10
________	20	(שְׁתַּיִם (shtah-yim) = 2)	עֶשְׂרִים (es-rim) 20
________	30	(שָׁלֹשׁ (shah-losh) = 3)	שְׁלֹשִׁים (shloh-shim) 30
________	40	(אַרְבַּע = 4)	אַרְבָּעִים (ar-bah-im) 40
________	50	(חָמֵשׁ (Hah-mesh) = 5)	חֲמִשִּׁים (Hah-mih-shim) 50
________	60	(שֵׁשׁ (shesh) = 6)	שִׁשִּׁים (shih-shim) 60
________	70	(שֶׁבַע (sheh-vah) = 7)	שִׁבְעִים (shih-vim) 70
________	80	(שְׁמוֹנֶה (shmoh-neh) = 8)	שְׁמוֹנִים (shmoh-nim) 80
________	90	(תֵּשַׁע (tay-shah) = 9)	תִּשְׁעִים (tish-im) 90
________	100		מֵאָה (may-ah) 100
________	500		חָמֵשׁ מֵאוֹת (Hah-mesh)(may-oht) 500
________	1000		אֶלֶף (el-ef) 1000

Now take a logical guess. אֵיךְ (ayH, how) would you write וְ say the following? הַתְּשׁוּבוֹת (hah-tshoo-voht, the answers) are at the bottom of הָעַמּוּד (hah-ah-mood).

________ 400 ________ 600

________ 800 ________ 300

הַתְּשׁוּבוֹת

אַרְבַּע מֵאוֹת = 400
שְׁמוֹנֶה מֵאוֹת = 800
שֵׁשׁ מֵאוֹת = 600
שְׁלֹשׁ מֵאוֹת = 300

The unit of currency (buh-yiss-rah-el) בְּיִשְׂרָאֵל (Israel in) is the (shek-el) שֶׁקֶל (shekel), abbreviated NIS which stands for "New Israeli Shekel." Bills are called (shtah-roht) שְׁטָרוֹת and coins are called (maht-bay-oht) מַטְבְּעוֹת. Just as an American (doh-lar) דוֹלָר (dollar) can be broken down into 100 pennies, a (shek-el) שֶׁקֶל can be broken down into 100 (ah-goh-roht) אֲגוֹרוֹת (agorot). Let's learn the various kinds of (shkah-lim) שְׁקָלִים (shekels) and (ah-goh-roht) אֲגוֹרוֹת. Always be sure to practice each (mih-lah) מִלָּה (word) out loud. You might want to exchange some money (aH-shahv) עַכְשָׁו (now) so that you can familiarize yourself (im) עִם (with) the various (shkah-lim) שְׁקָלִים and (ah-goh-roht) אֲגוֹרוֹת.

(shtah-roht) שְׁטָרוֹת (bills)

(maht-bay-oht) מַטְבְּעוֹת (coins)

Bills	Coins
(eh-Hahd) (shek-el) שֶׁקֶל אֶחָד (one)	(aH-aht) (ah-goh-rah) אֲגוֹרָה אַחַת (one)
(shkah-lim) (Hah-mish-ah) חֲמִשָּׁה שְׁקָלִים (five / shekels)	(ah-goh-roht) (Hah-mesh) חָמֵשׁ אֲגוֹרוֹת (five)
(shkah-lim) (ah-sah-rah) עֲשָׂרָה שְׁקָלִים (ten)	(ah-goh-roht) (es-er) עֶשֶׂר אֲגוֹרוֹת
(Hah-mih-shim) חֲמִשִּׁים שְׁקָלִים (fifty)	(shek-el) (Het-see) חֲצִי שֶׁקֶל (half)
(may-ah) מֵאָה שְׁקָלִים (hundred)	(eh-Hahd) (shek-el) שֶׁקֶל אֶחָד (one)

ד

flag	(deg-el)	דֶּגֶל
mailman	(dah-var)	דַּוָּר
diet	(dee-eh-tah)	דִיאֶטָה
dialogue	(dee-ah-lohg)	דִיאָלוֹג
fisherman	(dah-yahg)	דַּיָּג

Review הַמִּסְפָּרִים (hah-mis-pah-rim, numbers the) – עֶשֶׂר (es-er) through אֶלֶף (el-ef) again. עַכְשָׁו (aH-shahv) how do you say "twenty-two" אוֹ (oh, or) "fifty-three" בְּעִבְרִית (biv-rit)? You basically put the numbers together in a logical sequence, for example, 74 (70 + 4) = אַרְבַּע (ar-bah, four) וְ (vuh) שִׁבְעִים (shih-vim, seventy). See if you can say וְ write out הַמִּסְפָּרִים (hah-mis-pah-rim) on this עַמּוּד (ah-mood). הַתְּשׁוּבוֹת (hah-tshoo-voht, answers the) are at the bottom of הָעַמּוּד (hah-ah-mood).

a. 25 = ______________ (20 + 5)

b. 47 = ______________ (40 + 7)

c. 84 = ______________ (80 + 4)

d. 51 = ______________ (50 + 1)

e. 36 = ______________ (30 + 6)

f. 93 = ______________ (90 + 3)

g. 68 = ______________ (60 + 8)

h. 72 = ______________ (70 + 2)

To ask how much something costs בְּעִבְרִית (biv-rit), one asks כַּמָּה זֶה עוֹלֶה? (kah-mah, how much; zeh, it; oh-leh, costs) עַכְשָׁו (aH-shahv) answer the following questions based on הַמִּסְפָּרִים (hah-mis-pah-rim) in parentheses.

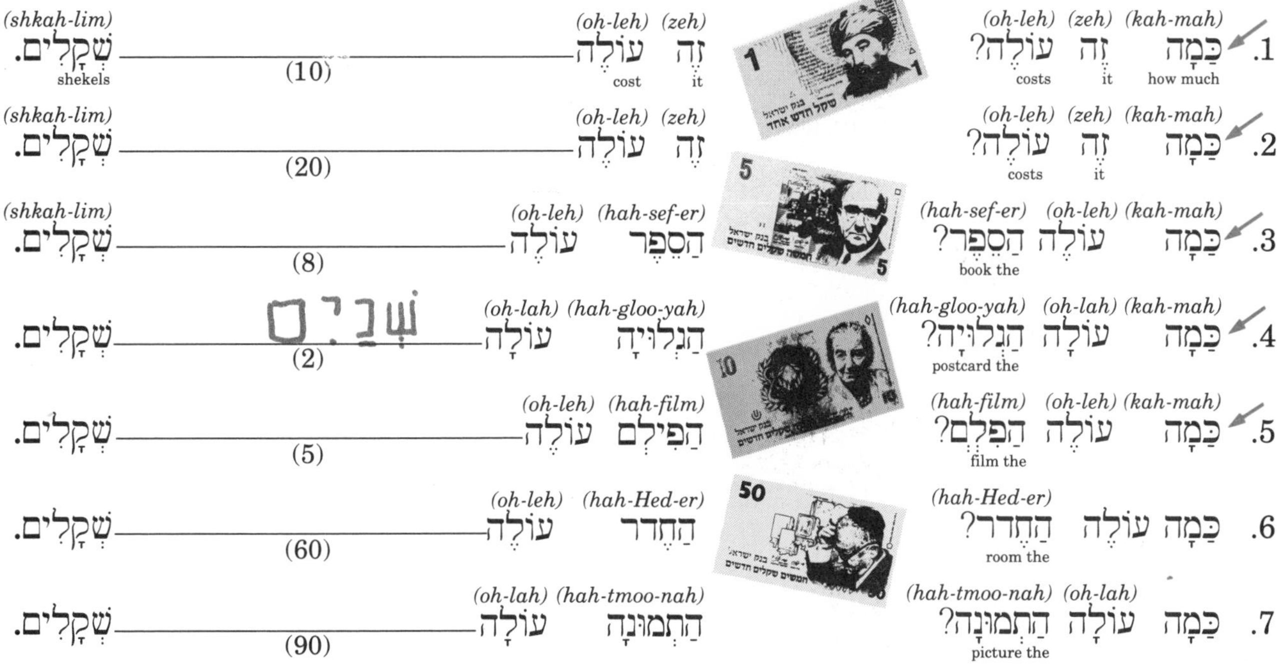

1. כַּמָּה זֶה עוֹלֶה? (kah-mah, how much; zeh, it; oh-leh, costs) — זֶה עוֹלֶה (zeh, it; oh-leh, cost) ______ (10) שְׁקָלִים. (shkah-lim, shekels)

2. כַּמָּה זֶה עוֹלֶה? (kah-mah; zeh, it; oh-leh, costs) — זֶה עוֹלֶה (zeh; oh-leh) ______ (20) שְׁקָלִים. (shkah-lim)

3. כַּמָּה עוֹלֶה הַסֵּפֶר? (kah-mah; oh-leh; hah-sef-er, book the) — הַסֵּפֶר עוֹלֶה (hah-sef-er; oh-leh) ______ (8) שְׁקָלִים. (shkah-lim)

4. כַּמָּה עוֹלָה הַגְּלוּיָה? (kah-mah; oh-lah; hah-gloo-yah, postcard the) — הַגְּלוּיָה עוֹלָה (hah-gloo-yah; oh-lah) שְׁנַיִם (2) שְׁקָלִים.

5. כַּמָּה עוֹלֶה הַפִּלְם? (kah-mah; oh-leh; hah-film, film the) — הַפִּילְם עוֹלֶה (hah-film; oh-leh) ______ (5) שְׁקָלִים.

6. כַּמָּה עוֹלֶה הַחֶדֶר? (hah-Hed-er, room the) — הַחֶדֶר עוֹלֶה (hah-Hed-er; oh-leh) ______ (60) שְׁקָלִים.

7. כַּמָּה עוֹלָה הַתְּמוּנָה? (oh-lah; hah-tmoo-nah, picture the) — הַתְּמוּנָה עוֹלָה (hah-tmoo-nah; oh-lah) ______ (90) שְׁקָלִים.

הַתְּשׁוּבוֹת

a. עֶשְׂרִים וְחָמֵשׁ
b. אַרְבָּעִים וְשֶׁבַע
c. שְׁמוֹנִים וְאַרְבַּע
d. חֲמִשִּׁים וְאַחַת
e. שְׁלֹשִׁים וָשֵׁשׁ
f. תִּשְׁעִים וְשָׁלֹשׁ
g. שִׁשִּׁים וּשְׁמוֹנֶה
h. שִׁבְעִים וּשְׁתַּיִם

1. עֲשָׂרָה
2. עֶשְׂרִים
3. שְׁמוֹנָה
4. שְׁנַיִם
5. חֲמִשָּׁה
6. שִׁשִּׁים
7. תִּשְׁעִים

Step 7

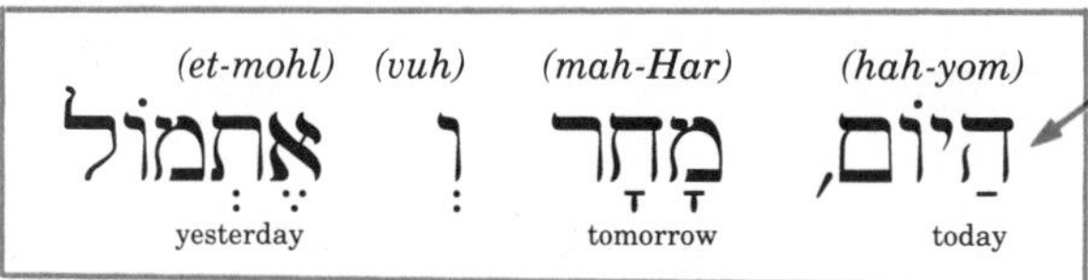

(hah-shah-nah) (loo-aH)
לוּחַ שָׁנָה
calendar

(yah-mim) (sheh-vah) (yesh) (buh-shah-voo-ah)
בְּשָׁבוּעַ יֵשׁ שֶׁבַע יָמִים
week in — seven — days

(shah-baht) יוֹם שַׁבָּת Saturday 7	(shee-shee) יוֹם שִׁשִּׁי Friday 6	(Hah-mish-ee) יוֹם חֲמִישִׁי Thursday 5	(reh-veh-ee)(yom) יוֹם רְבִיעִי Wednesday 4	(shlee-shee) (yom) יוֹם שְׁלִישִׁי Tuesday 3	(sheh-nee) (yom) יוֹם שֵׁנִי Monday 2	(rih-shon) (yom) יוֹם רִאשׁוֹן Sunday 1

It is very חָשׁוּב (Hah-shoov) (important) to know הַיָּמִים (hah-yah-mim) (days the) of the week וְ the various parts of the day. Let's learn them. Be sure to say them aloud before filling in the blanks below. בְּעִבְרִית (biv-rit) the names of the days mean simply "first day," "second day," "third day" and so on. The exception is Saturday — שַׁבָּת (shah-baht).

(rih-shon) (yom) יוֹם רִאשׁוֹן ______________	(sheh-nee) (yom) יוֹם שֵׁנִי ______________
(shlee-shee) (yom) יוֹם שְׁלִישִׁי ______________	(reh-veh-ee) (yom) יוֹם רְבִיעִי ______________
(Hah-mish-ee) יוֹם חֲמִישִׁי ______________	(shee-shee) יוֹם שִׁשִּׁי ___יוֹם שִׁשִּׁי___
(shah-baht) יוֹם שַׁבָּת ______________	

If הַיּוֹם (hah-yom) (today) is יוֹם רְבִיעִי (ruh-veh-ee) (yom) (Wednesday) then מָחָר (mah-Har) (tomorrow) is יוֹם חֲמִישִׁי (Hah-mish-ee) (yom) (Thursday) and אֶתְמוֹל (et-mohl) (yesterday) was יוֹם שְׁלִישִׁי (shlee-shee) (yom) (Tuesday).

Now, you supply the correct answers. If הַיּוֹם (hah-yom) (today) is יוֹם שֵׁנִי (sheh-nee) (yom) (Monday), then מָחָר (mah-Har) (tomorrow) is ______________ and אֶתְמוֹל (et-mohl) (yesterday) was______________. Or, if הַיּוֹם (hah-yom) (today) is יוֹם שֵׁנִי (sheh-nee) (yom) (Monday) then___מָחָר___ (tomorrow) is יוֹם שְׁלִישִׁי (shlee-shee) (Tuesday) and______________ (yesterday) was יוֹם רִאשׁוֹן (rih-shon) (Sunday).

What day is it today? .______________________ הַיּוֹם (hah-yom)

עַכְשָׁו (aH-shahv) peel off the next שֶׁבַע (sheh-vah) (seven) labels וְ put them on a לוּחַ שָׁנָה (loo-aH) (shah-nah) (calendar) you use every day. From now on, Monday is יוֹם שֵׁנִי (yom) (sheh-nee).

______________	ד	stewardess. . . . .(dah-yel-et) . . . . דַּיֶּלֶת
______________		gas. . . . .(del-ek) . . . . דֶּלֶק
______________		fuel tanker. . . . . . . (may-Hah-leet-del-ek) . . .מְכָלִית דֶּלֶק—
______________		gas pump. . . . . . .(mah-sheh-vaht-del-ek) . . מַשְׁאֵבַת דֶּלֶק—
______________		democracy. . . . . . .(deh-moh-krah-tee-yah). . . . . . . .דֶּמוֹקְרַטְיָה

There are אַרְבַּע (ar-bah) [four] parts to each יוֹם (yom) [day].

	Hebrew		English
______________________	בֹּקֶר (boh-ker)	=	morning
______________________	אַחֲרֵי (aH-ah-ray) הַצָּהֳרַיִם (hah-tsoh-hoh-rah-yim)	=	afternoon
עֶרֶב, עֶרֶב, עֶרֶב, עֶרֶב, עֶרֶב	עֶרֶב (eh-rev)	=	evening
______________________	לַיְלָה (lie-lah)	=	night

Notice that בְּ (buh) means "on" and בַּ (bah) means "in the." For example, בְּיוֹם (buh-yom) שִׁשִּׁי (shee-shee) means "on Friday," and בַּבֹּקֶר (bah-boh-ker) means "in the morning." עַכְשָׁו (aH-shahv) fill in the following blanks and then check your answers at the bottom of הָעַמּוּד (hah-ah-mood) [page the]. Don't forget to write from right to left! Follow the red arrows.

______________________	=	on Sunday (in the) morning	.a
______________________	=	on Friday evening	.b
______________________	=	on Saturday evening	.c
______________________	=	on Monday morning	.d
______________________	=	on Wednesday morning	.e
______________________	=	on Tuesday afternoon	.f
______________________	=	on Thursday afternoon	.g
______________________	=	on Thursday night	.h
______________________	=	yesterday evening	.i
______________________	=	yesterday afternoon	.j
______________________	=	yesterday morning	.k
______________________	=	tomorrow morning	.l
______________________	=	tomorrow afternoon	.m
______________________	=	tomorrow evening	.n

הַתְּשׁוּבוֹת

a. בְּיוֹם רִאשׁוֹן בַּבֹּקֶר
b. בְּיוֹם שִׁשִּׁי בָּעֶרֶב
c. בְּיוֹם שַׁבָּת בָּעֶרֶב
d. בְּיוֹם שֵׁנִי בַּבֹּקֶר
e. בְּיוֹם רְבִיעִי בַּבֹּקֶר
f. בְּיוֹם שְׁלִישִׁי אַחֲרֵי הַצָּהֳרַיִם
g. בְּיוֹם חֲמִישִׁי אַחֲרֵי הַצָּהֳרַיִם
h. בְּיוֹם חֲמִישִׁי בַּלַּיְלָה
i. אֶתְמוֹל בָּעֶרֶב
j. אֶתְמוֹל אַחֲרֵי הַצָּהֳרַיִם
k. אֶתְמוֹל בַּבֹּקֶר
l. מָחָר בַּבֹּקֶר
m. מָחָר אַחֲרֵי הַצָּהֳרַיִם
n. מָחָר בָּעֶרֶב

So, with merely אַחַת עֶשְׂרֵה (es-reh) (aH-aht) (eleven) words, you can specify any יוֹם (yom) of הַשָּׁבוּעַ (hah-shah-voo-ah) (week the) and any time of the יוֹם (yom). The words אֶתְמוֹל (et-mohl) (yesterday) וְ מָחָר (mah-Har) (tomorrow) הַיּוֹם, (hah-yom) (today) will be very important for you in making reservations וְ appointments, in getting כַּרְטִיסִים (kar-tih-sim) (tickets) for a קוֹנְצֶרְט (kohn-tsairt) (concert) and for many things you will wish to do. Knowing the parts of the יוֹם (yom) will help you to learn and understand the various עִבְרִית (iv-rit) greetings below. Practice these every day until your trip.

good morning	=	בֹּקֶר טוֹב (tohv) (boh-ker)	____________
good evening	=	עֶרֶב טוֹב (tohv) (eh-rev)	____________
good night	=	לַיְלָה טוֹב (tohv) (lie-lah)	____________
hello/goodbye	=	שָׁלוֹם (shah-lom)	שָׁלוֹם, שָׁלוֹם, שָׁלוֹם
goodbye	=	לְהִתְרָאוֹת (luh-hih-trah-oht)	____________
How are you?	=	מָה שְׁלוֹמְךָ? (shlohm-Hah) (mah) (♂)	____________
		מָה שְׁלוֹמֵךְ? (shloh-mayH) (mah) (♀)	____________

Take the next אַרְבַּע (ar-bah) labels וְ stick them on the appropriate דְּבָרִים (dvah-rim) in your בַּיִת (bah-yit) (house). How about the bathroom mirror for בֹּקֶר טוֹב (tohv) (boh-ker)? אוֹ (oh) (or) the front door for עֶרֶב טוֹב (tohv) (eh-rev)? אוֹ (oh) your alarm for לַיְלָה טוֹב (tohv) (lie-lah)? אוֹ (oh) your kitchen cabinet for שָׁלוֹם (shah-lom)? Remember that whenever you enter small shops וְ stores בְּיִשְׂרָאֵל (buh-yiss-rah-el) you will hear the appropriate greeting for the time of day. Don't be surprised. It is a מְאֹד (muh-ohd) (very) friendly וְ warm custom.

הַתְּשׁוּבוֹת TO THE CROSSWORD PUZZLE

ACROSS

.1	אֵיפֹה	.19	מְכוֹנִית	.31	כֶּלֶב
.3	בַּיִת	.20	כָּחוֹל	.32	שָׁלוֹם
.5	אוֹטוֹבּוּס	.21	חָתוּל	.33	עֵשֶׂב
.6	שְׁמוֹנֶה	.22	חֶדֶר	.34	אַרְבַּע
.9	סֵפֶר	.23	זֶה	.36	דְּבָרִים
.10	מַרְתֵּף	.24	מָלוֹן	.38	אֶתְמוֹל
.11	יִשְׂרָאֵל	.26	יוֹם	.39	יָרוֹק
.13	שַׁבָּת	.28	שָׁבוּעַ	.40	שְׁלֹשִׁים
.16	מִסְפָּרִים	.29	צָהוֹב	.41	עִבְרִית
.18	שֵׁשׁ	.30	כַּמָּה		

DOWN

.1	אָדוֹם	.11	יֵשׁ	.25	לָמָּה
.2	לָבָן	.12	לוּחַ שָׁנָה	.27	עַכְשָׁו
.3	בֹּקֶר	.13	שְׁקָלִים	.29	צְבָעִים
.4	תְּשׁוּבוֹת	.14	תְּמוּנָה	.30	כַּמָּה
.5	אָפוֹר	.15	מְנוֹרָה	.34	אוֹפַנַּיִם
.7	הַיּוֹם	.17	פְּרָחִים	.35	עֶשֶׂר
.8	שְׁתַּיִם	.18	שָׁחוֹר	.37	יוֹם שִׁשִּׁי
.10	מָחָר	.22	חָמֵשׁ		

CROSSWORD PUZZLE

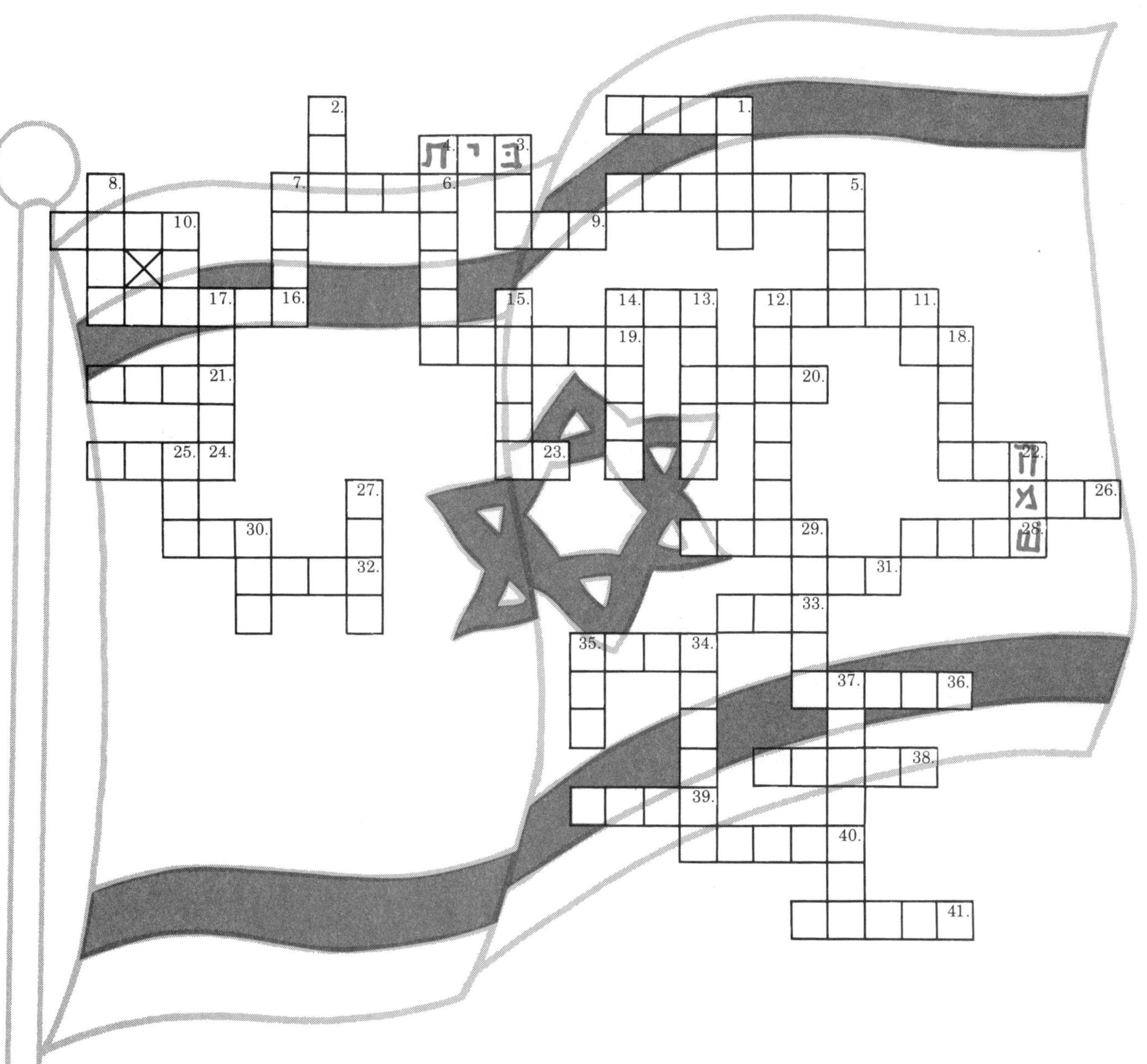

ACROSS

1. where
3. house
5. bus
6. eight
9. book
10. basement
11. Israel
13. Saturday
16. numbers
18. six
19. car
20. blue
21. cat
22. room
23. it is
24. hotel
26. day
28. week
29. yellow
30. how much/many
31. dog
32. hello/goodbye
33. grass
34. four
36. things
38. yesterday
39. green
40. thirty
41. Hebrew

DOWN

1. red
2. white
3. morning
4. answers
5. gray
7. today
8. two
10. tomorrow
11. there is/are
12. calendar
13. shekels
14. picture
15. lamp
17. flowers
18. black
22. five
25. why
27. now
29. colors
30. how much/many
34. bicycle
35. ten
37. Friday

Step 8

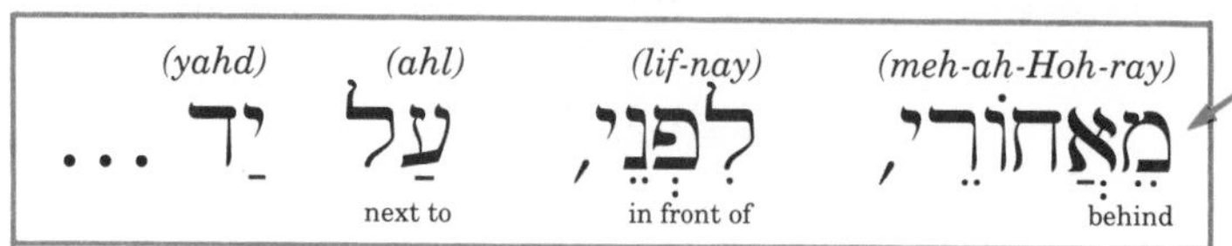

The (iv-rit) עִבְרִית prepositions (words like "in," "on," "through" and "next to") are easy to learn ן they allow you to be precise (im) עִם a minimum of effort. Instead of having to point (shesh) שֵׁשׁ (six) times at a piece of yummy pastry you wish to order, you can explain precisely which one you want by saying (zeh) זֶה ((is) it) behind, (zeh) זֶה ((is) it) in front of, (zeh) זֶה next to, זֶה under the piece of pastry that the salesperson is starting to pick up. Let's learn some of these little (mih-lim) מִלִּים which are as (Hah-shoo-voht) חֲשׁוּבוֹת (important) in (iv-rit) עִבְרִית as in (ahn-glit) אַנְגְלִית. Study the examples below.

from	=	(muh) מְ	also seen as (may) מֵ	under	=	(mee-tah-Haht) מִתַּחַת (lah) לַ
in	=	(buh) בְּ	also seen as (bah) בַּ	over	=	(may-ahl) מֵעַל (lah) לַ
to	=	(el) אֶל		next to	=	(ahl) עַל (yahd) יַד

(hah-ish) הָאִישׁ (man the) (hoh-leH) הוֹלֵךְ (goes) (el) אֶל (hah-mah-lon) הַמָּלוֹן.

(hah-ish-ah) הָאִשָּׁה (woman the) (bah-ah) בָּאָה (comes) (may) מֵ (hah-mah-lon) הַמָּלוֹן.

(hah-roh-feh) הָרוֹפֵא (doctor the) (bah-mah-lon) בַּמָּלוֹן (hotel the in (is)).

(hah-tmoo-nah) הַתְּמוּנָה (picture the) (ahl) עַל (yahd) יַד (hah-shah-on) הַשָּׁעוֹן (clock the).

(hah-shool-Hahn) הַשּׁוּלְחָן (table the) (may-ahl) מֵעַל (lah) לַ (the) (kel-ev) כֶּלֶב (dog).

(hah-kel-ev) הַכֶּלֶב (mee-tah-Haht) מִתַּחַת (lah) לַ (shool-Hahn) שׁוּלְחָן.

(hah-shool-Hahn) הַשּׁוּלְחָן (mee-tah-Haht) מִתַּחַת (lah) לַ (tmoo-nah) תְּמוּנָה.

(hah-shah-on) הַשָּׁעוֹן (ahl) עַל (yahd) יַד (hah-tmoo-nah) הַתְּמוּנָה.

ה

hall. . . . . (hohl) . . . . הוֹל
Holland. . . . .(hoh-lahnd) . . . . הוֹלַנְד
Dutch. . . . .(hoh-lahn-dee) . . . . הוֹלַנְדִי
historic. . . . . (hee-stoh-ree) . . . . הִיסְטוֹרִי
history. . . . .(hee-stoh-ree-yah) . . . . . הִיסְטוֹרִיָה

Fill in the blanks below (im) עִם the correct prepositions according to the pictures on the previous (ah-mood) עַמּוּד.

(hah-kel-ev) הַכֶּלֶב dog the ________ (under) (shool-Hahn) שׁוּלְחָן. (hah-ish) הָאִישׁ man the (hoh-leH) הוֹלֵךְ goes ________ (to) (hah-mah-lon) הַמָּלוֹן.

(hah-roh-feh) הָרוֹפֵא doctor the ________ (in) מָלוֹן. (hah-shah-on) הַשָּׁעוֹן clock the ________ (over) (shool-Hahn) שׁוּלְחָן.

(hah-tmoo-nah) הַתְּמוּנָה ________ (over) שׁוּלְחָן. (hah-shah-on) הַשָּׁעוֹן ________ (next to) (hah-tmoo-nah) הַתְּמוּנָה. picture the

הַתְּמוּנָה ________ (next to) (hah-shah-on) הַשָּׁעוֹן. (hah-shool-Hahn) הַשּׁוּלְחָן table the ________ (under) (tmoo-nah) תְּמוּנָה.

(hah-shool-Hahn) הַשּׁוּלְחָן ________ (over) (kel-ev) כֶּלֶב. (hah-ish-ah) הָאִשָּׁה woman the (bah-ah) בָּאָה comes __מ__ (from) (hah-mah-lon) הַמָּלוֹן.

(aH-shahv) עַכְשָׁו answer the (shuh-eh-loht) שְׁאֵלוֹת questions based on the (tmoo-noht) תְּמוּנוֹת pictures on the previous (ah-mood) עַמּוּד.

(ay-foh) אֵיפֹה where (hah-kel-ev) הַכֶּלֶב? dog the ____הַכֶּלֶב____

(ay-foh) אֵיפֹה (hah-shool-Hahn) הַשּׁוּלְחָן? ________

אֵיפֹה (hah-roh-feh) הָרוֹפֵא? ________

אֵיפֹה (hah-tmoo-nah) הַתְּמוּנָה? ________

(hah-im) הַאִם does (hah-ish-ah) הָאִשָּׁה woman the (bah-ah) בָּאָה come (may) מֵ from (hah-mah-lon) הַמָּלוֹן? hotel the ________

(hah-im) הַאִם does (hah-ish) הָאִישׁ man the (hoh-leH) הוֹלֵךְ go (el) אֶל to (hah-mah-lon) הַמָּלוֹן? hotel the ________

(hah-im) הַאִם is (hah-shah-on) הַשָּׁעוֹן (yah-rok) יָרוֹק? green ________

(hah-im) הַאִם is (hah-kel-ev) הַכֶּלֶב (ah-for) אָפוֹר? gray ________

________	dry river bed, wadi	(vah-dee)	וָאדִי
________	Washington	(vah-sheeng-tohn)	וַשִׁינְגְטוֹן
________ ו	viola	(vee-oh-lah)	וִיוֹלָה
________	virus	(vee-roos)	וִירוּס
________	virtuoso	(veer-too-oh-zee)	וִירְטוּאוֹזִי

(aH-shahv) *(iv-rit)*
עַכְשָׁו for some more practice with עִבְרִית prepositions!

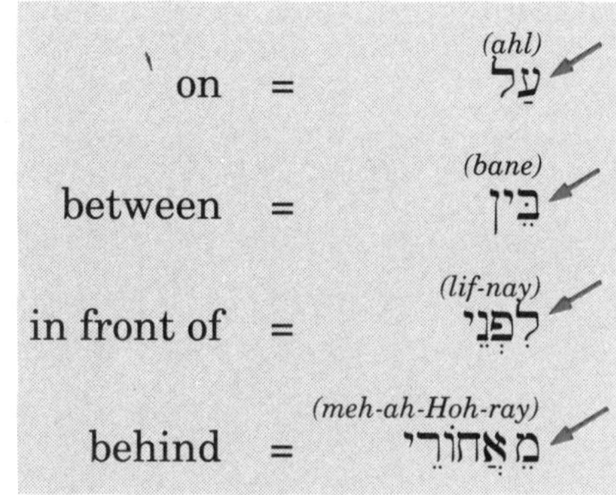

on	=	עַל *(ahl)*
between	=	בֵּין *(bane)*
in front of	=	לִפְנֵי *(lif-nay)*
behind	=	מֵאֲחוֹרֵי *(meh-ah-Hoh-ray)*

Now fill in the blanks based on the examples below.

(kohs) (hah-mah-yim) (ahl) (hah-shool-Hahn)
כּוֹס הַמַּיִם עַל הַשּׁוּלְחָן.
glass water on

(hah-tmoo-nah) (ahl) (hah-keer)
הַתְּמוּנָה עַל הַקִּיר.
the wall

(hah-mnoh-rah) (meh-ah-Hoh-ray)
הַמְּנוֹרָה מֵאֲחוֹרֵי הַשּׁוּלְחָן.
the lamp behind

(hah-shool-Hahn) (lif-nay) (hah-mee-tah)
הַשּׁוּלְחָן לִפְנֵי הַמִּיטָּה.
in front of the bed

(hah-mnoh-rah) (bane) (vuh-hah-mee-tah)
הַמְּנוֹרָה בֵּין הַשּׁוּלְחָן וְהַמִּיטָּה.
and the bed

(kohs) (hah-mah-yim) (hah-shool-Hahn)
כּוֹס הַמַּיִם ________ (on) הַשּׁוּלְחָן.

(hah-tmoo-nah) (hah-keer)
הַתְּמוּנָה ________ (on) הַקִּיר.

(hah-mnoh-rah)
הַמְּנוֹרָה ________ (behind) הַשּׁוּלְחָן.

(hah-mee-tah)
הַשּׁוּלְחָן __לִפְנֵי__ (in front of) הַמִּיטָּה.

(vuh-hah-mee-tah)
הַמְּנוֹרָה ________ (between) הַשּׁוּלְחָן וְהַמִּיטָּה.

Answer the following שְׁאֵלוֹת *(shuh-eh-loht)* (questions) based on the תְּמוּנוֹת *(tmoo-noht)* by filling in the blanks עִם *(im)* the correct prepositions. Choose the prepositions from those you have just learned.

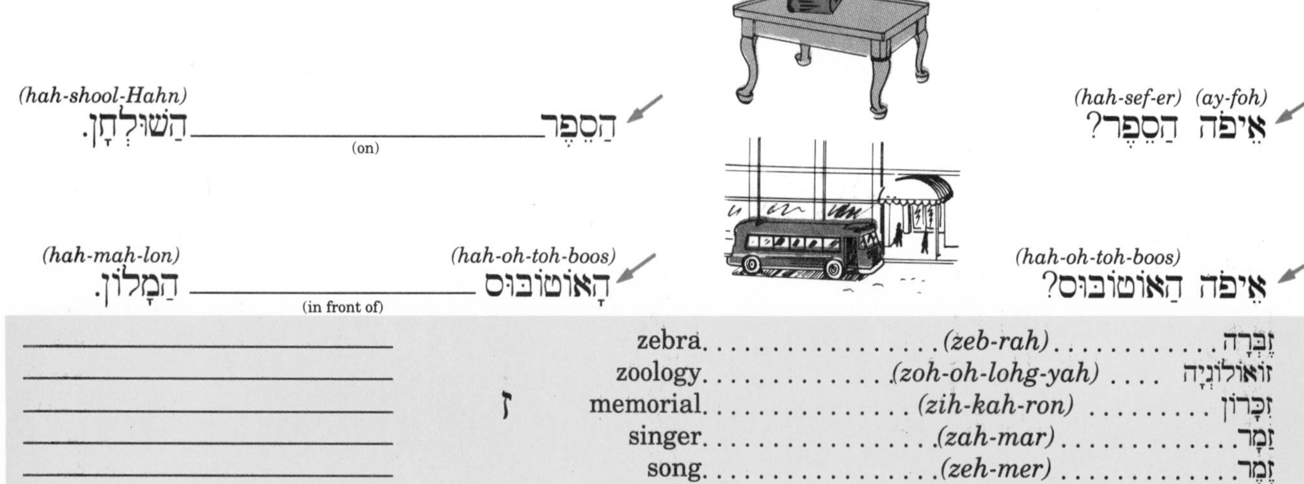

(ay-foh) (hah-sef-er)
אֵיפֹה הַסֵּפֶר?

(hah-shool-Hahn)
הַסֵּפֶר ________ (on) הַשּׁוּלְחָן.

(hah-oh-toh-boos)
אֵיפֹה הָאוֹטוֹבּוּס?

(hah-oh-toh-boos) (hah-mah-lon)
הָאוֹטוֹבּוּס ________ (in front of) הַמָּלוֹן.

ז

זֶבְּרָה	*(zeb-rah)*	zebra
זוֹאוֹלוֹגְיָה	*(zoh-oh-lohg-yah)*	zoology
זִכָּרוֹן	*(zih-kah-ron)*	memorial
זַמָּר	*(zah-mar)*	singer
זֶמֶר	*(zeh-mer)*	song

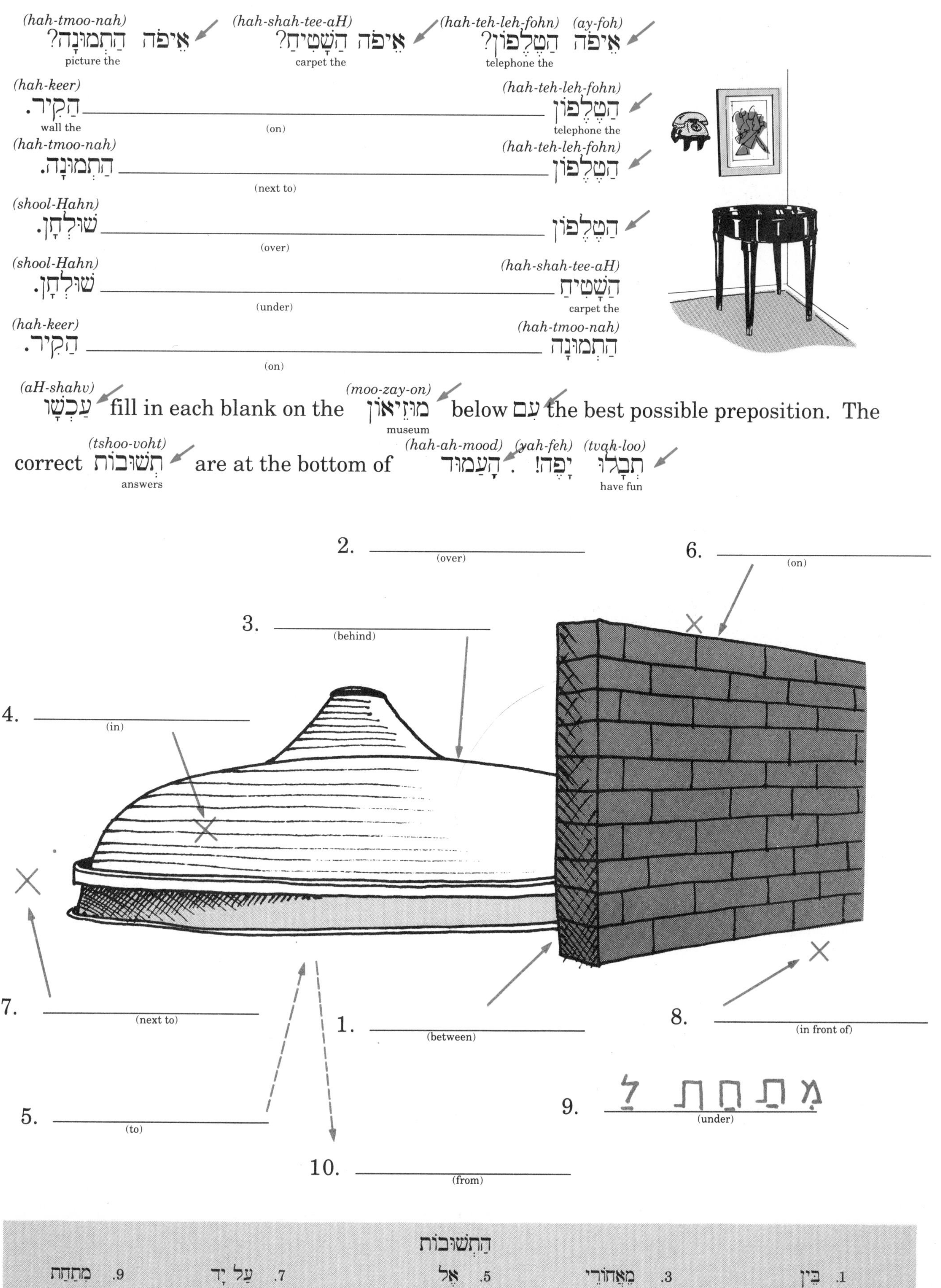

(ay-foh) (hah-teh-leh-fohn)
אֵיפֹה הַטֶלֶפוֹן?
telephone the

(hah-shah-tee-aH)
אֵיפֹה הַשָּׁטִיחַ?
carpet the

(hah-tmoo-nah)
אֵיפֹה הַתְּמוּנָה?
picture the

(hah-teh-leh-fohn) הַטֶלֶפוֹן (telephone the) ______ (on) הַקִּיר. (hah-keer) (wall the)

(hah-teh-leh-fohn) הַטֶלֶפוֹן ______ (next to) הַתְּמוּנָה. (hah-tmoo-nah)

הַטֶלֶפוֹן ______ (over) שׁוּלְחָן. (shool-Hahn)

(hah-shah-tee-aH) הַשָּׁטִיחַ (carpet the) ______ (under) שׁוּלְחָן. (shool-Hahn)

(hah-tmoo-nah) הַתְּמוּנָה ______ (on) הַקִּיר. (hah-keer)

(aH-shahv) עַכְשָׁו fill in each blank on the (moo-zay-on) מוּזֵיאוֹן (museum) below עִם the best possible preposition. The correct (tshoo-voht) תְּשׁוּבוֹת (answers) are at the bottom of (hah-ah-mood) הָעַמּוּד. (yah-feh) (tvah-loo) תְּבָלוּ יָפֶה! (have fun)

הַתְּשׁוּבוֹת

1. בֵּין
2. מֵעַל לְ
3. מֵאֲחוֹרֵי
4. בְּ
5. אֶל
6. עַל
7. עַל יַד
8. לִפְנֵי
9. מִתַּחַת
10. מִ

Step 9

(lah-Hoh-dah-shim) (sep-tem-bair) (ah-pril) (yoo-nee) (vuh-noh-vem-bair) (yah-mim) (shloh-shim)
לַחוֹדָשִׁים סֶפְּטֶמְבֶּר, אַפְּרִיל, יוּנִי וְנוֹבֶמְבֶּר יָמִים שְׁלֹשִׁים
months the in, September, April, June, November and, days, thirty

Sound familiar? You have learned the days of the week, so now it is time to learn the חוֹדָשִׁים (Hoh-dah-shim, months) of the שָׁנָה (shah-nah, year) and all the different kinds of מֶזֶג הָאֲוִיר (meh-zeg hah-ah-veer, weather). For example, you ask about the מֶזֶג הָאֲוִיר (meh-zeg hah-ah-veer, weather) in עִבְרִית (iv-rit) just as you would in אַנְגְלִית (bahn-glit).

אֵיךְ מֶזֶג הָאֲוִיר הַיוֹם? (ayH meh-zeg hah-ah-veer hah-yom — how (is) weather today) Practice all the possible תְּשׁוּבוֹת (tshoo-voht, answers) to this question and then write all the following תְּשׁוּבוֹת (tshoo-voht) in the blanks below.

אֵיךְ מֶזֶג הָאֲוִיר הַיוֹם? (ayH) (meh-zeg) (hah-ah-veer) (hah-yom) — weather, today

הַיוֹם יוֹרֵד גֶשֶׁם. (hah-yom yoh-red gesh-em — today comes down rain) ______

הַיוֹם יוֹרֵד שֶׁלֶג. (hah-yom yoh-red shel-eg — today comes down snow) ______

הַיוֹם חַם. (hah-yom Hahm — hot) ______

הַיוֹם קַר. (kar — cold) ______ היום קר.

הַיוֹם מֶזֶג הָאֲוִיר נָעִים. (meh-zeg hah-ah-veer nah-im — weather pleasant) ______

הַיוֹם מֶזֶג הָאֲוִיר רָע. (meh-zeg hah-ah-veer rah — bad) ______

הַיוֹם עֲרָפֶל. (ah-rah-fel — fog) ______

הַיוֹם רוּחַ חֲזָקָה. (roo-aH Hah-zah-kah — strong wind) ______

הַיוֹם חַמְסִין. (Hahm-seen — hot wind) ______

עַכְשָׁו practice הַמִלִים (hah-mih-lim) on the next עַמוּד (ah-mood) aloud, then fill in the blanks with the names of the חוֹדָשִׁים (Hoh-dah-shim, months) and the appropriate מֶזֶג הָאֲוִיר (meh-zeg hah-ah-veer, weather) report.

ח

life	(Hah-yim)	חַיִים
donkey	(Hah-mohr)	חֲמוֹר
clay	(Heh-mar)	חֵמָר
Mt. Hermon	(Har-mon)	חֶרְמוֹן
dark	(Hah-shooH)	חָשׁוּךְ

(shel-eg) (yoh-red) (byah-noo-ar) בְּיָנוּאַר יוֹרֵד שֶׁלֶג. ________ snow, down comes	(byah-noo-ar) בְּיָנוּאַר ________ January in
(gesh-em) (yoh-red) (buh-feb-roo-ar) בְּפֶבְּרוּאַר יוֹרֵד גֶּשֶׁם. ________ rain, down comes	(buh-feb-roo-ar) בְּפֶבְּרוּאַר ________ February in
(gesh-em) (yoh-red) (buh-mairts) בְּמֶרְץ יוֹרֵד גֶּשֶׁם. ________ rain, down comes	(buh-mairts) בְּמֶרְץ ________ March in
(nah-im) (hah-ah-veer) (meh-zeg) (bah-pril) בְּאַפְּרִיל מֶזֶג הָאֲוִיר נָעִים. ________ pleasant, weather	(bah-pril) בְּאַפְּרִיל ________ April in
(Hah-zah-kah) (roo-aH) (buh-my) בְּמַאי רוּחַ חֲזָקָה. ________ strong, wind	(buh-my) בְּמַאי ________ May in
(nah-im) (buh-yoo-nee) בְּיוּנִי נָעִים. ________ pleasant	(buh-yoo-nee) בְּיוּנִי בְּיוּנִי June in
(muh-ohd) (Hahm) (buh-yoo-lee) בְּיוּלִי חַם מְאֹד. ________ very, hot	(buh-yoo-lee) בְּיוּלִי ________ July in
(muh-ohd) (Hahm) (buh-oh-goost) בְּאוֹגוּסְט חַם מְאֹד. ________	(buh-oh-goost) בְּאוֹגוּסְט ________ August in
(nah-im) (buh-sep-tem-bair) בְּסֶפְּטֶמְבֶּר נָעִים. ________ pleasant	(buh-sep-tem-bair) בְּסֶפְּטֶמְבֶּר ________ September in
(ah-rah-fel) (buh-ohk-toh-bair) בְּאוֹקְטוֹבֶּר עֲרָפֶל. ________ fog	(buh-ohk-toh-bair) בְּאוֹקְטוֹבֶּר ________ October in
(kar) (buh-noh-vem-bair) בְּנוֹבֶמְבֶּר קַר. ________ cold	(buh-noh-vem-bair) בְּנוֹבֶמְבֶּר ________ November in
(rah) (buh-deh-tsem-bair) בְּדֶצֶמְבֶּר מֶזֶג הָאֲוִיר רַע. ________ bad	(buh-deh-tsem-bair) בְּדֶצֶמְבֶּר ________ December in

עַכְשָׁו answer the following questions based on הַתְּמוּנוֹת (hah-tmoo-noht) picture the to the right.

(buh-feb-roo-ar) (hah-ah-veer) (meh-zeg) (ayH)
אֵיךְ מֶזֶג הָאֲוִיר בְּפֶבְּרוּאַר? ________
weather

(bah-pril) (hah-ah-veer) (meh-zeg) (ayH)
אֵיךְ מֶזֶג הָאֲוִיר בְּאַפְּרִיל? ________

(buh-my)
אֵיךְ מֶזֶג הָאֲוִיר בְּמַאי? ________

(buh-oh-goost)
אֵיךְ מֶזֶג הָאֲוִיר בְּאוֹגוּסְט? ________

(rah) (oh) (tohv) (hah-yom) (hah-ah-veer) (meh-zeg)
מֶזֶג הָאֲוִיר הַיּוֹם טוֹב אוֹ רַע? ________
bad, or, good, today

ט

chef. . . . .(tah-baH) . . . . טַבָּח
Tiberias. . . . .(tveh-ree-yah) . . . . טְבֶרְיָה
windmill. . . . .(tah-Hah-naht-roo-aH) . . טַחֲנַת רוּחַ
pilot. . . . .(tah-yahs) . . . . טַיָּס
telescope. . . . .(teh-leh-skohp) . . . . טֶלֶסְקוֹפּ

עַכְשָׁו for the seasons of the (shah-nah) שָׁנָה (year) . . .

(Hoh-ref) חֹרֶף winter	(kah-yits) קַיִץ summer	(stahv) סְתָו autumn	(ah-veev) אָבִיב spring
______	______	______	______
(bah-Hof-ref) בַּחֹרֶף (winter in) (kar) קַר. (cold)	(bah-kah-yits) בַּקַּיִץ (summer in) (Hahm) חַם. (hot)	(bah-stahv) בַּסְּתָו (autumn in) (roo-aH) רוּחַ. (wind)	(bah-veev) בָּאָבִיב (spring in) (gesh-em) גֶּשֶׁם. (rain)

At this point, it is a (tohv) טוֹב idea to familiarize yourself with (yiss-ruh-eh-lee) יִשְׂרְאֵלִי temperatures. Study the thermometer because (tem-peh-rah-roht) טֶמְפֶּרָטוּרוֹת (temperatures) in (yiss-rah-el) יִשְׂרָאֵל are calculated on the basis of Centigrade (not Fahrenheit).

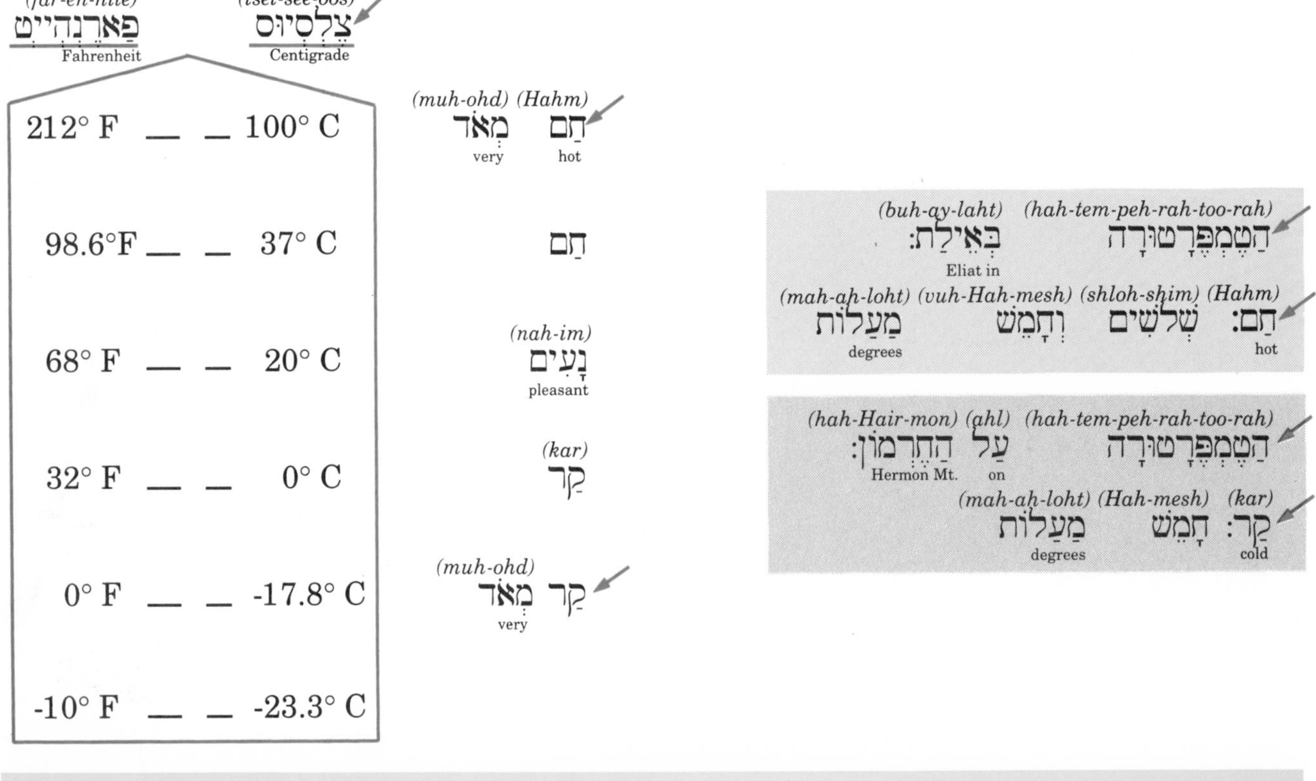

(far-en-hite) פָארֶנְהַייט Fahrenheit	(tsel-see-oos) צֶלְסִיוּס Centigrade	
212° F	100° C	(muh-ohd) מְאֹד (very) (Hahm) חַם (hot)
98.6°F	37° C	חַם
68° F	20° C	(nah-im) נָעִים (pleasant)
32° F	0° C	(kar) קַר
0° F	-17.8° C	(muh-ohd) קַר מְאֹד (very)
-10° F	-23.3° C	

(hah-tem-peh-rah-too-rah) הַטֶּמְפֶּרָטוּרָה (buh-ay-laht) בְּאֵילַת: (Eliat in)
(Hahm) חַם: (shloh-shim) שְׁלֹשִׁים (vuh-Hah-mesh) וְחָמֵשׁ (mah-ah-loht) מַעֲלוֹת (hot ... degrees)

(hah-tem-peh-rah-too-rah) הַטֶּמְפֶּרָטוּרָה (ahl) עַל (on) (hah-Hair-mon) הַחֶרְמוֹן: (Hermon Mt.)
(kar) קַר: (cold) (Hah-mesh) חָמֵשׁ (mah-ah-loht) מַעֲלוֹת (degrees)

ט

______	technician	(teH-nah-ee)	טֶכְנַאי
______	technology	(teH-noh-lohg-yah)	טֶכְנוֹלוֹגְיָה
______	(university) Technion	(teH-nee-ohn)	טֶכְנִיּוֹן
______	tennis	(teh-nis)	טֶנִיס
______	test	(test)	טֶסְט

Step 10

(vuh-hah-bah-yit) (hah-mish-pah-Hah)
וְהַבַּיִת הַמִּשְׁפָּחָה
house the and — family the

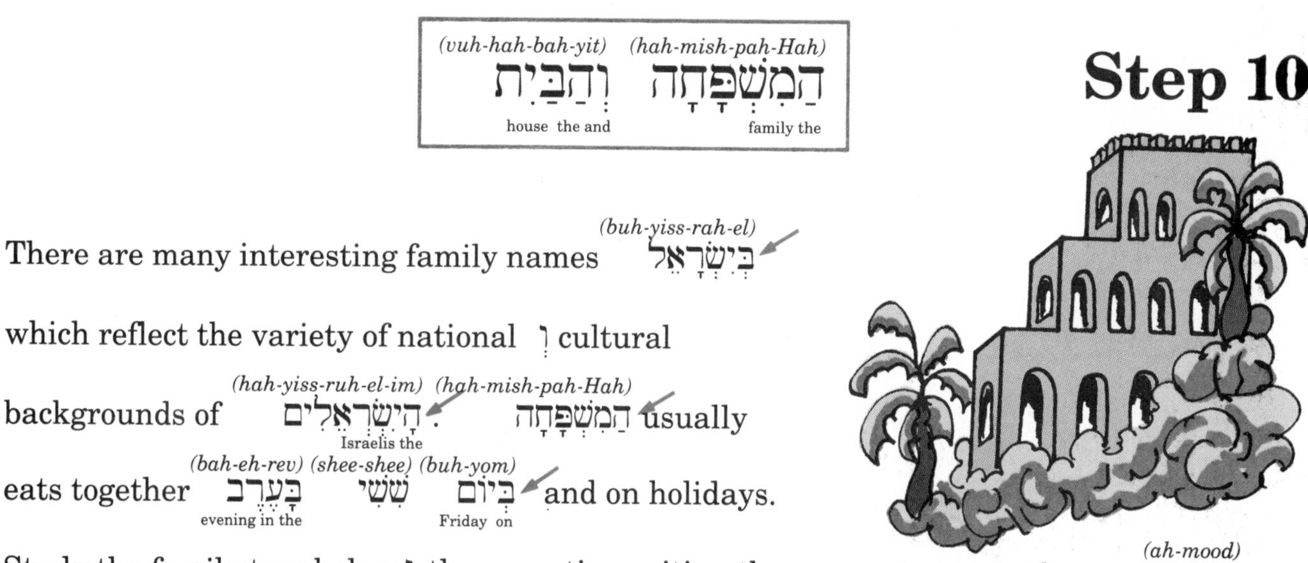

There are many interesting family names (buh-yiss-rah-el) בְּיִשְׂרָאֵל which reflect the variety of national וְ cultural backgrounds of (hah-yiss-ruh-el-im) הַיִּשְׂרְאֵלִים (Israelis the). (hah-mish-pah-Hah) הַמִּשְׁפָּחָה usually eats together (bah-eh-rev) בָּעֶרֶב (evening in the) (shee-shee) שִׁשִּׁי (buh-yom) בְּיוֹם (Friday on) and on holidays.

Study the family tree below וְ then practice writing these new names on the next (ah-mood) עַמּוּד.

(leh-vee) (Han-nah) לֵוִי חַנָּה — Levy, Hannah

(leh-vee) (shmoo-el) לֵוִי שְׁמוּאֵל — Levy, Samuel

(har-el) (dahn) הַרְאֵל דָּן — Harel, Dan

(har-el) (shoh-shah-nah) הַרְאֵל שׁוֹשַׁנָּה — Harel, Susan

(leh-vee) (dah-vid) לֵוִי דָּוִד — David

(leh-vee) (tah-mar) לֵוִי תָּמָר — Tamar

(har-el) (boh-ahz) הַרְאֵל בּוֹעַז — Boaz

(har-el) (roh-nit) הַרְאֵל רוֹנִית — Ronit

(oh-ded) לֵוִי עוֹדֵד — Oded

(mee-Hahl) לֵוִי מִיכַל — Michal

ט

text . . . . (text) . . . . טֶקְסְט
textiles . . . . (teks-teel) . . . . טֶקְסְטִיל
tragedy . . . . (trah-geh-dee-yah) . . . . . . טְרָגֶדְיָה
tropical . . . . (troh-pee) . . . . טְרוֹפִּי
tractor . . . . (trahk-tor) . . . . טְרַקְטוֹר

(kroh-vim) קְרוֹבִים relatives

(hoh-rim) הוֹרִים parents

(sah-bah) סַבָּא grandfather ______

(sahv-tah) סַבְתָּא grandmother ______

(ahv) אָב father ______

(em) אֵם mother ______

(yuh-lah-dim) יְלָדִים children

(kroh-vim) קְרוֹבִים relatives

(ben) בֵּן son ______

(baht) בַּת daughter ______

(dohd) דוֹד uncle ______

(doh-dah) דוֹדָה aunt ______

(ah-Hoht) אָחוֹת sister — (aH) אָח brother

(ish-ah) אִשָּׁה wife — (bah-ahl) בַּעַל husband

Let's learn how to identify (hah-mish-pah-Hah) הַמִּשְׁפָּחָה (family the) by (shem) שֵׁם (name). Study the following examples.

(hah-ahv) (shem) שֵׁם הָאָב (father the name)	______	(hah-ahv) (shem) (mah) מָה שֵׁם הָאָב? (father the name what)
(hah-em) (shem) שֵׁם הָאֵם (mother the)	______	(hah-em) (shem) (mah) מָה שֵׁם הָאֵם? (mother the)
(hah-ben) שֵׁם הַבֵּן (son the)	______	(hah-ben) (shem) (mah) מָה שֵׁם הַבֵּן? (son the)
(hah-baht) שֵׁם הַבַּת (daughter the)	______	(hah-baht) (shem) מָה שֵׁם הַבַּת? (daughter the)
(hah-dohd) שֵׁם הַדּוֹד (uncle the)	______	(hah-dohd) מָה שֵׁם הַדּוֹד? (uncle the)
(hah-doh-dah) שֵׁם הַדּוֹדָה (aunt the)	______	(hah-doh-dah) מָה שֵׁם הַדּוֹדָה? (aunt the)
(hah-sah-bah) שֵׁם הַסַּבָּא (grandfather the)	______	(hah-sah-bah) מָה שֵׁם הַסַּבָּא? (grandfather the)
(hah-sahv-tah) שֵׁם הַסַּבְתָּא (grandmother the)	______	(hah-sahv-tah) מָה שֵׁם הַסַּבְתָּא? (grandmother the)
(shmee) שְׁמִי (name my)	______	(shem-Hah) מָה שִׁמְךָ? (name your)

י

Greece	(yah-vahn)	יָוָן
jubilee	(yoh-vel)	יוֹבֵל
birthday	(yom-hoo-led-et)	יוֹם הוּלֶדֶת
yoga	(yoh-gah)	יוֹגָה
yoghurt	(yoh-goort)	יוֹגוּרְט

(mit-baH)
מִטְבָּח
kitchen

Study all these (tmoo-noht) תְּמוּנוֹת and then practice saying וְ writing out (hah-mih-lim) הַמִּלִּים.

This is (hah-mit-baH) הַמִּטְבָּח.
kitchen the

(muh-kah-reer) מְקָרֵר refrigerator	(tah-noor) תַּנּוּר stove	(yah-yin) יַיִן wine
(meets) מִיץ juice	(Hah-lahv) חָלָב milk	(Hem-ah) חֶמְאָה butter

Answer these questions aloud.

(hah-meets) אֵיפֹה הַמִּיץ? .... (hah-meets) הַמִּיץ (bah-muh-kah-reer) בַּמְקָרֵר.
juice the — refrigerator the in

(hah-yah-yin) (ay-foh) אֵיפֹה הַיַּיִן?
wine the

(hah-mah-yim) אֵיפֹה הַמַּיִם?
water the

(heh-Hah-lahv) אֵיפֹה הֶחָלָב?
milk the

(hah-bah-nah-nah) אֵיפֹה הַבָּנָנָה?

(hah-bee-rah) אֵיפֹה הַבִּירָה?
beer the

(hah-Hem-ah) אֵיפֹה הַחֶמְאָה?
butter the

diamond. . . . . (yah-hah-lohm) . . . . יַהֲלוֹם
sea. . . . . (yahm) . . . . יָם
Dead Sea. . . . . (yahm-hah-mel-aH). . . . . יָם הַמֶּלַח
Sea of Galilee. . . . . (yahm-kih-neh-ret). . . . . יָם כִּנֶּרֶת
forest. . . . . (yah-ahr). . . . . יַעַר

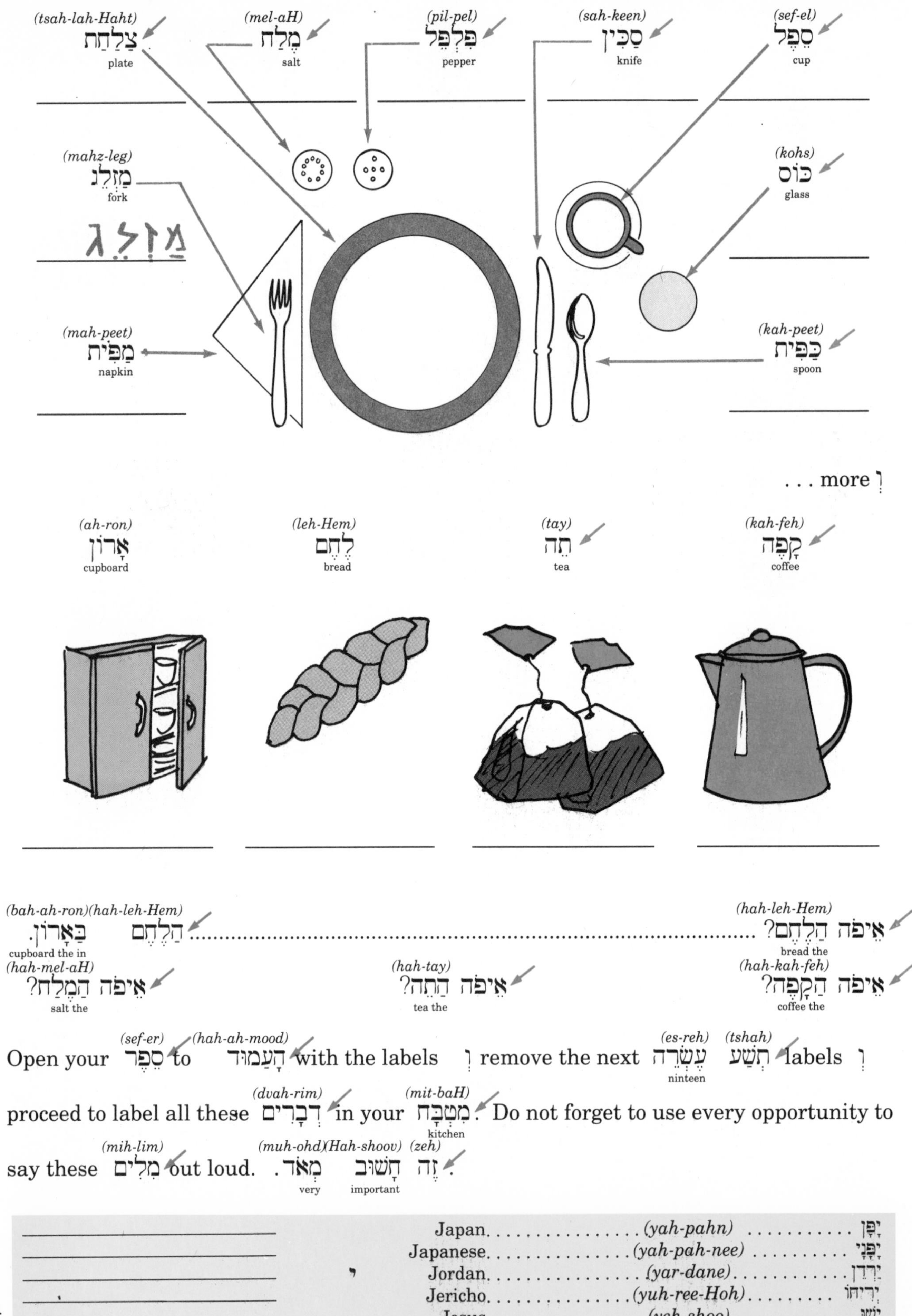

. . . more וְ

(hah-leh-Hem) אֵיפֹה הַלֶּחֶם? (bread the) .... (hah-leh-Hem) הַלֶּחֶם (bah-ah-ron) בָּאָרוֹן. (cupboard the in)

(hah-mel-aH) אֵיפֹה הַמֶּלַח? (salt the)

(hah-tay) אֵיפֹה הַתֵּה? (tea the)

(hah-kah-feh) אֵיפֹה הַקָּפֶה? (coffee the)

Open your (sef-er) סֵפֶר to (hah-ah-mood) הָעַמּוּד with the labels וְ remove the next (tshah) תְּשַׁע (es-reh) עֶשְׂרֵה (nineteen) labels וְ proceed to label all these (dvah-rim) דְּבָרִים in your (mit-baH) מִטְבָּח (kitchen). Do not forget to use every opportunity to say these (mih-lim) מִלִּים out loud. (zeh) זֶה (Hah-shoov) חָשׁוּב (important) (muh-ohd) מְאֹד (very).

______________		Japan	(yah-pahn)	יַפָּן
______________		Japanese	(yah-pah-nee)	יַפָּנִי
______________	י	Jordan	(yar-dane)	יַרְדֵּן
______________		Jericho	(yuh-ree-Hoh)	יְרִיחוֹ
______________		Jesus	(yeh-shoo)	יֵשׁוּ

(buh-yiss-rah-el) בְּיִשְׂרָאֵל religion is very important in everyday life. A person is usually one of the following.

(nohts-ree) נוֹצְרִי Christian

(moo-sluh-mee) מוּסְלְמִי Muslim

(yuh-hoo-dee) יְהוּדִי Jewish

(nohts-reet)(kness-ee-yah) כְּנֵסִיָּה נוֹצְרִית — church Christian

(moo-sluh-mee) (mis-gahd) מִסְגָּד מוּסְלְמִי — mosque Muslim

(yuh-hoo-dee) (kness-et) (bait) בֵּית כְּנֶסֶת יְהוּדִי — synagogue Jewish

You will see many beautiful (kness-ee-yoht) כְּנֵסִיּוֹת (churches) plus (mis-gah-dim) מִסְגָּדִים (mosques) and (kness-et)(bah-tay) בָּתֵּי כְּנֶסֶת (synagogues), some (Hah-dash-im) חֲדָשִׁים and others which are (ah-tee-kim) עַתִּיקִים (old), during your stay (buh-yiss-rah-el) בְּיִשְׂרָאֵל.

(aH-shahv) עַכְשָׁו let's learn how to say "I" (biv-rit) בְּעִבְרִית: ____________________ (ah-nee) אֲנִי = I

First practice saying (ah-nee) אֲנִי with the following (mih-lim) מִלִּים. Then write each sentence for more practice. Make sure you understand what you are saying.

(yuh-hoo-dee)(ah-nee) אֲנִי יְהוּדִי. (am) I, man Jewish ____________________

(yuh-hoo-dee-yah) (ah-nee) אֲנִי יְהוּדִיָּה. woman Jewish ____________________

(nohts-ree)(ah-nee) אֲנִי נוֹצְרִי. man Christian ____________________

(nohts-ree-yah) (ah-nee) אֲנִי נוֹצְרִיָּה. woman Christian ____________________

(moo-sluh-mee) אֲנִי מוּסְלְמִי. man Muslim ____________________

(moo-sluh-meet) אֲנִי מוּסְלְמִית. woman Muslim ____________________

(ah-meh-ree-kah-ee) אֲנִי אֲמֶרִיקָאִי. man American ____________________

(ah-meh-ree-kah-it) אֲנִי אֲמֶרִיקָאִית. woman American ____________________

____________	כ	fireman	(kah-by)	כַּבַּאי
____________		ball	(kah-door)	כַּדּוּר
____________		baseball	(kah-door-bah-sees)	כַּדּוּר בָּסִיס
____________		basketball	(kah-door-sahl)	כַּדּוּר סַל
____________		soccer	(kah-doo-reg-el)	כַּדּוּרֶגֶל

אֲנִי אַנְגְלִי. (ahn-glee) English man ______________________

אֲנִי אַנְגְלִיָּה. (ahn-glee-yah) English woman ______________________

אֲנִי הָאָב. (hah-ahv) father the ______________________

אֲנִי הָאֵם. (hah-em) mother the ______________________

אֲנִי בַּמִסְעָדָה. (bah-mis-ah-dah) restaurant the in ______________________

אֲנִי בַּמָלוֹן. (bah-mah-lon) hotel the in ______________________

עַכְשָׁו (aH-shahv) identify all הָאֲנָשִׁים (hah-ah-nah-shim) people the in הַתְּמוּנָה (hah-tmoo-nah) below by writing the correct עִבְרִית word for each person on the line with the corresponding number under הַתְּמוּנָה (hah-tmoo-nah).

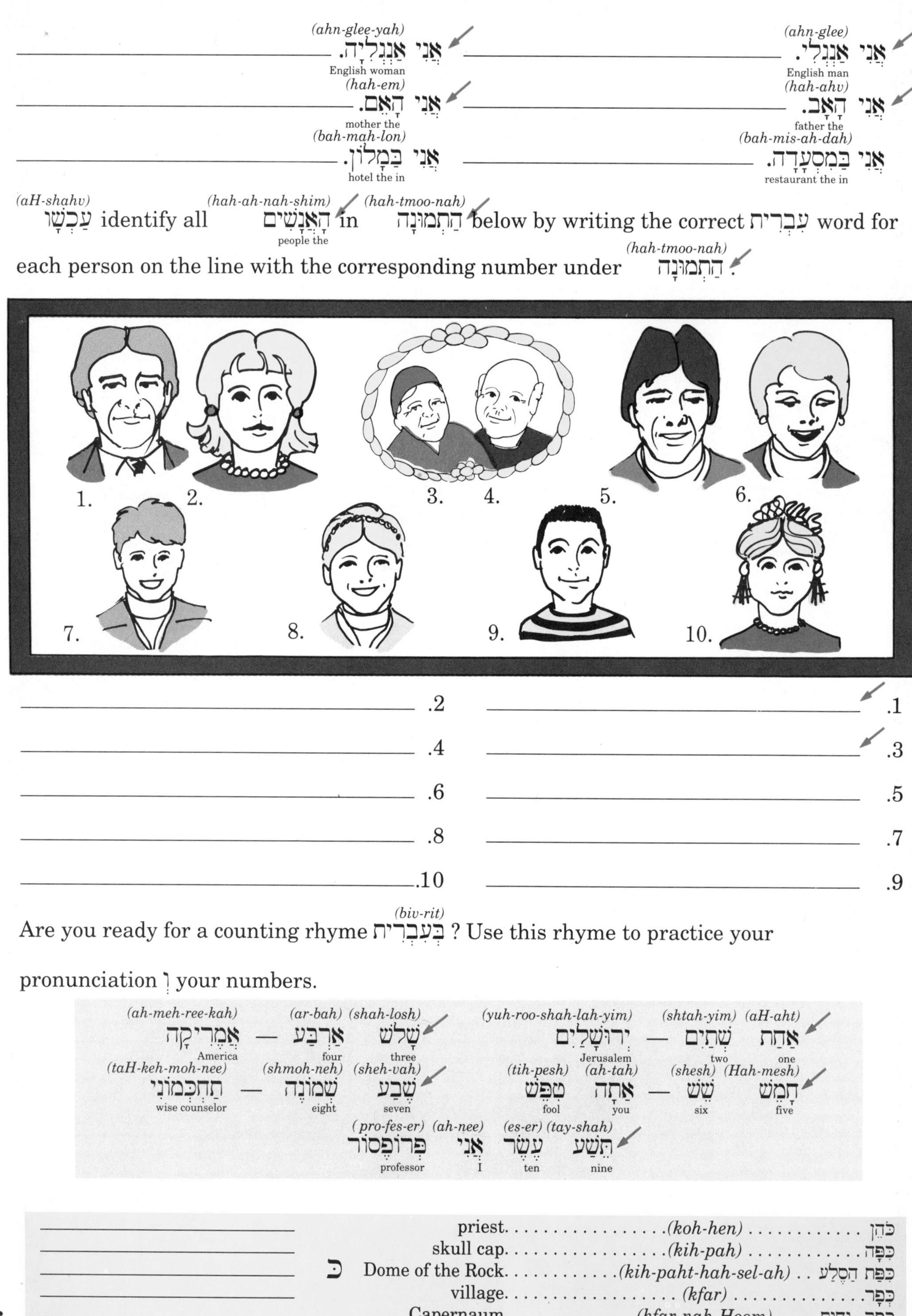

.1 ______________________ .2 ______________________

.3 ______________________ .4 ______________________

.5 ______________________ .6 ______________________

.7 ______________________ .8 ______________________

.9 ______________________ .10 ______________________

Are you ready for a counting rhyme בְּעִבְרִית (biv-rit)? Use this rhyme to practice your pronunciation וְ your numbers.

אַחַת (aH-aht) one שְׁתַּיִם (shtah-yim) two — יְרוּשָׁלַיִם (yuh-roo-shah-lah-yim) Jerusalem

שָׁלֹשׁ (shah-losh) three אַרְבַּע (ar-bah) four — אֲמֶרִיקָה (ah-meh-ree-kah) America

חָמֵשׁ (Hah-mesh) five שֵׁשׁ (shesh) six — אַתָּה (ah-tah) you טִפֵּשׁ (tih-pesh) fool

שֶׁבַע (sheh-vah) seven שְׁמוֹנֶה (shmoh-neh) eight — תַּחְכְּמוֹנִי (taH-keh-moh-nee) wise counselor

תֵּשַׁע (tay-shah) nine עֶשֶׂר (es-er) ten אֲנִי (ah-nee) I פְּרוֹפֶסוֹר (pro-fes-er) professor

כ

כֹּהֵן . . . . (koh-hen) . . . . priest ______________________

כִּפָּה . . . . (kih-pah) . . . . skull cap ______________________

כִּפַּת הַסֶּלַע . . (kih-paht-hah-sel-ah) . . . . Dome of the Rock ______________________

כְּפָר . . . . (kfar) . . . . village ______________________

כְּפַר נָחוּם . . . . (kfar-nah-Hoom) . . . . Capernaum ______________________

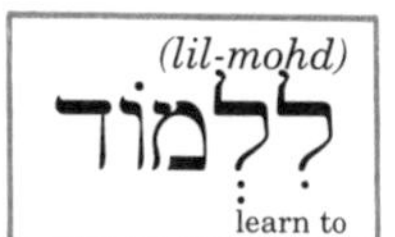

Step 11

You have already used "(roh-tseh) רוֹצֶה want (ah-nee) אֲנִי I" plus "(roh-tsim) רוֹצִים want (ah-naH-noo) אֲנַחְנוּ we". Although you might be able to get by with these verbs, let's assume you want to do better. First a quick review.

How do you say "I" (biv-rit) בְּעִבְרִית? __________ How do you say "we" (biv-rit) בְּעִבְרִית? ______

Learn these (mih-lim) מִלִּים (shiv-ah) שִׁבְעָה on the right (muh-ohd) מְאֹד very well. Use you (♂) when speaking to a man and you (♀) when speaking to a woman. Look for the figures (♂) and (♀) – they will help you remember which form to use.

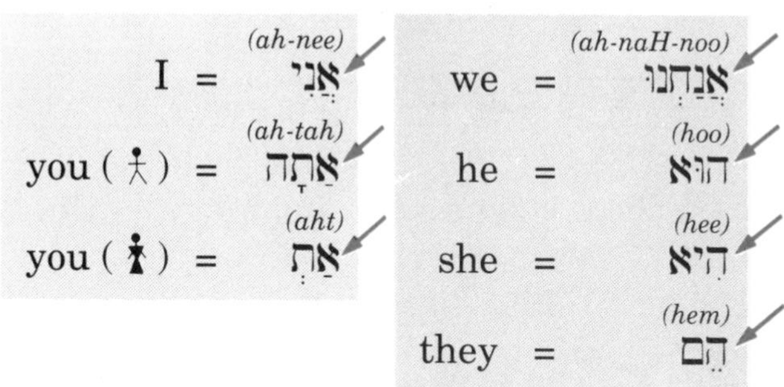

Not too hard, is it? When you're ready to test yourself, draw lines between the matching (ahn-glit) אַנְגְּלִית and (iv-rit) עִבְרִית words below to see if you can keep these (mih-lim) מִלִּים straight in your mind.

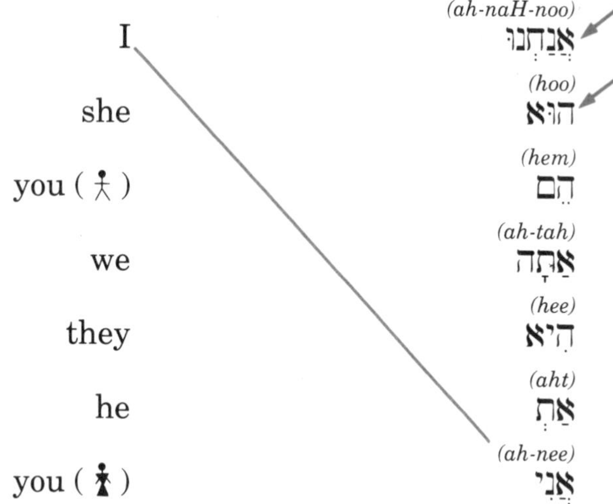

(aH-shahv) עַכְשָׁו close this (sef-er) סֵפֶר and write out both columns of the above practice on (nyar) נְיָר paper. (ayH) אֵיךְ did you do? (tohv) טוֹב good (oh) אוֹ (loh) לֹא not (tohv) טוֹב good? (tohv) טוֹב good (oh) אוֹ (rah) רַע bad? Once you know these (mih-lim) מִלִּים, you can say almost anything (biv-rit) בְּעִבְרִית with one basic formula: the "plug-in" formula. With this formula (ah-tah) אַתָּה you can correctly use any (mih-lim) מִלִּים you wish.

____________	כ	cotton. . . . . (koot-nah) . . . . כּוּתְנָה
____________		ticket. . . . . (kar-tis) . . . . כַּרְטִיס
____________		ticket collector. . . . . (kar-tee-sahn) . . . . כַּרְטִיסָן
____________		Carmel. . . . . (kar-mel) . . . . כַּרְמֶל
____________		kosher. . . . . (kah-sher) . . . . כָּשֵׁר

To demonstrate, let's take *(shih-shah)* שִׁשָּׁה (six) basic וְ practical verbs וְ see how the "plug-in" formula works. Write the verbs in the blanks below after you have practiced saying them.

to speak = *(luh-dah-bair)* לְדַבֵּר	to learn = *(lil-mohd)* לִלְמוֹד	to travel = *(lin-soh-ah)* לִנְסוֹעַ
______________	______________	______________
to come = *(lah-voh)* לָבוֹא	to buy = *(lik-noht)* לִקְנוֹת	to want = *(leer-tsoht)* לִרְצוֹת
לָבוֹא	______________	______________

At first verbs can be overwhelming. In English when we say "I come" we have one way of saying it. *(biv-rit)* בְּעִבְרִית there are two ways, depending on whether you are male (♂) *(oh)* אוֹ female (♀). Study the following pattern carefully. It looks confusing but you only have to learn one form.

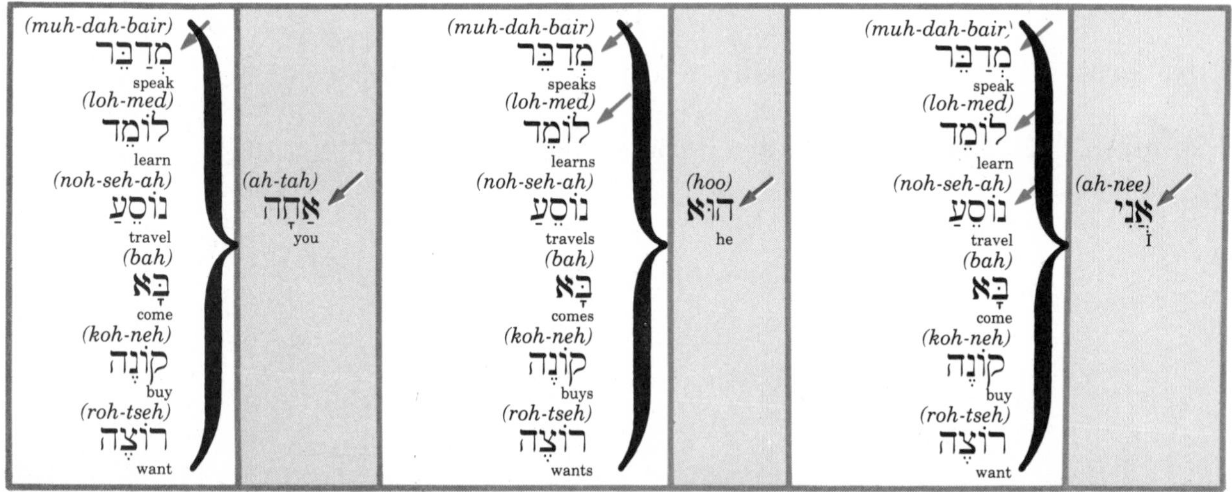

Verb	Pronoun	Verb	Pronoun	Verb	Pronoun
(muh-dah-bair) מְדַבֵּר speak		*(muh-dah-bair)* מְדַבֵּר speaks		*(muh-dah-bair)* מְדַבֵּר speak	
(loh-med) לוֹמֵד learn		*(loh-med)* לוֹמֵד learns		*(loh-med)* לוֹמֵד learn	
(noh-seh-ah) נוֹסֵעַ travel	*(ah-tah)* אַתָּה you	*(noh-seh-ah)* נוֹסֵעַ travels	*(hoo)* הוּא he	*(noh-seh-ah)* נוֹסֵעַ travel	*(ah-nee)* אֲנִי I
(bah) בָּא come		*(bah)* בָּא comes		*(bah)* בָּא come	
(koh-neh) קוֹנֶה buy		*(koh-neh)* קוֹנֶה buys		*(koh-neh)* קוֹנֶה buy	
(roh-tseh) רוֹצֶה want		*(roh-tseh)* רוֹצֶה wants		*(roh-tseh)* רוֹצֶה want	

Note:
- With all these verbs, the first thing you do is drop the first "ל" from the basic verb form.
- Notice that אַתָּה – הוּא – אֲנִי (♂) all use the same verb form so you only need to drill this one form.

There are always some verbs that will not conform to the rules! But don't worry *(yiss-ruh-eh-lim)* יִשְׂרְאֵלִים will be delighted that you have taken the time to learn their language.

	ל		
______________		Lebanon . . . . *(luh-vah-nohn)*	לְבָנוֹן
______________		linen, lingerie. . . . . *(luh-vah-nim)*	לְבָנִים
______________		London. . . . . *(lohn-dohn)*	לוֹנְדוֹן
______________		luxury. . . . . *(look-soos)*	לוּקְסוּס
______________		Latin. . . . . *(lah-tee-neet)*	לָטִינִית

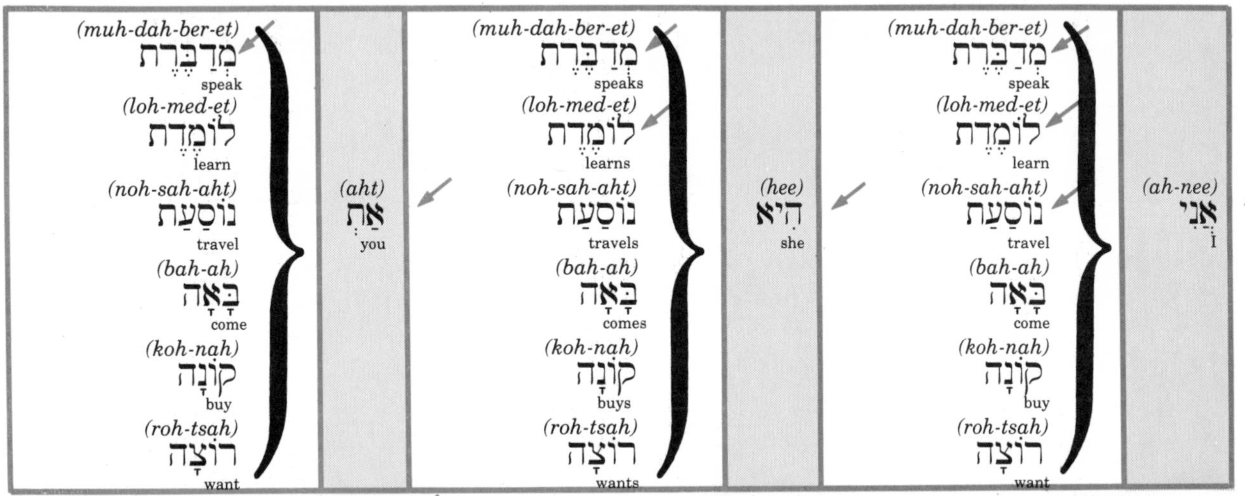

Note: • With אַתְּ – הִיא – אֲנִי ( ) you usually add ה or ת to the end of the masculine form.

• These three all use the same verb form ( ), so learning verbs is much easier for you!

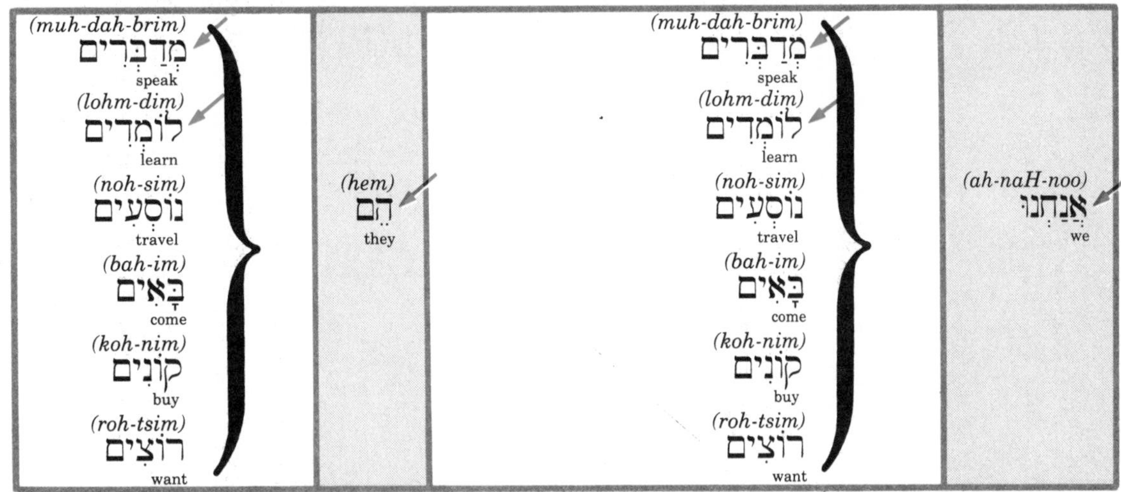

Note: • הֵם and אֲנַחְנוּ use the same verb form. This verb form always ends in ים . Easy, isn't it?

(lil-mohd)
לִלְמוֹד
learn to

(ah-nee) אֲנִי ____לוֹמֵד____ (iv-rit) עִבְרִית.
Hebrew

(hoo) הוּא ____לוֹמֵד____ עִבְרִית.
(ah-tah) אַתָּה

(hee) הִיא ____לוֹמֶדֶת____ עִבְרִית.
(aht) אַתְּ

(ah-naH-noo) אֲנַחְנוּ ____לוֹמְדִים____ עִבְרִית.
(hem) הֵם

(luh-dah-bair)
לְדַבֵּר
speak to

(ah-nee) אֲנִי ____מְדַבֵּר____ (iv-rit) עִבְרִית.

(hoo) הוּא ____מְדַבֵּר____ עִבְרִית.
(ah-tah) אַתָּה

(hee) הִיא ____מְדַבֶּרֶת____ עִבְרִית.
(aht) אַתְּ

(ah-naH-noo) אֲנַחְנוּ ____מְדַבְּרִים____ עִבְרִית.
(hem) הֵם

ל

לִיבֶּרָאלִי	(lee-beh-rah-lee)	liberal
לִיגָה	(lee-gah)	league
לִיטֶר	(lee-tair)	liter
לִימוֹן	(lee-mohn)	lemon
לִימוֹנָדָה	(lee-moh-nah-dah)	lemonade

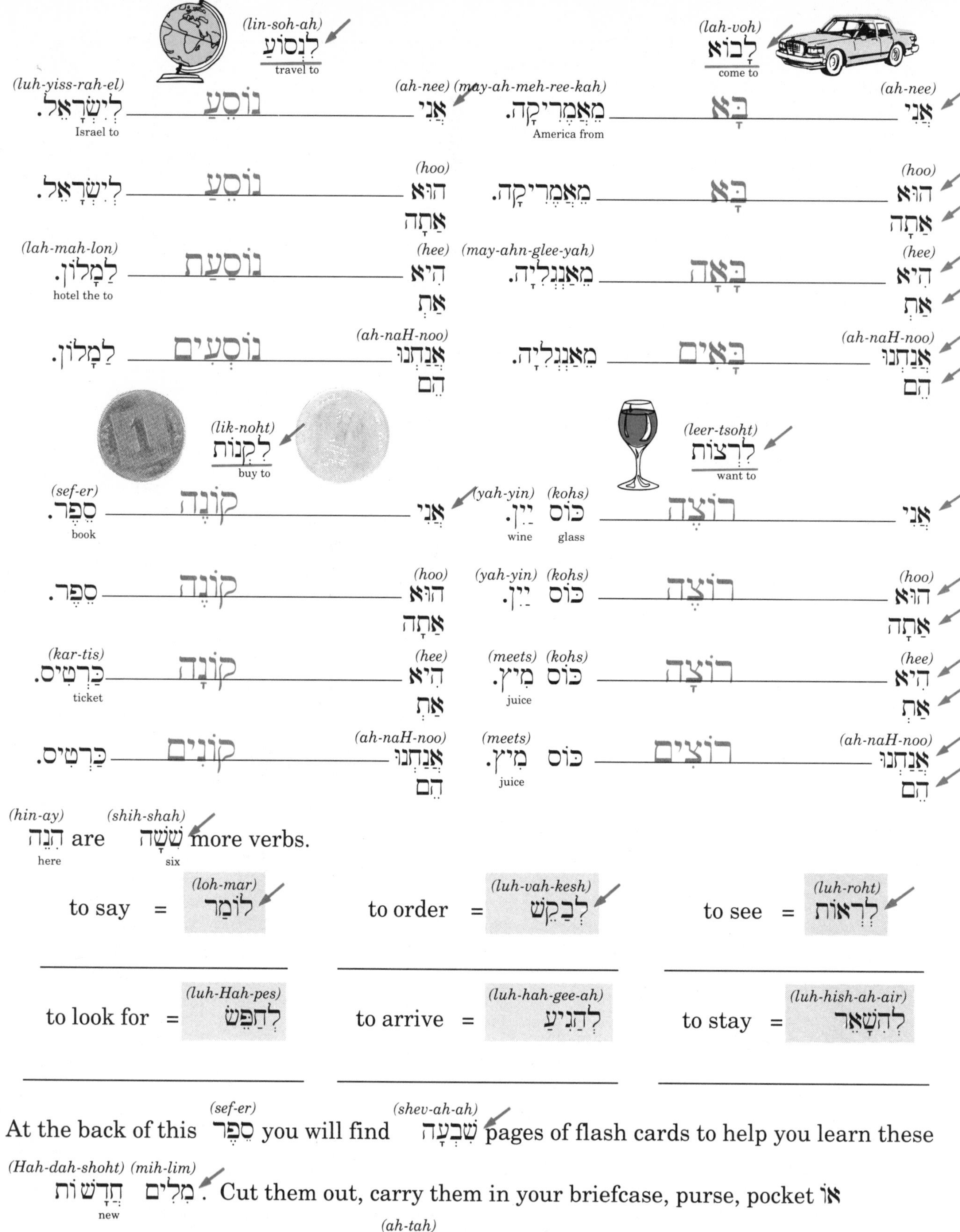

(lah-voh) לָבוֹא — come to

(lin-soh-ah) לִנְסוֹעַ — travel to

(ah-nee) אֲנִי בָּא (may-ah-meh-ree-kah) מֵאָמֶרִיקָה. (America from)	(ah-nee) אֲנִי נוֹסֵעַ (luh-yiss-rah-el) לְיִשְׂרָאֵל. (Israel to)
(hoo) הוּא / אַתָּה בָּא מֵאָמֶרִיקָה.	(hoo) הוּא / אַתָּה נוֹסֵעַ לְיִשְׂרָאֵל.
(hee) הִיא / אַתְּ בָּאָה (may-ahn-glee-yah) מֵאַנְגְלִיָה.	(hee) הִיא / אַתְּ נוֹסַעַת (lah-mah-lon) לַמָּלוֹן. (hotel the to)
(ah-naH-noo) אֲנַחְנוּ / הֵם בָּאִים מֵאַנְגְלִיָה.	(ah-naH-noo) אֲנַחְנוּ / הֵם נוֹסְעִים לַמָּלוֹן.

(leer-tsoht) לִרְצוֹת — want to

(lik-noht) לִקְנוֹת — buy to

אֲנִי רוֹצֶה (kohs) כּוֹס (yah-yin) יַיִן. (glass, wine)	אֲנִי קוֹנֶה (sef-er) סֵפֶר. (book)
(hoo) הוּא / אַתָּה רוֹצֶה (kohs) כּוֹס (yah-yin) יַיִן.	(hoo) הוּא / אַתָּה קוֹנֶה סֵפֶר.
(hee) הִיא / אַתְּ רוֹצָה (kohs) כּוֹס (meets) מִיץ. (juice)	(hee) הִיא / אַתְּ קוֹנָה (kar-tis) כַּרְטִיס. (ticket)
(ah-naH-noo) אֲנַחְנוּ / הֵם רוֹצִים כּוֹס (meets) מִיץ. (juice)	(ah-naH-noo) אֲנַחְנוּ / הֵם קוֹנִים כַּרְטִיס.

(hin-ay) הִנֵּה (here) are (shih-shah) שִׁשָּׁה (six) more verbs.

to say = (loh-mar) לוֹמַר	to order = (luh-vah-kesh) לְבַקֵּשׁ	to see = (luh-roht) לִרְאוֹת
to look for = (luh-Hah-pes) לְחַפֵּשׂ	to arrive = (luh-hah-gee-ah) לְהַגִּיעַ	to stay = (luh-hish-ah-air) לְהִשָּׁאֵר

At the back of this (sef-er) סֵפֶר you will find (shev-ah-ah) שִׁבְעָה pages of flash cards to help you learn these (mih-lim) מִלִּים (Hah-dah-shoht) חֲדָשׁוֹת (new). Cut them out, carry them in your briefcase, purse, pocket אוֹ knapsack, וְ review them whenever (ah-tah) אַתָּה have a free moment.

מ

tower	(mig-dahl)	מִגְדָּל
Tower of David	(mig-dahl-dah-vid)	מִגְדָּל דָּוִד
control tower	(mig-dahl-pih-koo-aH)	מִגְדָּל פִּקּוּחַ
scroll	(muh-gee-lah)	מְגִילָּה
Dead Sea Scrolls	(muh-gee-loht-yahm-hah-mel-aH)	מְגִילּוֹת יָם הַמֶּלַח

עַכְשָׁו fill in the following blanks (im) עִם the correct form of each verb. Be sure to say each sentence out loud until (ah-tah) אַתָּה have it down pat!

(luh-vah-kesh) לְבַקֵּשׁ
order to

(ah-nee) אֲנִי ___מְבַקֵּשׁ___ (kohs) כּוֹס (mah-yim) מַיִם.
water

(hoo) הוּא / אַתָּה ___מְבַקֵּשׁ___ כּוֹס (meets) מִיץ.

(hee) הִיא / אַתְּ ___מְבַקֶּשֶׁת___ כּוֹס (Hah-lahv) חָלָב.

(ah-naH-noo) אֲנַחְנוּ / הֵם ___מְבַקְשִׁים___ כּוֹס (yah-yin) יַיִן.

(loh-mar) לוֹמַר
say to

אֲנִי ___אוֹמֵר___ (shah-lom) שָׁלוֹם.

(hoo) הוּא / אַתָּה ___אוֹמֵר___ שָׁלוֹם.

(hee) הִיא / אַתְּ ___אוֹמֶרֶת___ (boh-ker) בֹּקֶר (tohv) טוֹב.
morning good

(ah-naH-noo) אֲנַחְנוּ / הֵם ___אוֹמְרִים___ (boh-ker) בֹּקֶר (tohv) טוֹב.

(luh-Hah-pes) לְחַפֵּשׂ
for look to

אֲנִי ___מְחַפֵּשׂ___ (sef-er) סֵפֶר.
book

(hoo) הוּא / אַתָּה ___מְחַפֵּשׂ___ (mah-lon) מָלוֹן.
hotel

(hee) הִיא / אַתְּ ___מְחַפֶּשֶׂת___ (oh-toh-boos) אוֹטוֹבּוּס.

(ah-naH-noo) אֲנַחְנוּ / הֵם ___מְחַפְּשִׂים___ (bahnk) בַּנְק.

(luh-roht) לִרְאוֹת
see to

אֲנִי ___רוֹאֶה___ (sef-er) סֵפֶר.

הוּא / אַתָּה ___רוֹאֶה___ (mah-lon) מָלוֹן.

הִיא / אַתְּ ___רוֹאָה___ (muh-Hoh-nit) מְכוֹנִית.

אֲנַחְנוּ / הֵם ___רוֹאִים___ (bahnk) בַּנְק.

(luh-hish-ah-air) לְהִשָּׁאֵר
stay to

אֲנִי ___נִשְׁאָר___ (buh-yiss-rah-el) בְּיִשְׂרָאֵל.
Israel in

(hoo) הוּא / אַתָּה ___נִשְׁאָר___ (buh-tel) בְּתֵל (ah-veev) אָבִיב.
Tel in Aviv

(hee) הִיא / אַתְּ ___נִשְׁאֶרֶת___ (bee-roo-shah-lah-yim) בִּירוּשָׁלַיִם.
Jerusalem in

(ah-naH-noo) אֲנַחְנוּ / הֵם ___נִשְׁאָרִים___ (buh-ay-roh-pah) בְּאֵירוֹפָּה.
Europe in

(luh-hah-gee-ah) לְהַגִּיעַ
arrive to

אֲנִי ___מַגִּיעַ___ (buh-yiss-rah-el) בְּיִשְׂרָאֵל.

הוּא / אַתָּה ___מַגִּיעַ___ (buh-tel) בְּתֵל (ah-veev) אָבִיב.

הִיא / אַתְּ ___מַגִּיעָה___ (bee-roo-shah-lah-yim) בִּירוּשָׁלַיִם.

אֲנַחְנוּ / הֵם ___מַגִּיעִים___ (buh-Hay-fah) בְּחֵיפָה.
Haifa in

מ

desert. . . . .(mid-bar) . . . . מִדְבָּר
sidewalk. . . . .(mid-rah-Hah) . . . . מִדְרָכָה.
museum. . . . . (moo-zay-on) . . . . מוּזֵיאוֹן
Islam Museum. . . . .(moo-zay-on-hah-iss-lahm) . . מוּזֵיאוֹן הָאִסְלָאם.
Israel Museum. . . . . . .(moo-zay-on-yiss-rah-el). . . . מוּזֵיאוֹן יִשְׂרָאֵל.

(aH-shahv) עַכְשָׁו take a deep breath. See if (ah-tah) אַתָּה can fill in the blanks (luh-mah-tah) לְמַטָּה (below). The correct (tshoo-voht) תְּשׁוּבוֹת (answers) are at the bottom of this (ah-mood) עַמּוּד.

1. I (♀) speak Hebrew. ________________

2. He comes from America. ________________

3. We learn Hebrew. ________________

4. You (♂) arrive in Israel. ________________

5. She wants a glass of juice. ________________

6. We look for a hotel. ________________

7. I (♂) stay in Tel Aviv. ________________

8. He says "Shalom." ________________

9. You (♀) buy a book. אַתְּ קוֹנָה סֵפֶר.

10. He orders a glass of juice. ________________

(ken) כֵּן, it is hard to get used to all those new (mih-lim) מִלִּים. But just keep it up וְ before (ah-tah) אַתָּה know it, you'll be using them naturally.

In the following Steps, אַתָּה will be introduced to more וְ more verbs וְ you should drill them in exactly the same way as אַתָּה did in this section. Look up the new מִלִּים in your (mih-lon) מִלּוֹן (dictionary) and make up your own sentences using the same type of pattern. Try out your new (mih-lim) מִלִּים for that's how אַתָּה make them yours to use on your holiday. Remember, the more אַתָּה practice (aH-shahv) עַכְשָׁו, the more enjoyable your trip will be. (buh-hahts-lah-Hah) בְּהַצְלָחָה! (luck good)

עַכְשָׁו is a perfect time to turn to the back of this (sef-er) סֵפֶר, clip out your verb flash cards וְ start flashing. Be sure to check off your free (mih-lim) מִלִּים in the box provided as (ah-tah) אַתָּה (you) (loh-med) לוֹמֵד (learn) each one.

הַתְּשׁוּבוֹת

1. אֲנִי מְדַבֶּרֶת עִבְרִית.
2. הוּא בָּא מֵאֲמֶרִיקָה.
3. אֲנַחְנוּ לוֹמְדִים עִבְרִית.
4. אַתָּה מַגִּיעַ לְיִשְׂרָאֵל.
5. הִיא רוֹצָה כּוֹס מִיץ.
6. אֲנַחְנוּ מְחַפְּשִׂים מָלוֹן.
7. אֲנִי נִשְׁאָר בְּתֵל אָבִיב.
8. הוּא אוֹמֵר "שָׁלוֹם."
9. אַתְּ קוֹנָה סֵפֶר.
10. הוּא מְבַקֵּשׁ כּוֹס מִיץ.

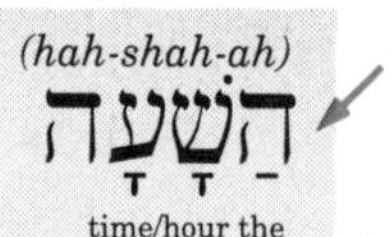

Step 12

אַתָּה know אֵיךְ (ayH) how to tell הַיָּמִים (hah-yah-mim) days the of הַשָּׁבוּעַ (hah-shah-voo-ah) week the and הֶחֳדָשִׁים (hah-Hoh-dash-im) months the of הַשָּׁנָה (hah-shah-nah) year the, so now let's learn to tell time. As a traveler בְּיִשְׂרָאֵל (buh-yiss-rah-el) you need to be able to tell time in order to make reservations and to catch אוֹטוֹבּוּסִים (oh-toh-boos-im) buses. Here are the "basics."

(hah-shah-ah)(mah) מָה הַשָּׁעָה?	=	What time is it?
לִפְנֵי, לִפְנֵי, לִפְנֵי — (luh) לְ or (lif-nay) לִפְנֵי	=	before
(ah-Hah-ray) אַחֲרֵי	=	after
(vah-Het-see) וָחֵצִי	=	half past

(shesh)(hah-shah-ah) הַשָּׁעָה שֵׁשׁ. (hour the, six)

(Hah-mesh)(hah-shah-ah) הַשָּׁעָה חָמֵשׁ. (hour the, five)

5:40 = (luh-shesh)(es-rim)(hah-shah-ah) הַשָּׁעָה עֶשְׂרִים לְשֵׁשׁ (hour the, twenty, six before)

5:10 = (vuh-es-er)(Hah-mesh)(hah-shah-ah) הַשָּׁעָה חָמֵשׁ וְעֶשֶׂר (hour the, five, ten and)

5:50 = (luh-shesh)(es-er)(hah-shah-ah) הַשָּׁעָה עֶשֶׂר לְשֵׁשׁ (ten, six before)

5:20 = (vuh-es-rim)(Hah-mesh)(hah-shah-ah) הַשָּׁעָה חָמֵשׁ וְעֶשְׂרִים (five, twenty and)

5:55 = (luh-shesh)(Hah-mesh) הַשָּׁעָה חָמֵשׁ לְשֵׁשׁ (five)

5:30 = (vah-Het-see)(Hah-mesh) הַשָּׁעָה חָמֵשׁ וָחֵצִי (half past)

עַכְשָׁו (aH-shahv) fill in the blanks according to הַשָּׁעָה indicated on הַשְּׁעוֹנִים (hah-shoh-nim) clocks the. הַתְּשׁוּבוֹת (hah-tshoo-voht) answers the are below.

1. ______________.

2. ______________.

3. ______________.

4. ______________.

5. ______________.

6. ______________.

7. ______________.

8. ______________.

הַתְּשׁוּבוֹת

1. הַשָּׁעָה עֶשֶׂר וָעֶשֶׂר.
2. הַשָּׁעָה עֶשְׂרִים אַחֲרֵי שְׁתַּיִם.
3. הַשָּׁעָה שֶׁבַע וָחֵצִי.
4. הַשָּׁעָה עֶשְׂרִים לְשָׁלוֹשׁ.
5. הַשָּׁעָה שֵׁשׁ וְחָמֵשׁ.
6. הַשָּׁעָה עֶשֶׂר לִשְׁמוֹנֶה.
7. הַשָּׁעָה אַרְבַּע וָחֵצִי.
8. הַשָּׁעָה חָמֵשׁ.

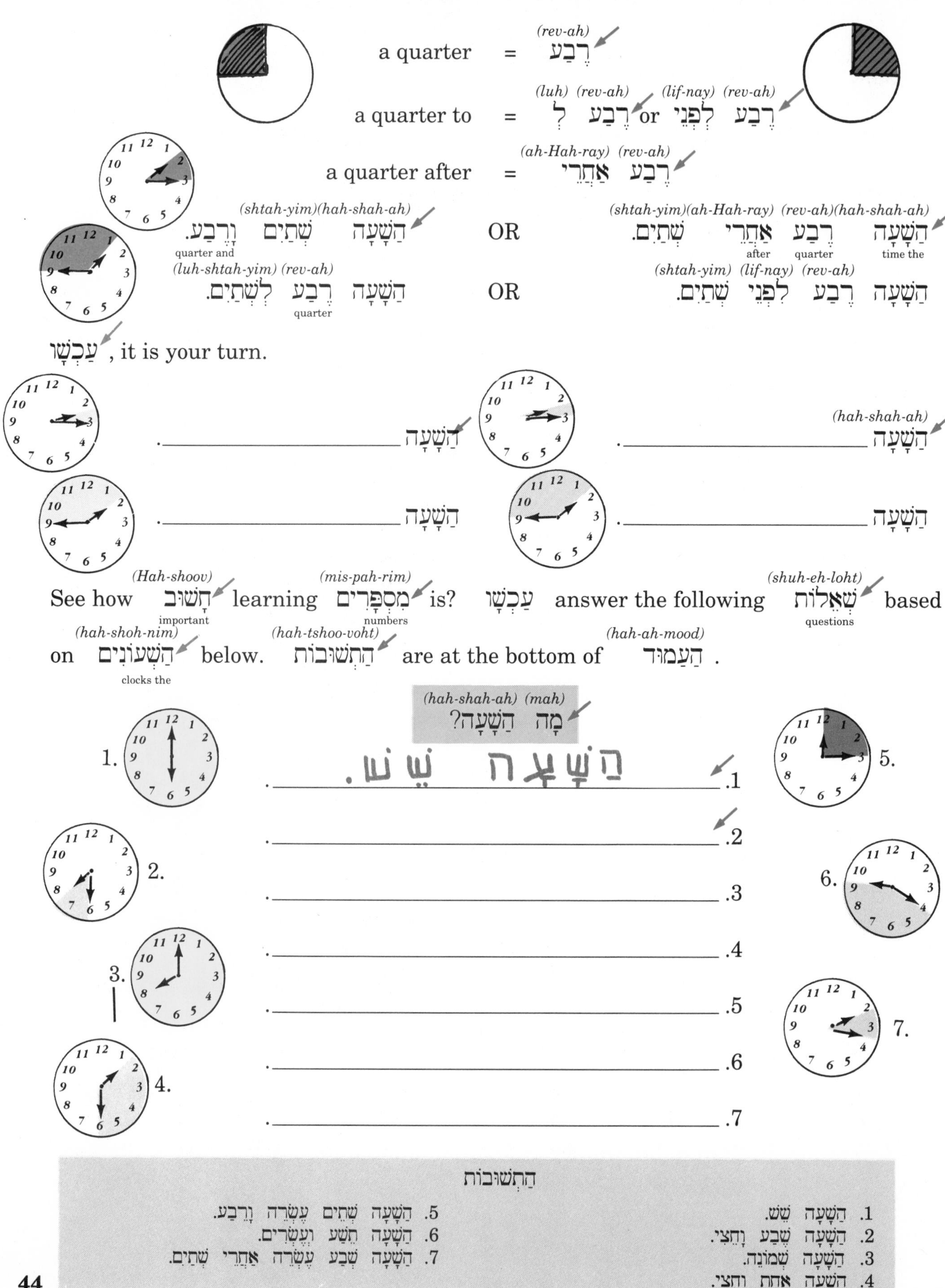

(hin-ay) הִנֵּה are more time-telling (mih-lim) מִלִּים to add to your vocabulary.

a quarter = (rev-ah) רֶבַע

a quarter to = (luh) (rev-ah) רֶבַע לְ or (lif-nay) (rev-ah) רֶבַע לִפְנֵי

a quarter after = (ah-Hah-ray) (rev-ah) רֶבַע אַחֲרֵי

(shtah-yim)(hah-shah-ah) הַשָּׁעָה שְׁתַּיִם וָרֶבַע. (quarter and) OR (shtah-yim)(ah-Hah-ray) (rev-ah)(hah-shah-ah) הַשָּׁעָה רֶבַע אַחֲרֵי שְׁתַּיִם. (time the / quarter / after)

(luh-shtah-yim) (rev-ah) הַשָּׁעָה רֶבַע לִשְׁתַּיִם. (quarter) OR (shtah-yim) (lif-nay) (rev-ah) הַשָּׁעָה רֶבַע לִפְנֵי שְׁתַּיִם.

עַכְשָׁו, it is your turn.

(hah-shah-ah) הַשָּׁעָה __________________.

הַשָּׁעָה __________________.

הַשָּׁעָה __________________.

הַשָּׁעָה __________________.

See how (Hah-shoov) חָשׁוּב (important) learning (mis-pah-rim) מִסְפָּרִים (numbers) is? עַכְשָׁו answer the following (shuh-eh-loht) שְׁאֵלוֹת (questions) based on (hah-shoh-nim) הַשְּׁעוֹנִים (clocks the) below. (hah-tshoo-voht) הַתְּשׁוּבוֹת are at the bottom of (hah-ah-mood) הָעַמּוּד.

(hah-shah-ah) (mah) מָה הַשָּׁעָה?

1. הַשָּׁעָה שֵׁשׁ.
2. __________________.
3. __________________.
4. __________________.
5. __________________.
6. __________________.
7. __________________.

הַתְּשׁוּבוֹת

1. הַשָּׁעָה שֵׁשׁ.
2. הַשָּׁעָה שֶׁבַע וָחֵצִי.
3. הַשָּׁעָה שְׁמוֹנֶה.
4. הַשָּׁעָה אַחַת וָחֵצִי.
5. הַשָּׁעָה שְׁתֵּים עֶשְׂרֵה וָרֶבַע.
6. הַשָּׁעָה תֵּשַׁע וְעֶשְׂרִים.
7. הַשָּׁעָה שְׁבַע עֶשְׂרֵה אַחֲרֵי שְׁתַּיִם.

When אַתָּה answer a (mah-tie) מָתַי (when) question, say (buh) בְּ (at) before אַתָּה give the time.

אוֹטוֹבּוּס
18:00

(bah)(mah-tie) מָתַי בָּא (comes) הָאוֹטוֹבּוּס? בְּשָׁעָה שֵׁשׁ.

עַכְשָׁו answer the following (shuh-eh-loht) שְׁאֵלוֹת (questions) based on (hah-shoh-nim) הַשְּׁעוֹנִים (clocks the) below. Be sure to practice saying each (sheh-lah) שְׁאֵלָה (question) out loud several times.

(hah-kohn-tsairt)(mah-tie) מָתַי (is) when) הַקּוֹנְצֶרְט (concert the)? ______ בְּ

(hah-oh-toh-boos)(mah-gee-ah)(mah-tie) מָתַי מַגִּיעַ (arrives) הָאוֹטוֹבּוּס? ______ בְּ

(ptoo-Hah)(hah-mis-ah-dah)(mah-tie) מָתַי הַמִּסְעָדָה (restaurant the) פְּתוּחָה (open)? ______ בְּ

(sgoo-rah) מָתַי הַמִּסְעָדָה סְגוּרָה (closed)? ______

(pah-too-aH)(hah-moo-zay-on) מָתַי הַמּוּזֵיאוֹן (museum the) פָּתוּחַ (open)? ______

(sah-goor)(hah-moo-zay-on) מָתַי הַמּוּזֵיאוֹן סָגוּר (closed)? ______

(ohm-rim)(bah-boh-ker)(shmoh-neh)(buh-shah-ah) בְּשָׁעָה שְׁמוֹנֶה בַּבֹּקֶר (morning the in) אוֹמְרִים,

(leh-vee)(gveh-ret)(tohv)(boh-ker) "בֹּקֶר טוֹב, גְּבֶרֶת (Mrs.) לֵוִי (Levy)!"

(ohm-rim)(bah-eh-rev)(shmoh-neh)(buh-shah-ah) בְּשָׁעָה (hour at) שְׁמוֹנֶה (eight) בָּעֶרֶב (evening the in) אוֹמְרִים (say (we)),

(har-el)(mahr)(tohv)(eh-rev) "עֶרֶב טוֹב, מַר (Mr.) הַרְאֵל (Harel)!"

(ohm-rim)(bah-lie-lah)(es-er)(buh-shah-ah) בְּשָׁעָה עֶשֶׂר בַּלַּיְלָה אוֹמְרִים,

(mee-Hahl)(tohv)(lie-lah) "לַיְלָה טוֹב, מִיכַל!"

(ohm-rim)(shah-baht)(buh-yom) בְּיוֹם (on) שַׁבָּת (Saturday) אוֹמְרִים,

(shah-lohm)(shah-baht) "שַׁבָּת שָׁלוֹם!"

מ

______	music.	(moo-see-kah)	מוּסִיקָה
______	Moses.	(moh-sheh)	מֹשֶׁה
______	Muhammed.	(moo-Hah-mahd)	מוּחָמַד
______	cooperative farm/moshav.	(moh-shahv)	מוֹשָׁב
______	orchard.	(mah-tah)	מַטָּע

Remember:

What time is it? = מָה הַשָּׁעָה? *(mah) (hah-shah-ah)*

When? = מָתַי *(mah-tie)*

Can אַתָּה pronounce וְ understand the following paragraph?

(buh-shah-losh) (mah-gee-ah) (mee-Hay-fah)
הָאוֹטוֹבּוּס מֵחֵיפָה מַגִּיעַ בְּשָׁלֹשׁ.
arrives — Haifa from

(mah-gee-ah) (vuh-es-rim)(shah-losh)
עַכְשָׁו שָׁלֹשׁ וְעֶשְׂרִים. הָאוֹטוֹבּוּס מַגִּיעַ
arrives

(mah-Har) (vah-Het-see) (Hah-mesh)(buh-shah-ah)(hah-yom)
הַיּוֹם בְּשָׁעָה חָמֵשׁ וָחֵצִי. מָחָר
tomorrow — past half — today

(buh-shah-losh) (mah-gee-ah)
הָאוֹטוֹבּוּס מַגִּיעַ בְּשָׁלֹשׁ.

הִנֵּה are some more practice exercises. Answer הַשְּׁאֵלוֹת *(hah-shuh-eh-loht)* based on הַשָּׁעוֹת *(hah-shah-oht)* (times the) given לְמַטָּה *(luh-mah-tah)* (below).

מָה הַשָּׁעָה? *(mah) (hah-shah-ah)*

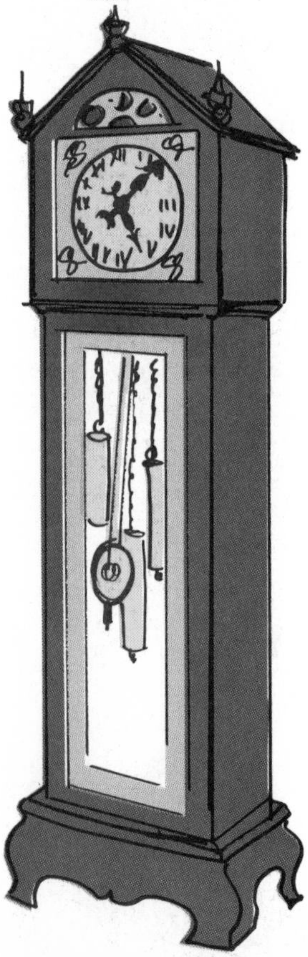

1. (10:30) ______________________
2. (6:30) ______________________
3. (2:15) ______________________
4. (11:40) ______________________
5. (12:18) ______________________
6. (7:20) ______________________
7. (3:10) ______________________
8. (4:05) ______________________
9. (5:35) ______________________
10. (11:50) ______________________

מ

מֶטֶר	*(met-air)*	meter
מִילְק שֵׁייק	*(milk-shake)*	milkshake
מַיִם	*(mah-yim)*	water
מַפַּל מַיִם	*(mah-pahl-mah-yim)*	waterfall
מִינִימוּם	*(mee-nee-moom)*	minimum

הִנֵּה is a quick quiz. Fill in the blanks with the correct מִסְפָּרִים (mis-pah-rim) numbers. הַתְּשׁוּבוֹת (hah-tshoo-voht) are below.

1. בְּדַקָּה (buh-dah-kah) minute in יֵשׁ (yesh) (are) there ________ (?) שְׁנִיּוֹת. (shnee-yoht) seconds

2. בְּשָׁעָה (buh-shah-ah) hour in יֵשׁ (yesh) (are) there ________ (?) דַּקּוֹת. (dah-koht) minutes

3. בְּיוֹם (buh-yom) day in יֵשׁ ________ (?) שָׁעוֹת. (shah-oht) hours

4. בְּשָׁבוּעַ (buh-shah-voo-ah) week in יֵשׁ ________ (?) יָמִים. (yah-mim) days

5. בְּחוֹדֶשׁ (buh-Hoh-desh) month in יֵשׁ (yesh) (are) there ________ (?) יָמִים. (yah-mim) days

6. בְּשָׁנָה (buh-shah-nah) year in יֵשׁ (yesh) ________ (?) חוֹדָשִׁים. (Hoh-dah-shim) months

7. בְּשָׁנָה (buh-shah-nah) יֵשׁ ________ (?) שָׁבוּעוֹת. (shah-voo-oht) weeks

8. בְּשָׁנָה (buh-shah-nah) יֵשׁ ________ (?) יָמִים. (yah-mim) days

הִנֵּה is a sample עַמּוּד (ah-mood) from a אוֹטוֹבּוּס (oh-toh-boos) schedule.

(mah-gee-ah) מַגִּיעַ arrives	אוֹטוֹבּוּס	(yoh-tseh) יוֹצֵא departs
8:50	**50**	8:00
9:05	**19**	8:15
9:20	**10**	8:30
9:35	**4**	8:45
9:50	**22**	9:00

Table title: (yuh-roo-shah-lah-yim) יְרוּשָׁלַיִם — (ah-veev) (tel) תֵּל אָבִיב

Note: • All those dots and dashes known as vowels are only used to help you when you first begin to learn Hebrew. When you arrive in Israel you will see these same familiar words but without most of the dots and dashes.

הַתְּשׁוּבוֹת

1. שִׁשִּׁים
2. שִׁשִּׁים
3. עֶשְׂרִים וְאַרְבַּע
4. שִׁבְעָה
5. שְׁלֹשִׁים
6. שְׁנֵים עָשָׂר
7. חֲמִשִּׁים וּשְׁנַיִם
8. שְׁלֹשׁ מֵאוֹת שִׁשִּׁים וַחֲמִשָּׁה

(hin-ay)
הִנֵּה are the new verbs for Step 12.
here

to live/reside = לָגוּר (lah-goor) to eat = לֶאֱכֹל (leh-eh-Hohl) to drink = לִשְׁתּוֹת (lish-toht)

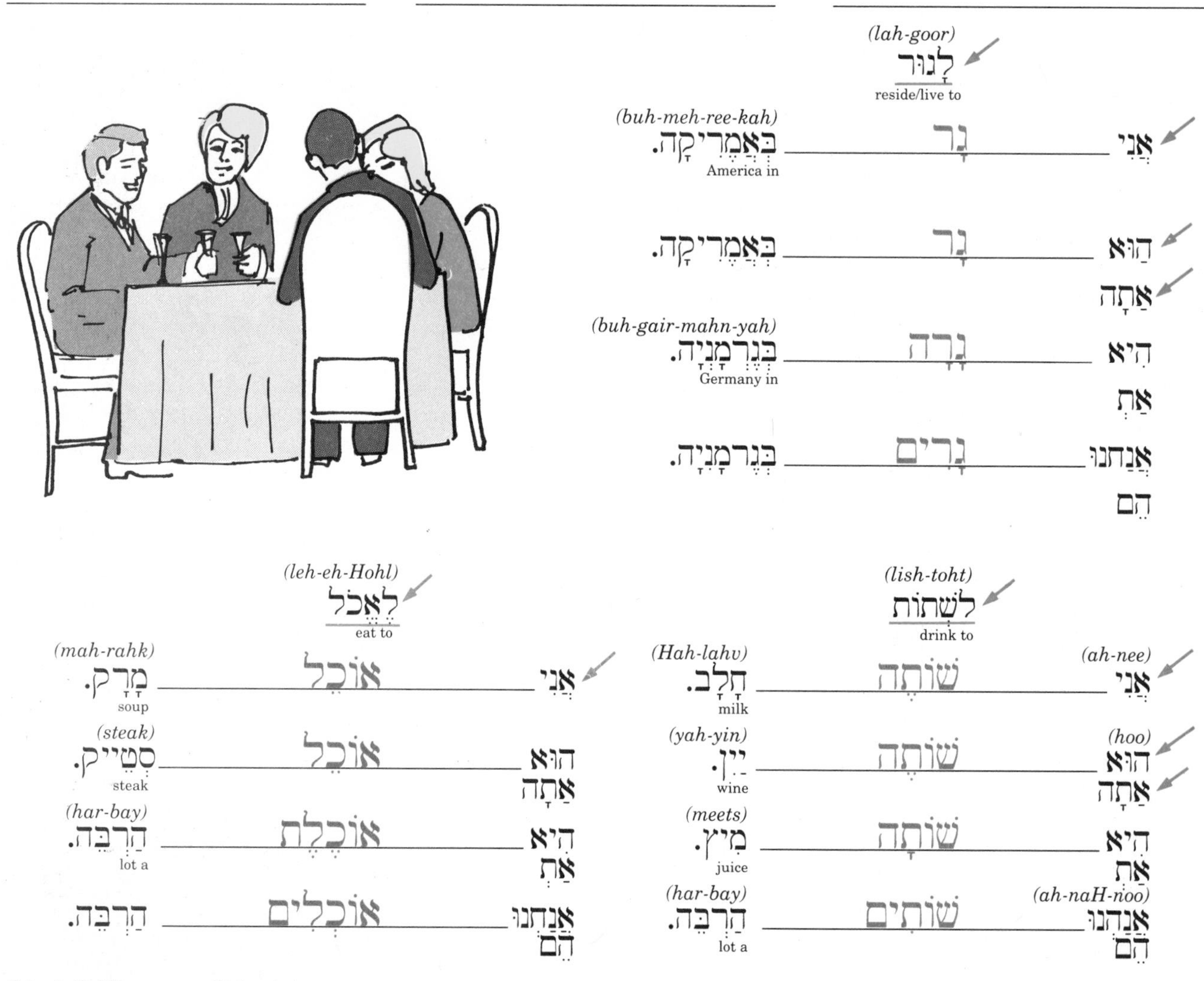

לָגוּר (lah-goor)
reside/live to

אֲנִי ______ גָּר ______ בְּאָמֶרִיקָה. (buh-meh-ree-kah) America in
הוּא ______ גָּר ______ בְּאָמֶרִיקָה.
אַתָּה
הִיא ______ גָּרָה ______ בְּגֶרְמַנְיָה. (buh-gair-mahn-yah) Germany in
אַתְּ
אֲנַחְנוּ ______ גָּרִים ______ בְּגֶרְמַנְיָה.
הֵם

לֶאֱכֹל (leh-eh-Hohl)
eat to

אֲנִי ______ אוֹכֵל ______ מָרָק. (mah-rahk) soup
הוּא ______ אוֹכֵל ______ סְטֵייק. (steak) steak
אַתָּה
הִיא ______ אוֹכֶלֶת ______ הַרְבֵּה. (har-bay) lot a
אַתְּ
אֲנַחְנוּ ______ אוֹכְלִים ______ הַרְבֵּה.
הֵם

לִשְׁתּוֹת (lish-toht)
drink to

אֲנִי (ah-nee) ______ שׁוֹתֶה ______ חָלָב. (Hah-lahv) milk
הוּא (hoo) ______ שׁוֹתֶה ______ יַיִן. (yah-yin) wine
אַתָּה
הִיא ______ שׁוֹתָה ______ מִיץ. (meets) juice
אַתְּ
אֲנַחְנוּ (ah-naH-noo) ______ שׁוֹתִים ______ הַרְבֵּה. (har-bay) lot a
הֵם

לֶאֱכֹל (leh-oh-Hohl) and לִשְׁתּוֹת (lish-toht) will be very important for you during your stay בְּיִשְׂרָאֵל (buh-yiss-rah-el). Learn them well! If אַתָּה are visiting יִשְׂרָאֵל on a special occasion, אַתָּה may want to use one of the following greetings.

Congratulations!	=	מַזָּל (mah-zahl) טוֹב! (tohv)
Good Sabbath!	=	שַׁבָּת (shah-baht) שָׁלוֹם! (shah-lom)
Happy Holiday!	=	חַג (Hahg) שָׂמֵחַ! (sah-may-aH)
Happy New Year!	=	שָׁנָה (shah-nah) טוֹבָה! (toh-vah)

מ

mechanic	(muh-Hoh-nah-ee)	מְכוֹנַאי
dirty	(muh-looH-laH)	מְלוּכְלָךְ
million	(mee-lee-yohn)	מִלְיוֹן
millionair	(mee-lee-oh-nair)	מִילְיוֹנֶר
missionary	(mees-yoh-nair)	מִסְיוֹנֶר

(tmoo-nah) תְּמוּנָה	(sah-lon) סָלוֹן	(tay-shah) תֵּשַׁע 9	(tohv) (eh-rev) עֶרֶב טוֹב
(tik-rah) תִּקְרָה	(moo-saH) מוּסָךְ	(es-er) עֶשֶׂר 10	(tohv) (lie-lah) לַיְלָה טוֹב
(pee-nah) פִּינָה	(mar-tef) מַרְתֵּף	(lah-vahn) לָבָן	(shah-lom) שָׁלוֹם
(Hah-lon) חַלּוֹן	(muh-Hoh-nit) מְכוֹנִית	(shah-Hor) שָׁחוֹר	(luh-hih-trah-oht) לְהִתְרָאוֹת
(mnoh-rah) מְנוֹרָה	(oh-fah-nah-yim) אוֹפַנַּיִם	(tsah-hohv) צָהוֹב	(muh-kah-reer) מְקָרֵר
(or) אוֹר	(kel-ev) כֶּלֶב	(ah-dohm) אָדוֹם	(tah-noor) תַּנּוּר
(sah-pah) סַפָּה	(Hah-tool) חָתוּל	(kah-Hohl) כָּחוֹל	(yah-yin) יַיִן
(kis-eh) כִּסֵּא	(gahn) גַּן	(ah-for) אָפוֹר	(meets) מִיץ
(shah-tee-aH) שָׁטִיחַ	(doh-ar) דּוֹאַר	(Hoom) חוּם	(Hah-lahv) חָלָב
(shool-Hahn) שׁוּלְחָן	(doh-ar) (tay-vaht) תֵּיבַת דּוֹאַר	(yah-rok) יָרוֹק	(Hem-ah) חֶמְאָה
(del-et) דֶּלֶת	(praH-im) פְּרָחִים	(vah-rohd) וָרוֹד	(tsah-lah-Haht) צַלַּחַת
(shah-on) שָׁעוֹן	(pah-ah-mon) פַּעֲמוֹן	(kah-tohm) כָּתוֹם	(mel-aH) מֶלַח
(vee-lon) וִילוֹן	(aH-aht) אַחַת 1	(rih-shon) (yom) יוֹם רִאשׁוֹן	(pil-pel) פִּלְפֵּל
(keer) קִיר	(shtah-yim) שְׁתַּיִם 2	(sheh-nee) (yom) יוֹם שֵׁנִי	(sah-keen) סַכִּין
(bah-yit) בַּיִת	(shah-losh) שָׁלֹשׁ 3	(shlee-shee) (yom) יוֹם שְׁלִישִׁי	(sef-el) סֵפֶל
(ah-voh-dah) (Hah-dar) חֲדַר עֲבוֹדָה	(ar-bah) אַרְבַּע 4	(ruh-veh-ee) (yom) יוֹם רְבִיעִי	(mahz-leg) מַזְלֵג
(ahm-baht-yah) (Hah-dar) חֲדַר אַמְבַּטְיָה	(Hah-mesh) חָמֵשׁ 5	(Hah-mish-ee) (yom) יוֹם חֲמִישִׁי	(kohs) כּוֹס
(mit-baH) מִטְבָּח	(shesh) שֵׁשׁ 6	(shee-shee) (yom) יוֹם שִׁשִּׁי	(mah-peet) מַפִּית
(shay-nah) (Hah-dar) חֲדַר שֵׁינָה	(sheh-vah) שֶׁבַע 7	(shah-baht) (yom) יוֹם שַׁבָּת	(kah-peet) כַּפִּית
(oh-Hel) (Hah-dar) חֲדַר אֹכֶל	(shmoh-neh) שְׁמוֹנֶה 8	(tohv) (boh-ker) בֹּקֶר טוֹב	(ah-ron) אָרוֹן

STICKY LABELS

This book has over 150 special sticky labels for you to use as you learn new words. When you are introduced to a word, remove the corresponding label from these pages. Be sure to use each of these unique labels by adhering them to a picture, window, lamp, or whatever object it refers to. The sticky labels make learning to speak Hebrew much more fun and a lot easier than you ever expected.

For example, when you look in the mirror and see the label, say

(ruh-ee)
"רְאִי".

Don't say it just once, say it again and again.
And once you label the refrigerator, you should never again open that door without saying

By using the sticky labels, you not only learn new words but friends and family learn along with you!

(leh-Hem) לֶחֶם	(it-on) עִתּוֹן	(muh-eel) מְעִיל	(Hool-tsah) חוּלְצָה
(tay) תֵּה	(mish-kah-fah-yim) מִשְׁקָפַיִם	(gesh-em) (muh-eel) מְעִיל גֶּשֶׁם	(Hah-tsah-it) חֲצָאִית
(kah-feh) קָפֶה	(tel-eh-vee-zee-yah) טֶלֶוִויזְיָה	(mit-ree-aH) מִטְרִיָּה	(sved-air) סְוֶדֶר
(mee-tah) מִיטָה	(nyar-oht) (sahl) סַל נְיָרוֹת	(kfah-foht) כְּפָפוֹת	(Hah-zee-yah) חֲזִיָּה
(smee-Hah) שְׂמִיכָה	(dar-kon) דַּרְכּוֹן	(koh-vah) כּוֹבַע	(taH-toh-nit) תַּחְתּוֹנִית
(kar) כַּר	(kar-tees) כַּרְטִיס	(mah-gah-fah-yim) מַגָּפַיִם	(taH-toh-nim) תַּחְתּוֹנִים
(muh-oh-reer) (shah-on) שָׁעוֹן מְעוֹרֵר	(miz-vah-dah) מִזְוָדָה	(nah-ah-lah-yim) נַעֲלַיִם	(goo-fee-yah) גוּפִיָּה
(kee-yor) כִּיּוֹר	(teek) תִּיק	(gar-bah-yim) גַּרְבַּיִם	(teh-leh-fohn) טֶלֶפוֹן
(mik-lah-Haht) מִקְלַחַת	(kes-ef) (ar-nahk) אַרְנָק כֶּסֶף	(gar-bee-oh-nim) גַּרְבִּיוֹנִים	(jah-ket) ז׳קֶט
(shim-oosh) (bait) בֵּית שִׁמּוּשׁ	(kes-ef) כֶּסֶף	(pee-jah-mah) פִּיגָ׳מָה	(miH-nah-sah-yim) מִכְנָסַיִם
(ruh-ee) רְאִי	(mahts-leh-mah) מַצְלֵמָה	(lie-lah) (koo-toh-net) כּוּתֹנֶת לַיְלָה	(mah-im) מַיִם
(mah-geh-vet) מַגֶּבֶת	(film) פִילְם	(Hah-look) חָלוּק	(shah-nah) (loo-aH) לוּחַ שָׁנָה
(ip-ah-ron) עִפָּרוֹן	(yahm) (beg-ed) בֶּגֶד יָם	(bah-yit) (nah-ah-lay) נַעֲלֵי בַּיִת	(sim-lah) שִׂמְלָה
(et) עֵט	(sahn-dah-lim) סַנְדָּלִים	(Hah-lee-fah) חֲלִיפָה	(buh-tay-ah-von) בְּתֵאָבוֹן!
(nyar) נְיָר	(sah-bon) סַבּוֹן	(ah-nee-vah) עֲנִיבָה	(luh-Hah-im) לְחַיִּים!
(miH-tahv) מִכְתָּב	(shin-ah-yim) (miv-resh-et) מִבְרֶשֶׁת שִׁנַּיִם	(mim-Hah-tah) מִמְחָטָה	(slee-Hah) סְלִיחָה
(gloo-yah) גְּלוּיָה	(shin-ah-yim)(mish-Haht) מִשְׁחַת שִׁנַּיִם	(koo-toh-net) כּוּתֹנֶת	(ah-meh-ree-kah-ee) (ah-nee) אֲנִי אֲמֶרִיקָאִי
(bool) בּוּל	(git-oo-aH)(sah-keen) סַכִּין גִּלּוּחַ	(iv-rit) (lil-mohd) (roht-seh) (ah-nee) אֲנִי רוֹצֶה לִלְמוֹד עִבְרִית.	
(sef-air) סֵפֶר	(day-oh-doh-rahnt) דֵּיאוֹדוֹרַנְט	(shlohm-Hah) (mah) מַה שְּׁלוֹמְךָ?	
(shah-voo-on) שָׁבוּעוֹן	(mahs-rek) מַסְרֵק	(shmee) שְׁמִי . . .	

PLUS . . .

Your book includes a number of other innovative features. At the back of the book, you'll find seven pages of flash cards. Cut them out and flip through them at least once a day.

On pages 112 and 113, you'll find a beverage guide and a menu guide. Don't wait until your trip to use them. Clip out the menu guide and use it tonight at the dinner table. And use the beverage guide to practice ordering your favorite drinks.

By using the special features in this book, you will be speaking Hebrew before you know it.

(buh-mah-zahl) (tohv)
בְּמַזָּל טוֹב!

Step 13

(tsah-fon)		(dar-om)	(miz-raH)		(mah-ah-rahv)
צָפוֹן	-	דָּרוֹם,	מִזְרָח	-	מַעֲרָב
north		south	east		west

If (ah-tah) אַתָּה are looking at a (mah-pah) מַפָּה (map) and you see the following (mih-lim) מִלִּים, it should not be too difficult to figure out (mah) מָה (what) they mean. Take an educated guess. (hah-tshoo-voht) הַתְּשׁוּבוֹת (luh-mah-tah) לְמַטָּה. (below)

(tsfon) צְפוֹן (ah-meh-ree-kah) אֲמֶרִיקָה	(drom) דְּרוֹם (ah-meh-ree-kah) אֲמֶרִיקָה	(miz-raH) מִזְרַח (gair-mahn-yah) גֶּרְמַנְיָה
(tsfon) צְפוֹן (koh-ray-ah) קוֹרֵיאָה	(drom) דְּרוֹם (koh-ray-ah) קוֹרֵיאָה	(mah-ah-rahv) מַעֲרַב (gair-mahn-yah) גֶּרְמַנְיָה
(drom) דְּרוֹם (ah-free-kah) אַפְרִיקָה	(miz-raH) מִזְרַח (bair-leen) בֶּרְלִין	(mah-ah-rahv) מַעֲרַב (bair-leen) בֶּרְלִין

Do you recognize (hah-mih-lah) הַמִּלָּה for west - (mah-ah-rahv) מַעֲרָב - in (hah-koh-tel) הַכֹּתֶל (hah-mah-ah-rah-vee) הַמַּעֲרָבִי (Wall Western)? (hah-koh-tel) הַכֹּתֶל (hah-mah-ah-rah-vee) הַמַּעֲרָבִי (bee-roo-shah-lah-yim) בִּירוּשָׁלַיִם. (Jerusalem in)

______________ northern	=	(tsfoh-nee) צְפוֹנִי
______________ southern	=	(droh-mee) דְּרוֹמִי
______________ eastern	=	(miz-rah-Hee) מִזְרָחִי
______________ western	=	(mah-ah-rah-vee) מַעֲרָבִי

______________ north	=	(tsah-fon) צָפוֹן
דרום south	=	(dar-om) דָּרוֹם
______________ east	=	(miz-raH) מִזְרָח
______________ west	=	(mah-ah-rahv) מַעֲרָב

But what about more basic directions such as "left," "right," וְ "straight ahead"? Let's learn these (mih-lim) מִלִּים today.

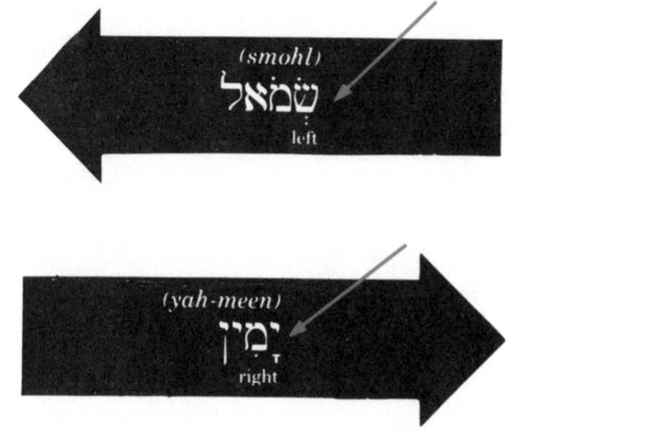

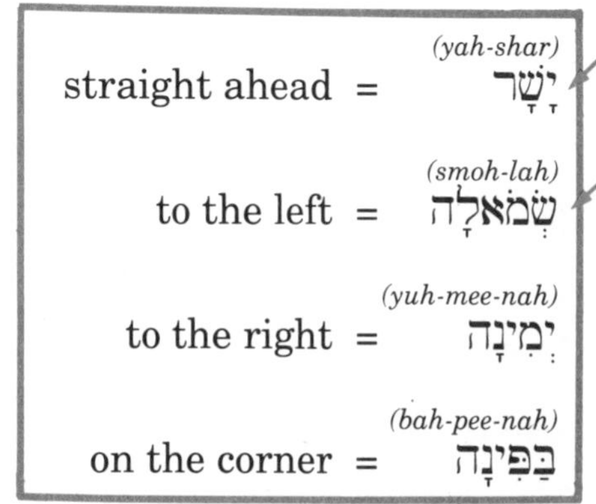

straight ahead	=	(yah-shar) יָשָׁר
to the left	=	(smoh-lah) שְׂמֹאלָה
to the right	=	(yuh-mee-nah) יְמִינָה
on the corner	=	(bah-pee-nah) בַּפִּינָה

הַתְּשׁוּבוֹת

East Germany	South America	North America
West Germany	South Korea	North Korea
West Berlin	East Berlin	South Africa

Just as בְּאַנְגְלִית (bahn-glit) English in these מִלִּים (mih-lim) אַרְבָּעָה (ar-bah-ah) go a long way.

_____ please	= בְּבַקָּשָׁה (buh-vah-kah-shah)
_____ thank you	= תּוֹדָה (toh-dah)
סְלִיחָה _____ excuse me	= סְלִיחָה (slee-Hah)
_____ you're welcome	= עַל לֹא דָבָר (ahl) (loh) (dah-var)

הִנֵּה (hin-ay) are שְׁתֵּי (shtay) two typical שִׂיחוֹת (see-Hoht) for someone who is trying to find something.

דָּוִד: (dah-vid) סְלִיחָה, (slee-Hah) אֵיפֹה הַמָּלוֹן (hah-mah-lon) "יְרוּשָׁלַיִם"? (yuh-roo-shah-lah-yim)

גַּד: (gahd) לֵךְ (leH) go שְׁנֵי (shnay) two רְחוֹבוֹת. (reh-Hoh-voht) streets פְּנֵה (pneh) turn שְׂמֹאלָה (smoh-lah) left the to בָּרְחוֹב (bah-ruh-Hohv) street the in הַשֵּׁנִי. (hah-sheh-nee) second מָלוֹן (mah-lon) "יְרוּשָׁלַיִם" (yuh-roo-shah-lah-yim) מִיָּמִין. (mee-yah-meen) right on

עוֹדֵד: (oh-ded) סְלִיחָה, אֵיפֹה מוּזֵיאוֹן (moo-zay-on) museum "הָאִיסְלַאם"? (hah-iss-lahm) Islam

רוּת: (root) פְּנֵה (pneh) turn יָמִינָה. (yuh-mee-nah) right the to לֵךְ (leH) go עֶשְׂרִים (es-rim) מֶטְרִים. (met-rim) meters פְּנֵה (pneh) שְׂמֹאלָה. (smoh-lah) left the to וְהַמּוּזֵיאוֹן (vuh-hah-moo-zay-on) בַּפִּינָה. (bah-pee-nah) corner the on

Are אַתָּה (ah-tah) lost? There is no need to be lost if אַתָּה have learned the basic direction words. Do not try to memorize these שִׂיחוֹת (see-Hoht) conversations because אַתָּה will never be looking for precisely these places. One day, אַתָּה might need to ask for directions to הַכְּנֶסֶת (hah-kness-et) Knesset the or הַשּׁוּק (hah-shook) market the. Learn the key direction words and be sure אַתָּה can find your destination. אַתָּה may want to לִקְנוֹת (lik-noht) buy a guidebook to start planning what places אַתָּה would like to visit. מָה (mah) what if the person responding to your שְׁאֵלָה (shuh-eh-lah) question answers too quickly for אַתָּה to understand the entire reply? Just ask פַּעַם (pahm) more עוֹד (ohd) once saying,

_____	מ	maximum . . . . (mahk-see-moom)	מַקְסִימוּם
_____		margerine . . . . (mar-gah-ree-nah)	מַרְגָרִינָה
_____		marzipan . . . . (mar-tsee-pahn)	מַרְצִיפָּן
_____		Messiah . . . . (mah-shee-aH)	מָשִׁיחַ
_____		mathematics . . . . (mah-tay-mah-tee-kah)	מָתֶמָטִיקָה

סְלִיחָה, אֲנִי אֲמֶרִיקָאִי. (ah-meh-ree-kah-ee) אֲנִי מְדַבֵּר (muh-dah-bair) speak רַק (rahk) only קְצָת (ktsaht) little עִבְרִית. (iv-rit) בְּבַקָּשָׁה (buh-vah-kah-shah) לְדַבֵּר (luh-dah-bair) speak

לְאַט (luh-aht) slowly וְלַחֲזוֹר. repeat and תּוֹדָה. (toh-dah)

כֵּן (ken), it is difficult at first but don't give up! עַכְשָׁו when the directions are repeated, אַתָּה will be able to understand if אַתָּה have learned the key מִלִּים for directions. Quiz yourself by filling in the blanks below with the correct עִבְרִית words.

בּוֹעַז: (boh-ahz) סְלִיחָה (slee-Hah) גְּבֶרֶת, (gveh-ret) Madam אֵיפֹה הַמִּסְעָדָה (hah-mis-ah-dah) restaurant "הַפִּיל"? (hah-pil) elephant the

חַנָּה: (Hah-nah) לֵךְ (leH) go ______ ahead straight. בָּרְחוֹב (bah-ruh-Hohv) street the in הַשְּׁלִישִׁי (hah-shlee-shee) third פְּנֵה (pneh) turn ______ right the to.

יֵשׁ (yesh) שָׁם (shahm) בַּנְק. (bahnk) אַחֲרֵי (ah-Hah-ray) הַבַּנְק (hah-bahnk) פְּנֵה (pneh) ______ right the to.

הַמִּסְעָדָה (hah-mis-ah-dah) "הַפִּיל" ______ corner the on. בְּהַצְלָחָה! (buh-hahts-lah-Hah) luck good

Here are אַרְבַּע (ar-bah) new verbs. Quick — מָה (mah) is the עִבְרִית (iv-rit) word for "they"? For "we"? For "she"?

לְחַכּוֹת (luh-Hah-koht) לְ (luh)	= to wait for	______
לְהָבִין (luh-hah-veen)	= to understand	______
לַחֲזוֹר (lah-Hah-zor) עַל (ahl)	= to repeat	______
צָרִיךְ (tsah-reeH)	= I need	______

מ

מְנַצֵּחַ	(muh-nah-tsay-aH) . . . . (orchestra) conductor ______
מַפְתֵּחַ	(mahf-tay-aH) . . . . key ______
מֶלֶךְ	(mel-eH) . . . . king ______
מְלוֹן הַמֶּלֶךְ דָּוִד	(mah-lon-hah-mel-eH-dah-vid) . . King David Hotel ______
מַשָּׂאִית	(mah-sah-eet) . . . . truck ______

As always, say each sentence out loud. Say each ְ every (mih-lah) מִלָּה carefully, pronouncing each (iv-rit) עִבְרִית sound as well as אַתָּה can.

(luh-hah-veen) לְהָבִין understand to

(ah-nee) אֲנִי	מֵבִין	(iv-rit) עִבְרִית.
הוּא / אַתָּה	מֵבִין	עִבְרִית.
הִיא / אַתְּ	מְבִינָה	(ah-rah-vit) עֲרָבִית. Arabic
אֲנַחְנוּ / הֵם	מְבִינִים	(ee-tahl-kit) אִיטַלְקִית. Italian

(luh)(luh-Hah-koht) לְחַכּוֹת לְ for wait to

אֲנִי	מְחַכֶּה לְ	(oh-toh-boos) אוֹטוֹבּוּס.
הוּא / אַתָּה	מְחַכֶּה לְ	אוֹטוֹבּוּס.
הִיא / אַתְּ	מְחַכָּה לְ	(tahk-see) טַקְסִי. taxi the
אֲנַחְנוּ / הֵם	מְחַכִּים לְ	טַקְסִי.

(ahl) (lah-Hah-zor) לַחֲזוֹר עַל repeat to

אֲנִי	חוֹזֵר עַל	(hah-mih-lah) הַמִּלָּה.
הוּא / אַתָּה	חוֹזֵר עַל	(hah-tshoo-vah) הַתְּשׁוּבָה. answer the
הִיא / אַתְּ	חוֹזֶרֶת עַל	(hah-shem) הַשֵּׁם. name the
אֲנַחְנוּ / הֵם	חוֹזְרִים עַל	(hah-mis-pah-rim) הַמִּסְפָּרִים.

(tsah-reeH) צָרִיךְ need I

אֲנִי	צָרִיךְ	(tahk-see) טַקְסִי. taxi
הוּא / אַתָּה	צָרִיךְ	(bahnk) בַּנְק. bank
הִיא / אַתְּ	צְרִיכָה	(mah-lon) מָלוֹן. hotel
אֲנַחְנוּ / הֵם	צְרִיכִים	(sef-el) (kah-feh) סֵפֶל קָפֶה. cup coffee

עַכְשָׁו see if אַתָּה can translate the following thoughts into עִבְרִית. (luh-mah-tah) (hah-tshoo-voht) הַתְּשׁוּבוֹת לְמַטָּה. answers the

1. She repeats the name. ______________________
2. You (♂) need tickets. ______________________
3. He waits for the taxi. ______________________
4. I understand Hebrew. ______________________
5. I understand Arabic. ______________________
6. They wait for the bus. ______________________

הַתְּשׁוּבוֹת

1. הִיא חוֹזֶרֶת עַל הַשֵּׁם.
2. אַתָּה צָרִיךְ כַּרְטִיסִים.
3. הוּא מְחַכֶּה לְטַקְסִי.
4. אֲנַחְנוּ מְבִינִים עִבְרִית.
5. אֲנִי מֵבִין עֲרָבִית.
6. הֵם מְחַכִּים לְאוֹטוֹבּוּס.

Step 14

(luh-mah-tah) (luh-mah-uh-lah)
לְמַטָּה - לְמַעְלָה
downstairs/below upstairs/above

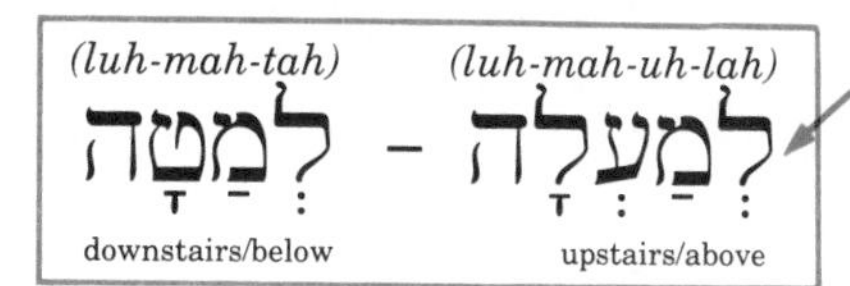

(lif-nay) לִפְנֵי (before) you begin Step 14, review Step 8. עַכְשָׁו we will learn more (mih-lim) מִלִּים.

(buh-yiss-rah-el) (bah-yit) (hin-ay)
הִנֵּה בַּיִת בְּיִשְׂרָאֵל.

(luh-mah-uh-lah) (shay-nah) (Hah-dar)
חֲדַר שֵׁינָה לְמַעְלָה.
bedroom above

(ahm-baht-yah) (Hah-dar)(gahm)
גַּם חֲדַר אַמְבַּטְיָה לְמַעְלָה.
also bathroom

(luh-mah-tah) (sah-lon)
סָלוֹן לְמַטָּה.
below

(ah-voh-dah)(Hah-dar)(gahm)
גַּם חֲדַר עֲבוֹדָה לְמַטָּה.
also study

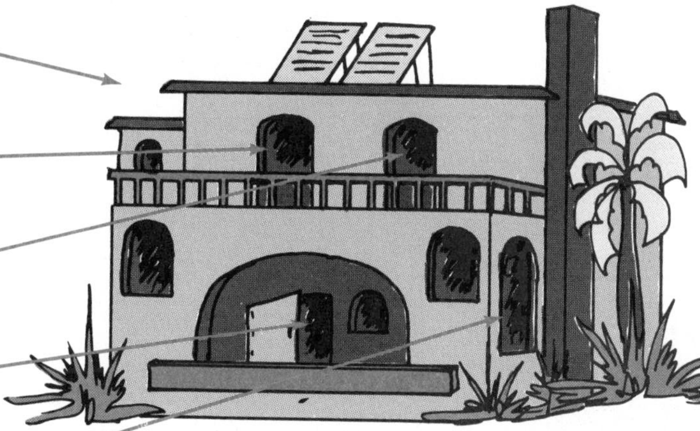

עַכְשָׁו go to your (shay-nah) (Hah-dar) חֲדַר שֵׁינָה (bedroom) and look around the (Hed-er) חֶדֶר. Let's learn the names of the things (hah-shay-nah) (buh-Hah-dar) בְּחֲדַר הַשֵּׁינָה (in the bedroom), just like (ah-naH-noo) אֲנַחְנוּ (we) learned the various parts of (hah-bah-yit) הַבַּיִת. Be sure to practice saying (hah-mih-lim) הַמִּלִּים as אַתָּה write them in the spaces (luh-mah-tah) לְמַטָּה. Also say out loud the sample sentences (lah-tmoo-noht) (mee-tah-Haht) מִתַּחַת (under) לַתְּמוּנוֹת (the pictures).

(mee-tah) מִיטָּה (bed)

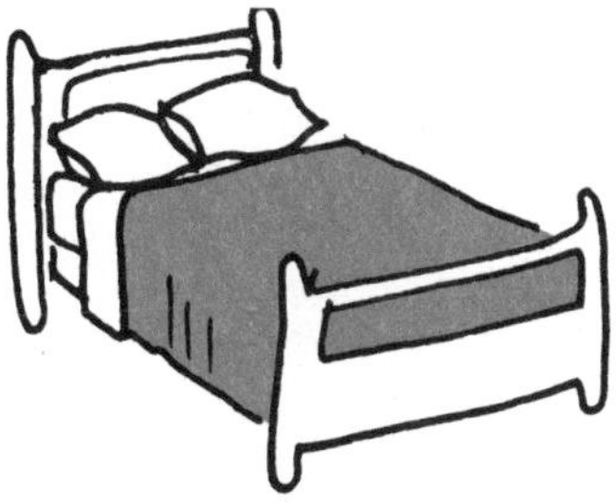

(smee-Hah) שְׂמִיכָה (blanket)

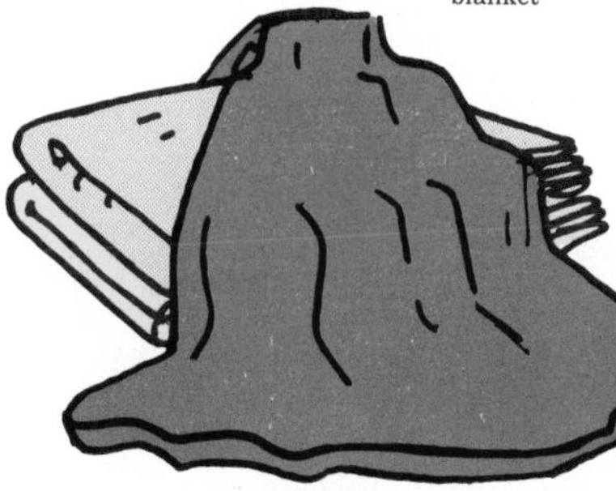

(kar) כַּר (pillow)

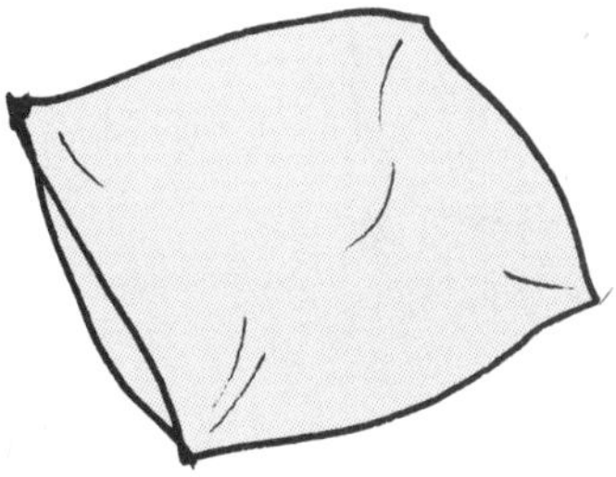

(gdoh-lah) (hah-mee-tah)
הַמִּיטָּה גְּדוֹלָה.
the bed big

(smee-Hah) (tsah-reeH)
אֲנִי צָרִיךְ שְׂמִיכָה.

(kar)(tsah-reeH)
אֲנִי צָרִיךְ כַּר.
need

מ

police. . . . . (mish-tah-rah) . . . . מִשְׁטָרָה
police car. . (muh-Hoh-nit-mish-tah-rah) מְכוֹנִית מִשְׁטָרָה —
gift. . . . . (mah-tah-nah) . . . . מַתָּנָה
teacher. . . . . (moh-rah) . . . . מוֹרָה
Egypt. . . . . (mits-rah-yim) . . . . מִצְרַיִם

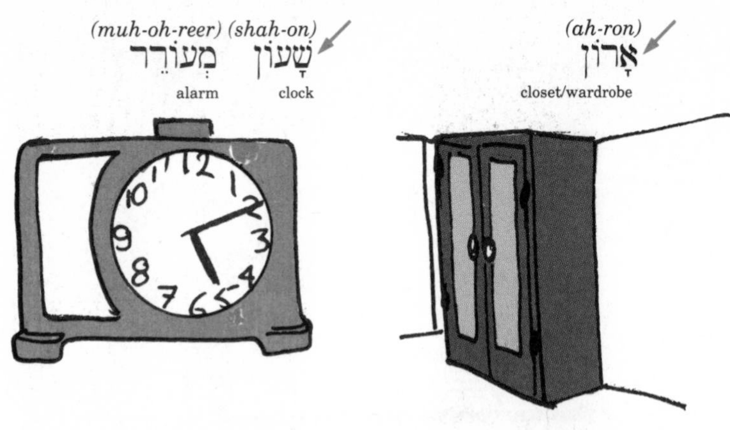

(Hah-mesh) (dvah-rim) (shay-nah)(Hah-dar)

עַכְשָׁו remove the next חָמֵשׁ stickers וְ label these דְּבָרִים in your חֲדַר שֵׁינָה (bedroom).

(muh-oh-reer) (shah-on) (tsah-reeH) (ah-ron) (yesh)(shay-nah) (buh-Hah-dar)

בְּחֲדַר שֵׁינָה יֵשׁ אָרוֹן. אֲנִי צָרִיךְ שָׁעוֹן מְעוֹרֵר.

(bedroom in; need)

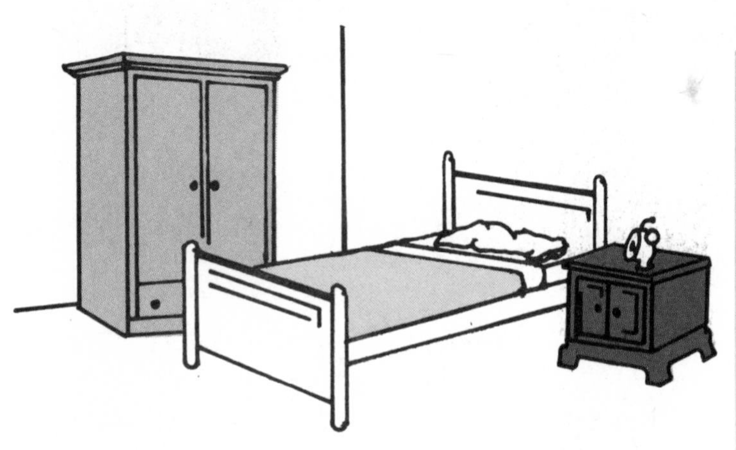

(buh-yiss-rah-el)(buh-mah-lon)(shay-nah)(Hah-dar)

חֲדַר שֵׁינָה בְּמָלוֹן בְּיִשְׂרָאֵל

(lee-shon) לִישׁוֹן = to sleep. This is an important verb for the תַּיָּר עָיֵף (ah-yef)(tah-yar) (tired tourist). Study the following שְׁאֵלוֹת (shuh-eh-loht) (questions) and their תְּשׁוּבוֹת (tshoo-voht) (answers) based on הַתְּמוּנָה (hah-tmoo-nah) to the left.

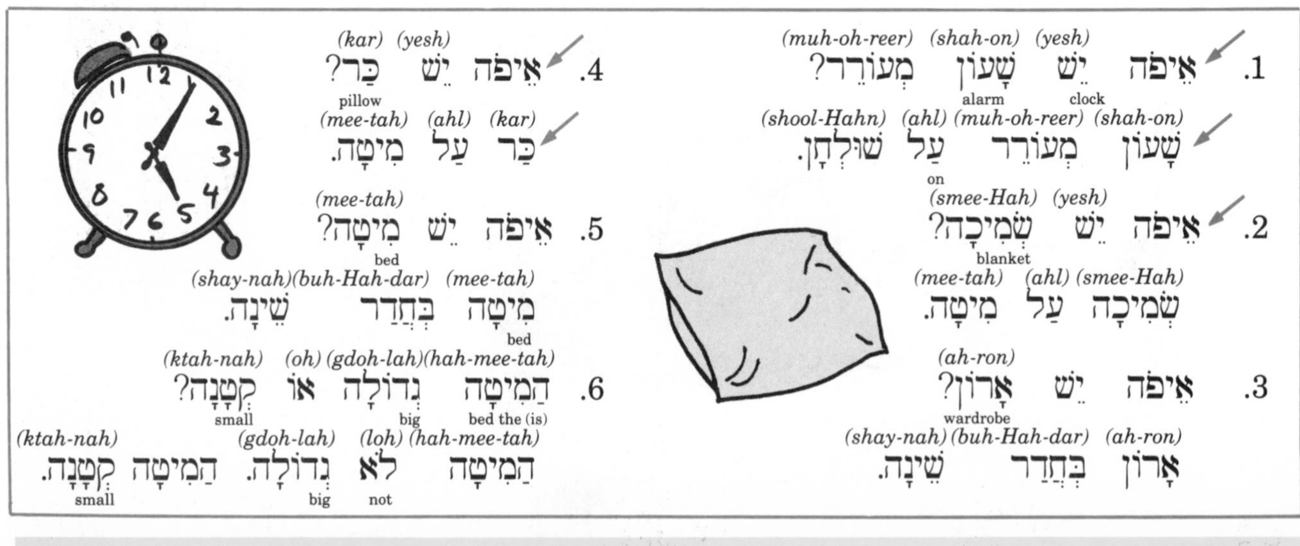

1. (muh-oh-reer) (shah-on) (yesh) אֵיפֹה יֵשׁ שָׁעוֹן מְעוֹרֵר? (alarm clock)
   (shool-Hahn) (ahl) (muh-oh-reer) (shah-on) שָׁעוֹן מְעוֹרֵר עַל שׁוּלְחָן. (on)
2. (smee-Hah) (yesh) אֵיפֹה יֵשׁ שְׂמִיכָה? (blanket)
   (mee-tah) (ahl) (smee-Hah) שְׂמִיכָה עַל מִיטָּה.
3. (ah-ron) אֵיפֹה יֵשׁ אָרוֹן? (wardrobe)
   (shay-nah) (buh-Hah-dar) (ah-ron) אָרוֹן בְּחֲדַר שֵׁינָה.
4. (kar) (yesh) אֵיפֹה יֵשׁ כַּר? (pillow)
   (mee-tah) (ahl) (kar) כַּר עַל מִיטָּה.
5. (mee-tah) אֵיפֹה יֵשׁ מִיטָּה? (bed)
   (shay-nah)(buh-Hah-dar) (mee-tah) מִיטָּה בְּחֲדַר שֵׁינָה. (bed)
6. (ktah-nah) (oh) (gdoh-lah)(hah-mee-tah) הַמִּיטָּה גְּדוֹלָה אוֹ קְטַנָּה? (bed the (is) big small)
   (ktah-nah) (gdoh-lah) (loh) (hah-mee-tah) הַמִּיטָּה לֹא גְּדוֹלָה. הַמִּיטָּה קְטַנָּה. (not big small)

נ

prophet	(nah-vee)	נָבִיא
carpenter	(nah-gahr)	נַגָּר
river	(nah-har)	נָהָר
Nahariya	(nah-hah-ree-yah)	נַהֲרִיָּה
stream	(nah-Hahl)	נַחַל

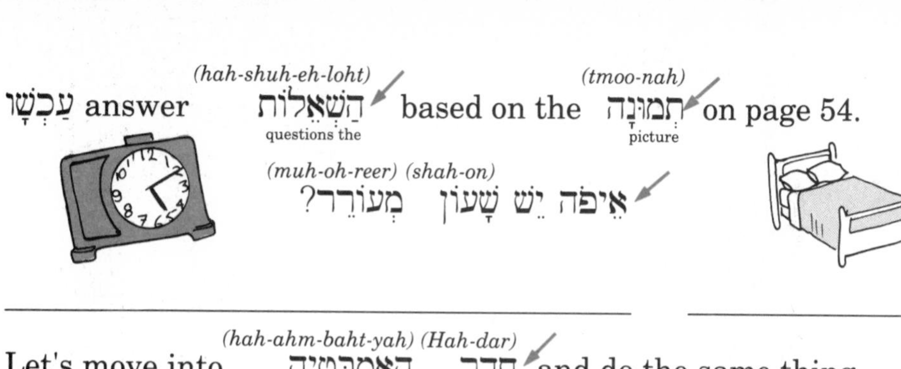

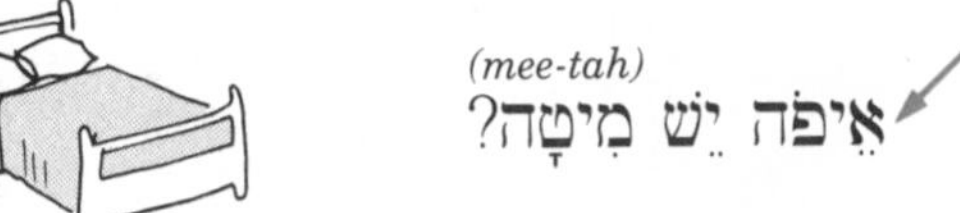

עַכְשָׁו answer *(hah-shuh-eh-loht)* הַשְּׁאֵלוֹת (questions the) based on the *(tmoo-nah)* תְּמוּנָה (picture) on page 54.

(muh-oh-reer) (shah-on) אֵיפֹה יֵשׁ שָׁעוֹן מְעוֹרֵר?

(mee-tah) אֵיפֹה יֵשׁ מִיטָּה?

Let's move into *(hah-ahm-baht-yah) (Hah-dar)* חֲדַר הָאַמְבַּטְיָה (bathroom the) and do the same thing.

(kee-yor) כִּיּוֹר — washstand

(mik-lah-Haht) מִקְלַחַת — shower

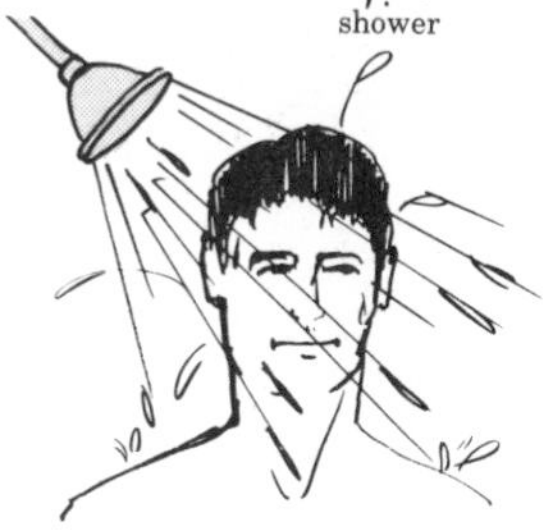

(shim-oosh) (bait) בֵּית שִׁמּוּשׁ — toilet

(hah-ahm-baht-yah) (buh-Hah-dar) בַּחֲדַר הָאַמְבַּטְיָה
(yah-rok) (kee-yor) יֵשׁ כִּיּוֹר יָרוֹק. (green)

בַּחֲדַר הָאַמְבַּטְיָה
(ah-foh-rah) (mik-lah-Haht) יֵשׁ מִקְלַחַת אֲפוֹרָה. (gray)

(hah-ahm-baht-yah) (buh-Hah-dar) בַּחֲדַר הָאַמְבַּטְיָה
(shim-oosh) (bait) (yesh) יֵשׁ בֵּית שִׁמּוּשׁ
(lah-vahn) (yah-rok) יָרוֹק לָבָן. (white, green)

(ruh-ee) רְאִי ____________

(mah-gah-voht) מַגָּבוֹת (towels) ____ מַגָּבוֹת ____

(ah-doo-mah)(mah-geh-vet) מַגֶּבֶת אֲדוּמָּה (towel, red) ____________

(Hoo-mah) (mah-geh-vet) מַגֶּבֶת חוּמָה (brown) ____________

(ktoo-mah) מַגֶּבֶת כְּתוּמָה (orange) ____________

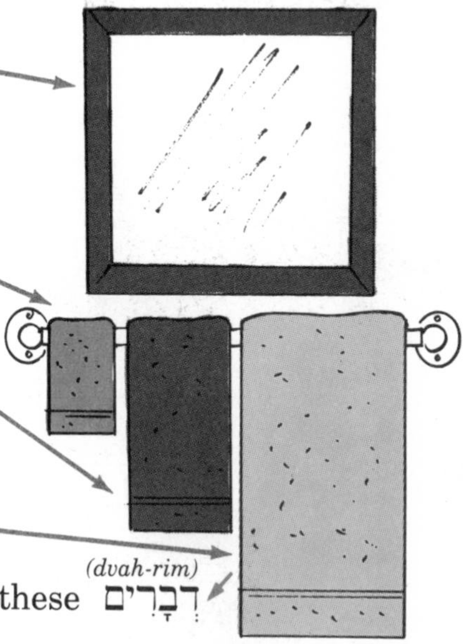

Do not forget to remove the next *(sheh-vah)* שֶׁבַע stickers וְ label these *(dvah-rim)* דְּבָרִים in your *(ahm-baht-yah) (Hah-dar)* חֲדַר אַמְבַּטְיָה (bathroom).

נ

New Zealand	*(new-zee-lahnd)*	נְיוּ - זִילַנְד
harbor	*(nah-mahl)*	נָמָל
Nazareth	*(nah-tseh-ret)*	נָצֶרֶת
candle	*(nair)*	נֵר
Netanya	*(nuh-tahn-yah)*	נְתַנְיָה

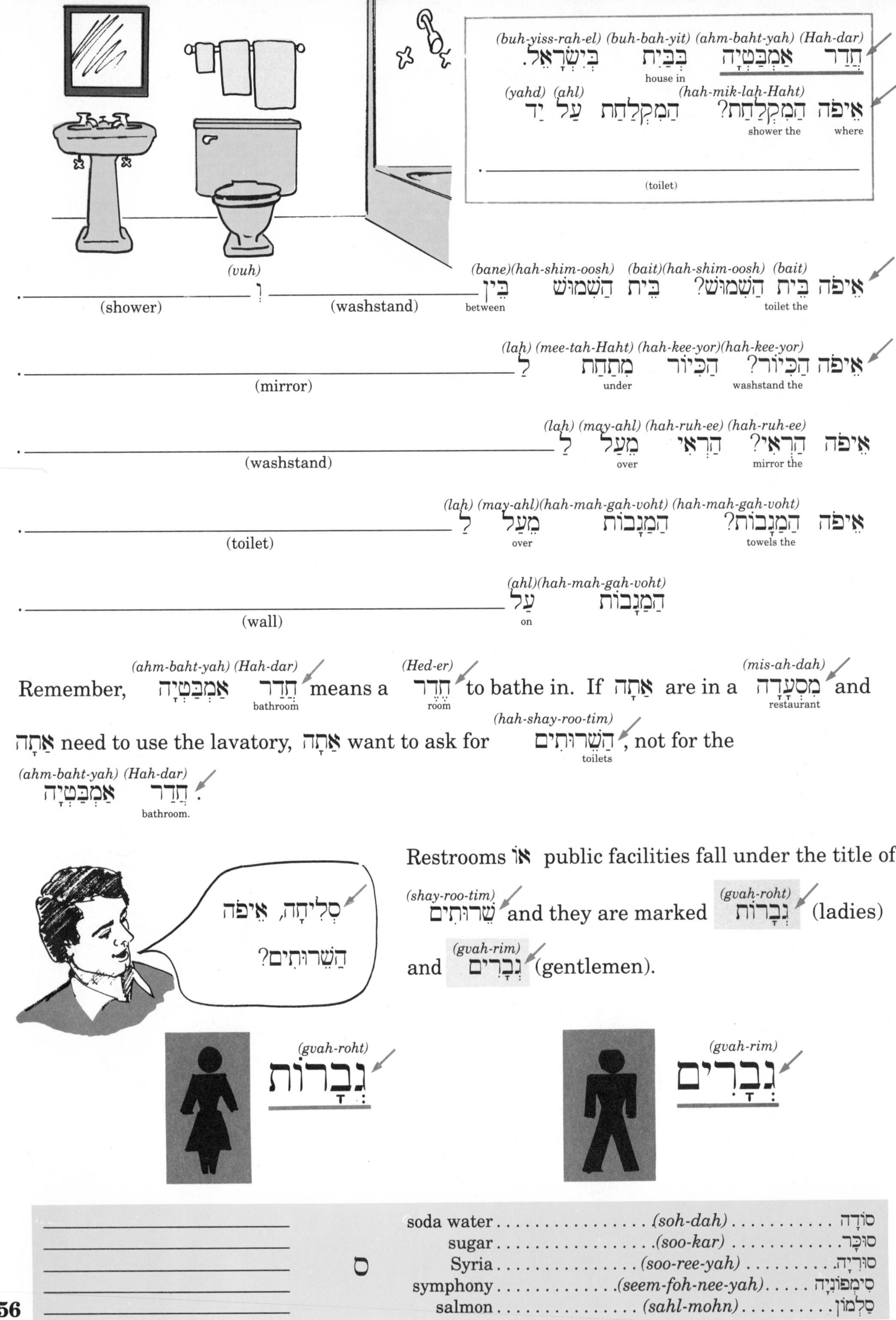

(buh-yiss-rah-el) (buh-bah-yit) (ahm-baht-yah) (Hah-dar)
חֶדֶר אַמְבַּטְיָה בְּבַיִת בְּיִשְׂרָאֵל.
house in

(yahd) (ahl) (hah-mik-lah-Haht)
אֵיפֹה הַמִּקְלַחַת? הַמִּקְלַחַת עַל יַד ______________.
where shower the
(toilet)

(bane)(hah-shim-oosh) (bait)(hah-shim-oosh) (bait)
אֵיפֹה בֵּית הַשִּׁמּוּשׁ? בֵּית הַשִּׁמּוּשׁ בֵּין ______________ (washstand) וְ (vuh) ______________ (shower).
toilet the — between

(lah) (mee-tah-Haht) (hah-kee-yor)(hah-kee-yor)
אֵיפֹה הַכִּיּוֹר? הַכִּיּוֹר מִתַּחַת לַ ______________ (mirror).
washstand the — under

(lah) (may-ahl) (hah-ruh-ee) (hah-ruh-ee)
אֵיפֹה הָרְאִי? הָרְאִי מֵעַל לַ ______________ (washstand).
mirror the — over

(lah) (may-ahl)(hah-mah-gah-voht) (hah-mah-gah-voht)
אֵיפֹה הַמַּגָּבוֹת? הַמַּגָּבוֹת מֵעַל לַ ______________ (toilet).
towels the — over

(ahl)(hah-mah-gah-voht)
הַמַּגָּבוֹת עַל ______________ (wall).
on

Remember, חֶדֶר אַמְבַּטְיָה (Hah-dar) (ahm-baht-yah) (bathroom) means a חֶדֶר (Hed-er) (room) to bathe in. If אַתָּה are in a מִסְעָדָה (mis-ah-dah) (restaurant) and אַתָּה need to use the lavatory, אַתָּה want to ask for הַשֵּׁרוּתִים (hah-shay-roo-tim) (toilets), not for the חֶדֶר אַמְבַּטְיָה (Hah-dar) (ahm-baht-yah) (bathroom).

Restrooms אוֹ public facilities fall under the title of שֵׁרוּתִים (shay-roo-tim) and they are marked גְּבָרוֹת (gvah-roht) (ladies) and גְּבָרִים (gvah-rim) (gentlemen).

ס

soda water . . . . (soh-dah) . . . . סוֹדָה
sugar . . . . (soo-kar) . . . . סוּכָּר
Syria . . . . (soo-ree-yah) . . . . סוּרְיָה
symphony . . . . (seem-foh-nee-yah) . . . . סִימְפוֹנְיָה
salmon . . . . (sahl-mohn) . . . . סַלְמוֹן

Next stop — חֲדַר הָעֲבוֹדָה *(Hah-dar) (hah-ah-voh-dah)* [study the], specifically שׁוּלְחַן הַכְּתִיבָה *(shool-Hahn) (hah-ktee-vah)* [desk the].

מָה עַל שׁוּלְחַן הַכְּתִיבָה? *(mah) (ahl) (shool-Hahn) (hah-ktee-vah)* [what]

Let's identify הַדְּבָרִים *(hah-dvah-rim)* that one normally finds on שׁוּלְחַן הַכְּתִיבָה *(shool-Hahn) (hah-ktee-vah)* [desk the] or strewn about הַבַּיִת *(hah-bah-yit)*.

ס

China . . . . *(seen)* . . . . סִין
Chinese . . . . *(see-nee)* . . . . סִינִי
boat . . . . *(see-rah)* . . . . סִירָה
fishing boat . . . . *(see-raht-dah-yig)* . . . . . סִירַת דַּיִג
celery . . . . *(seh-leh-ree)* . . . . סֶלֶרִי

עַכְשָׁו label these *(dvah-rim)* דְּבָרִים in your *(ah-voh-dah)(Hah-dar)* עֲבוֹדָה חֲדַר (study) with your stickers. Do not forget to say these *(mih-lim)* מִלִּים out loud whenever אַתָּה write them, אַתָּה see them or אַתָּה apply the stickers. עַכְשָׁו identify *(hah-dvah-rim)* הַדְּבָרִים in *(hah-tmoo-nah)* הַתְּמוּנָה (picture the) below by filling in each blank עִם the correct *(iv-rit)* עִבְרִית *(mih-lah)* מִלָּה.

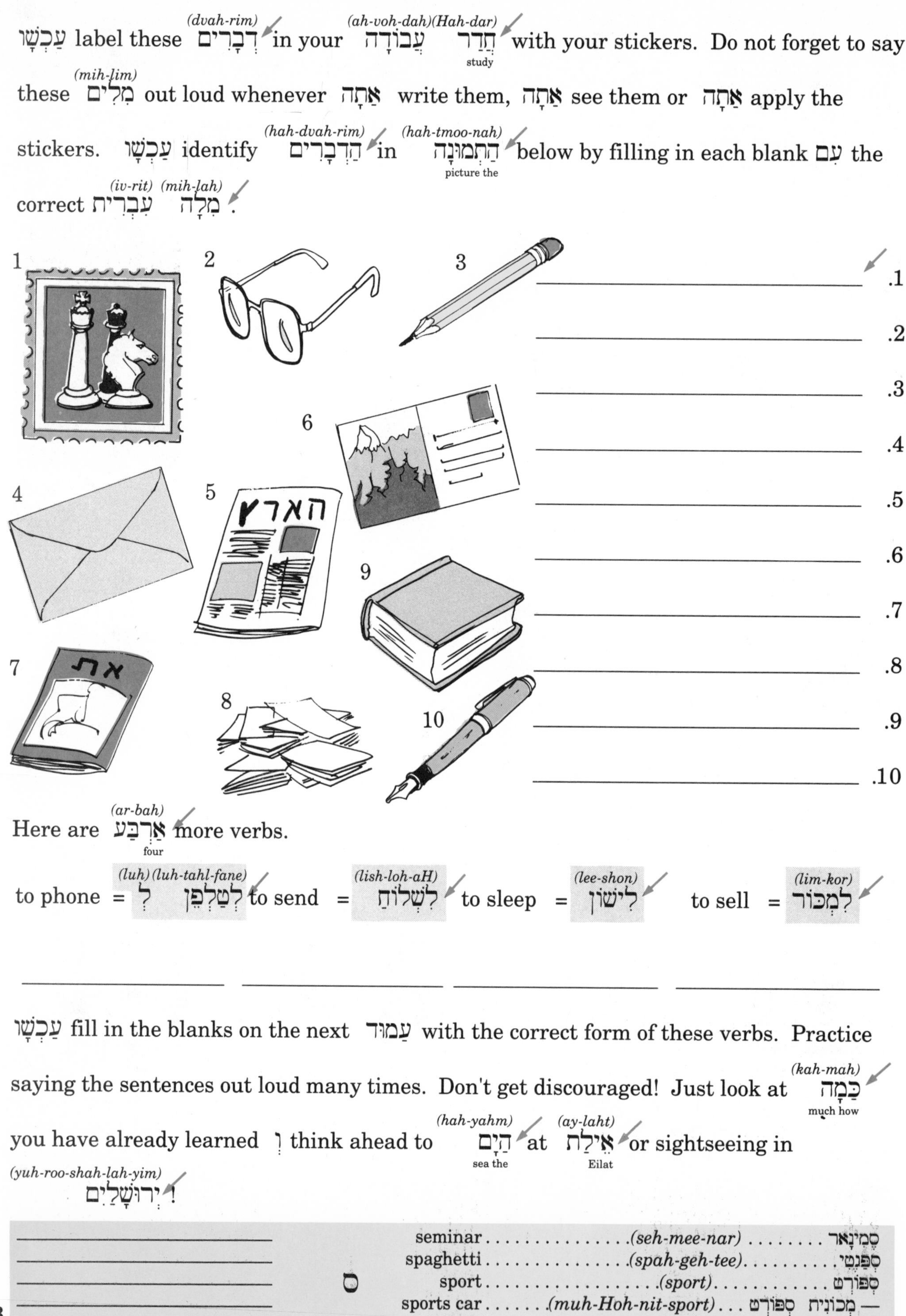

1 ____________________ .1

2 ____________________ .2

3 ____________________ .3

4 ____________________ .4

5 ____________________ .5

6 ____________________ .6

7 ____________________ .7

8 ____________________ .8

9 ____________________ .9

10 ____________________ .10

Here are *(ar-bah)* אַרְבַּע (four) more verbs.

to phone = *(luh)* לְ *(luh-tahl-fane)* לְטַלְפֵן to send = *(lish-loh-aH)* לִשְׁלוֹחַ to sleep = *(lee-shon)* לִישׁוֹן to sell = *(lim-kor)* לִמְכּוֹר

____________________ ____________________ ____________________ ____________________

עַכְשָׁו fill in the blanks on the next עַמּוּד with the correct form of these verbs. Practice saying the sentences out loud many times. Don't get discouraged! Just look at *(kah-mah)* כַּמָּה (much how) you have already learned וְ think ahead to *(hah-yahm)* הַיָּם (sea the) at *(ay-laht)* אֵילַת (Eilat) or sightseeing in *(yuh-roo-shah-lah-yim)* יְרוּשָׁלַיִם!

____________________	ס	seminar	*(seh-mee-nar)*	סֶמִינָר
____________________		spaghetti	*(spah-geh-tee)*	סְפָּגֶטִי
____________________		sport	*(sport)*	סְפּוֹרְט
____________________		sports car	*(muh-Hoh-nit-sport)*	מְכוֹנִית סְפּוֹרְט —
____________________		ski	*(skee)*	סְקִי

(lish-loh-aH)
לִשְׁלוֹחַ
send to

(ah-nee) אֲנִי ____ שׁוֹלֵחַ ____ מִכְתָּב. (miH-tahv) letter

(hoo) הוּא ____ שׁוֹלֵחַ ____ גְלוּיָה. (gloo-yah) postcard
אַתָּה

(hee) הִיא ____ שׁוֹלַחַת ____ סֵפֶר. (sef-er)
אַתְ

(ah-naH-noo) אֲנַחְנוּ ____ שׁוֹלְחִים ____ אַרְבַּע גְלוּיוֹת. (ar-bah) (gloo-yoht) postcards
הֵם

(luh)(luh-tahl-fane)
לְטַלְפֵן לְ
phone to

אֲנִי ____ מְטַלְפֵן לְ ____ מָלוֹן. (mah-lon) hotel

הוּא ____ מְטַלְפֵן לְ ____ מִסְעָדָה. (mis-ah-dah) restaurant
אַתָּה

הִיא ____ מְטַלְפֶנֶת לְ ____ אֲמֶרִיקָה. (ah-meh-ree-kah)
אַתְ

אֲנַחְנוּ ____ מְטַלְפְנִים לְ ____ תֵל אָבִיב. (tel) (ah-veev)
הֵם

(lim-kor)
לִמְכּוֹר
sell to

אֲנִי ____ מוֹכֵר ____ בּוּלִים. (boo-lim) stamps

(hoo) הוּא ____ מוֹכֵר ____ עִתּוֹנִים. (ih-toh-nim) newspapers
אַתָּה

הִיא ____ מוֹכֶרֶת ____ מִשְׁקָפַיִם. (mish-kah-fah-yim) eyeglasses
אַתְ

(ah-naH-noo) אֲנַחְנוּ ____ מוֹכְרִים ____ פְּרָחִים. (praH-im) flowers
הֵם

(lee-shon)
לִישׁוֹן
sleep to

אֲנִי ____ יָשֵׁן ____ בְּחֶדֶר שֵׁינָה. (buh-Hah-dar)(shay-nah) bedroom in

הוּא ____ יָשֵׁן ____ בַּמִיטָה. (bah-mee-tah) bed the in
אַתָּה

הִיא ____ יְשֵׁנָה ____ בַּמָלוֹן. (bah-mah-lon)
אַתְ

אֲנַחְנוּ ____ יְשֵׁנִים ____ בַּבַּיִת. (bah-bah-yit)
הֵם

The word (loh) לֹא (not) is extremely useful בְּעִבְרִית. Add לֹא before a verb וְ you negate the sentence.

I send a letter. = אֲנִי שׁוֹלֵחַ מִכְתָּב. (shoh-lay-aH)(miH-tahv)

I do not send a letter. = אֲנִי לֹא שׁוֹלֵחַ מִכְתָּב. (loh)

Simple, isn't it? עַכְשָׁו you negate the following sentences.

אֲנִי רוֹצֶה כּוֹס מַיִם. (roh-tseh) (kohs) glass (mah-yim) water ______________________________

אֲנַחְנוּ נוֹסְעִים לְיִשְׂרָאֵל. (ah-naH-noo)(noh-sim) travel (luh-yiss-rah-el) ______________________________

אֲנִי מְדַבֵּר עִבְרִית. (muh-dah-bair) speak ______________________________

ס

סְפָרַד .... (sfah-rahd) .... Spain	______________
סְפָרַדִי .... (sfah-rah-dee) .... Spanish	______________
סְקַנְדִינַבְיָה .... (skahn-dee-nahv-yah) .... Scandinavia	______________
סְקַנְדִינַבִי .... (skahn-dee-nah-vee) .... Scandinavian	______________
סַרְדִינִים .... (sar-dee-neem) .... sardines	______________

Step 15

(doh-ar) דוֹאַר mail

אַתָּה know עַכְשָׁו how to count, (ayH) אֵיךְ how to ask (shuh-eh-loht) שְׁאֵלוֹת questions, how to use verbs with the "plug-in" formula, אֵיךְ to make statements וְ how to describe something, be it the location of a מָלוֹן or the color of a (bah-yit) בַּיִת. Let's now take the basics that אַתָּה have learned וְ expand them in special areas that will be most helpful in your travels. מָה does everyone do on a holiday? Send (gloo-yoht) גְלוּיוֹת postcards, of course! Let's learn exactly (ayH) אֵיךְ the (hah-doh-ar) (mis-rahd) מִשְׂרַד הַדוֹאַר office post works (buh-yiss-rah-el) בְּיִשְׂרָאֵל.

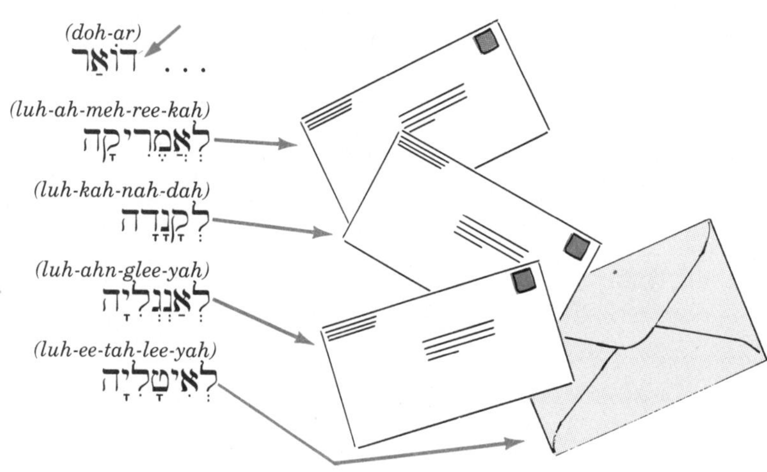

(doh-ar) דוֹאַר . . .
(luh-ah-meh-ree-kah) לְאַמֶרִיקָה
(luh-kah-nah-dah) לְקָנָדָה
(luh-ahn-glee-yah) לְאַנְגְלִיָה
(luh-ee-tah-lee-yah) לְאִיטַלְיָה

(hah-doh-ar) (mis-rahd) מִשְׂרַד הַדוֹאַר office post is where אַתָּה need to go (buh-yiss-rah-el) בְּיִשְׂרָאֵל to buy a (bool) בּוּל stamp, mail a package, send a telegram or use (hah-teh-leh-fohn) הַטֶלֶפוֹן telephone the. Here are some necessary (mih-lim) מִלִים for (hah-doh-ar) (mis-rahd) מִשְׂרַד הַדוֹאַר. Be sure to practice them out loud וְ then write (hah-mih-lah) הַמִלָה below (hah-tmoo-nah) הַתְּמוּנָה.

(miH-tahv) מִכְתָּב
letter

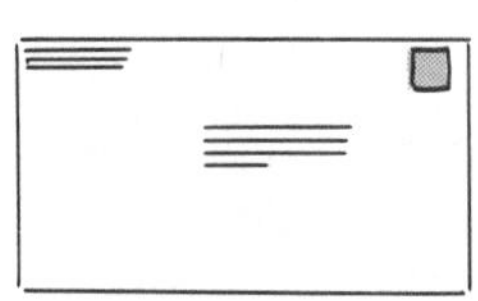

(gloo-yah) גְלוּיָה
postcard

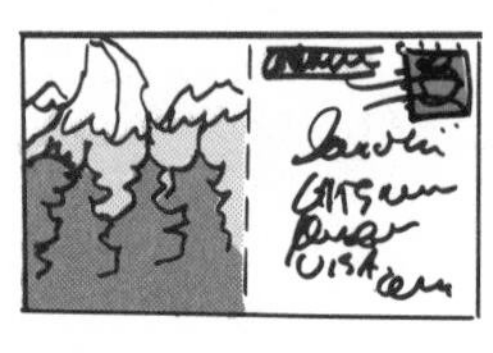

(bool) בּוּל
stamp

(miv-rahk) מִבְרָק
telegram

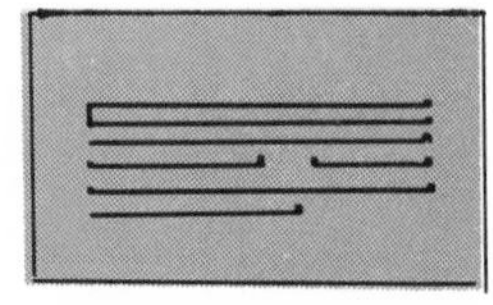

_______________ _______________ _______________ _______________

ע

cloud	(ah-nahn)	עָנָן
tree	(ehts)	עֵץ
Arab	(ah-rah-vee)	עֲרָבִי
Arabic	(ah-rah-veet)	עֲרָבִית
antique	(ah-teek)	עַתִּיק

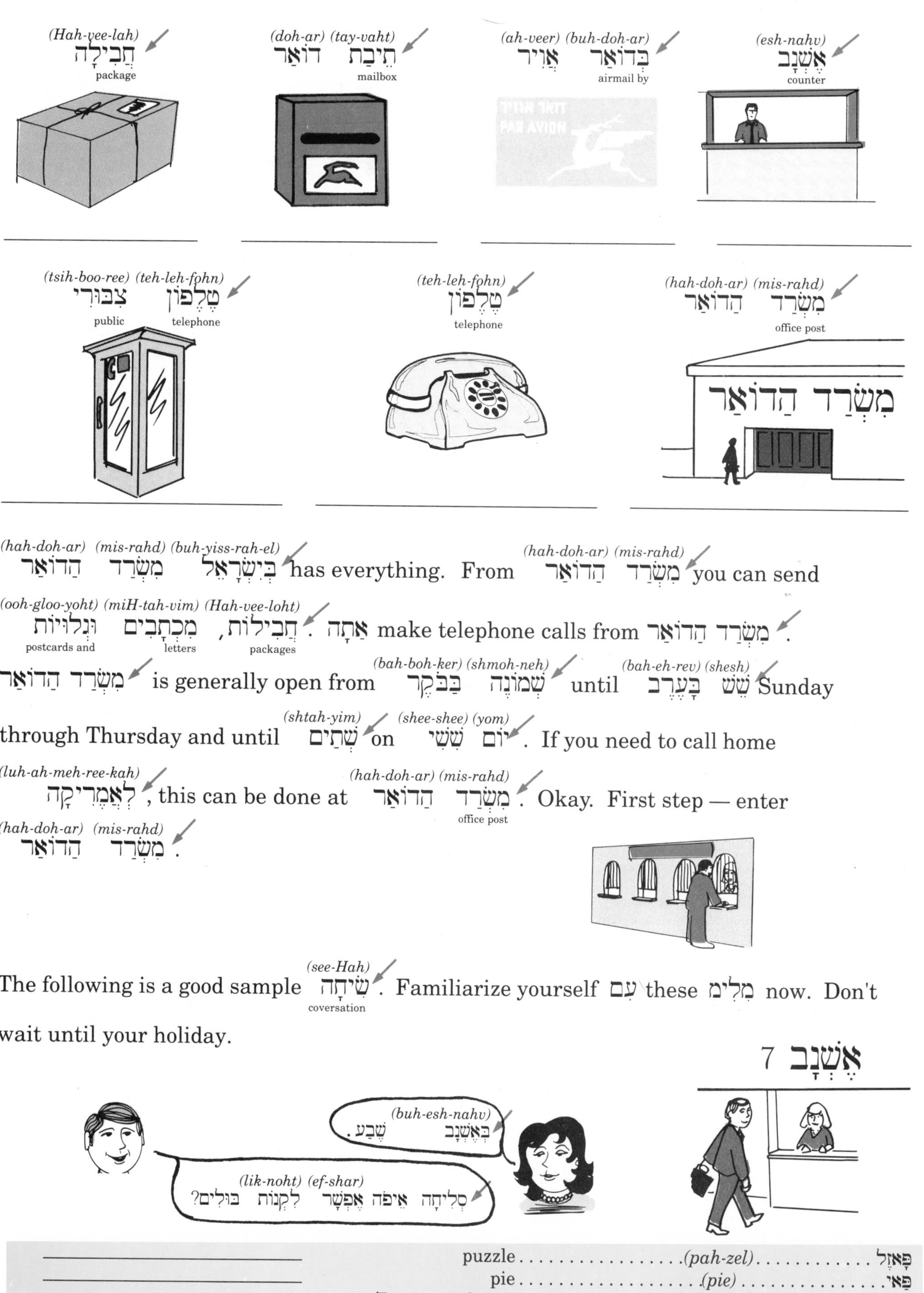

(Hah-vee-lah) חֲבִילָה — package

(doh-ar) (tay-vaht) תֵּיבַת דּוֹאַר — mailbox

(ah-veer) (buh-doh-ar) בְּדוֹאַר אֲוִיר — airmail by

(esh-nahv) אֶשְׁנָב — counter

(tsih-boo-ree) (teh-leh-fohn) טֶלֶפוֹן צִבּוּרִי — public telephone

(teh-leh-fohn) טֶלֶפוֹן — telephone

(hah-doh-ar) (mis-rahd) מִשְׂרַד הַדּוֹאַר — office post

מִשְׂרַד הַדּוֹאַר בְּיִשְׂרָאֵל (buh-yiss-rah-el) (mis-rahd) (hah-doh-ar) has everything. From מִשְׂרַד הַדּוֹאַר (mis-rahd) (hah-doh-ar) you can send חֲבִילוֹת (Hah-vee-loht, packages), מִכְתָּבִים (miH-tah-vim, letters) וּגְלוּיוֹת (ooh-gloo-yoht, postcards and). אַתָּה make telephone calls from מִשְׂרַד הַדּוֹאַר. מִשְׂרַד הַדּוֹאַר is generally open from שְׁמוֹנֶה בַּבֹּקֶר (shmoh-neh) (bah-boh-ker) until שֵׁשׁ בָּעֶרֶב (shesh) (bah-eh-rev) Sunday through Thursday and until שְׁתַּיִם (shtah-yim) on יוֹם שִׁשִּׁי (yom) (shee-shee). If you need to call home לְאָמֶרִיקָה (luh-ah-meh-ree-kah), this can be done at מִשְׂרַד הַדּוֹאַר (mis-rahd) (hah-doh-ar) (office post). Okay. First step — enter מִשְׂרַד הַדּוֹאַר (mis-rahd) (hah-doh-ar).

The following is a good sample שִׂיחָה (see-Hah, coversation). Familiarize yourself עִם these מִלִּים now. Don't wait until your holiday.

פ

puzzle . . . . (pah-zel) . . . . פָּאזֶל
pie . . . . (pie) . . . . פַּאי
political . . . . (poh-lee-tee) . . . . פּוֹלִיטִי
politics . . . . (poh-lee-tee-kah) . . . . . . פּוֹלִיטִיקָה
policy . . . . (poh-lee-sah) . . . . פּוֹלִיסָה

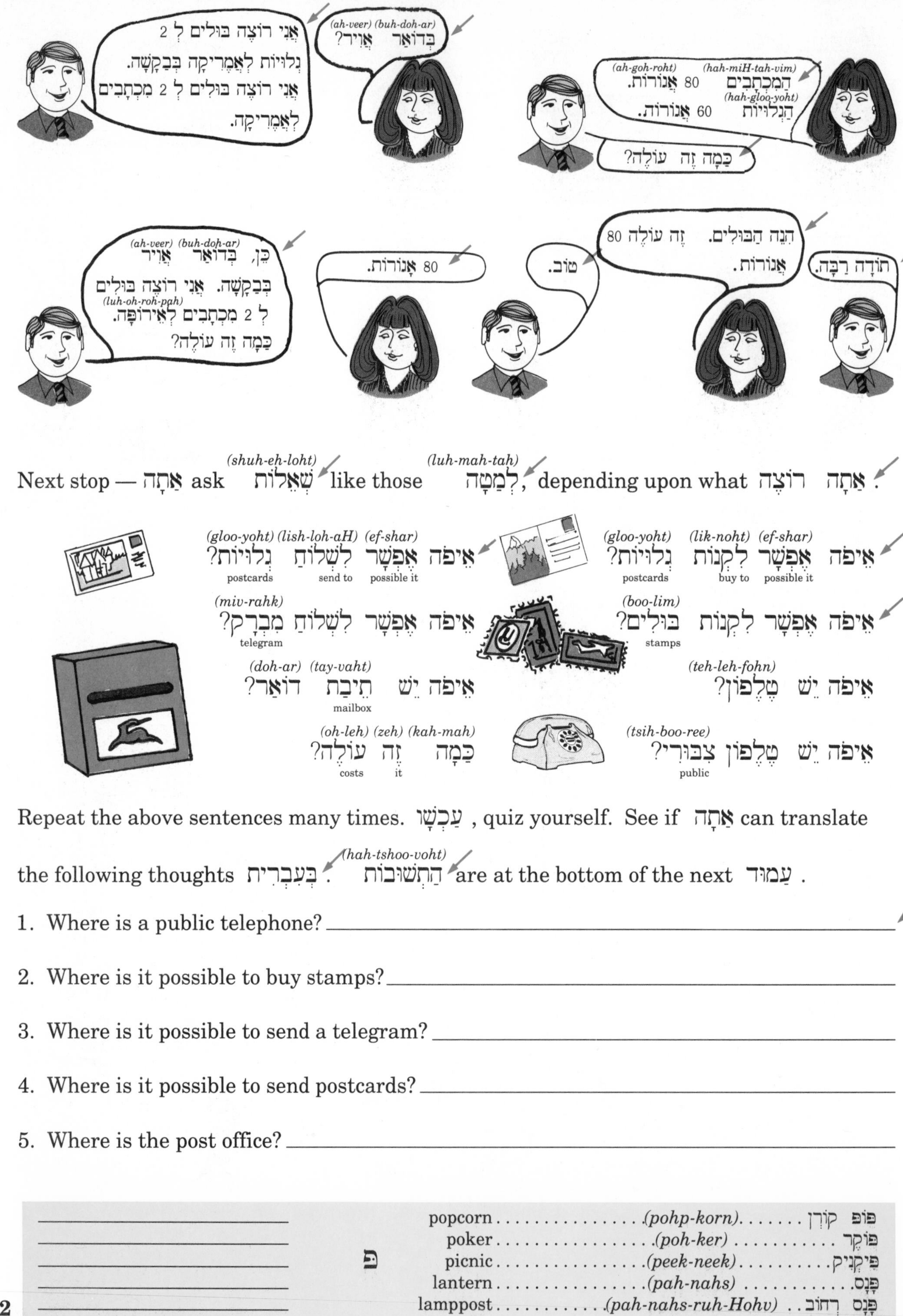

Next stop — אַתָּה ask (shuh-eh-loht) שְׁאֵלוֹת like those (luh-mah-tah) לְמַטָּה, depending upon what אַתָּה רוֹצֶה.

אֵיפֹה אֶפְשָׁר לִקְנוֹת גְלוּיוֹת? (ef-shar / lik-noht / gloo-yoht) — possible it / buy to / postcards	אֵיפֹה אֶפְשָׁר לִשְׁלוֹחַ גְלוּיוֹת? (ef-shar / lish-loh-aH / gloo-yoht) — possible it / send to / postcards
אֵיפֹה אֶפְשָׁר לִקְנוֹת בּוּלִים? (boo-lim) — stamps	אֵיפֹה אֶפְשָׁר לִשְׁלוֹחַ מִבְרָק? (miv-rahk) — telegram
אֵיפֹה יֵשׁ טֶלֶפוֹן? (teh-leh-fohn)	אֵיפֹה יֵשׁ תֵּיבַת דוֹאַר? (tay-vaht / doh-ar) — mailbox
אֵיפֹה יֵשׁ טֶלֶפוֹן צִבּוּרִי? (tsih-boo-ree) — public	כַּמָּה זֶה עוֹלֶה? (kah-mah / zeh / oh-leh) — it / costs

Repeat the above sentences many times. עַכְשָׁו, quiz yourself. See if אַתָּה can translate the following thoughts בְּעִבְרִית. (hah-tshoo-voht) הַתְּשׁוּבוֹת are at the bottom of the next עַמּוּד.

1. Where is a public telephone? ____________________

2. Where is it possible to buy stamps? ____________________

3. Where is it possible to send a telegram? ____________________

4. Where is it possible to send postcards? ____________________

5. Where is the post office? ____________________

פ

popcorn	(pohp-korn)	פּוֹפּ קוֹרְן
poker	(poh-ker)	פּוֹקֶר
picnic	(peek-neek)	פִּיקְנִיק
lantern	(pah-nahs)	פָּנָס
lamppost	(pah-nahs-ruh-Hohv)	פָּנָס רְחוֹב

6. Where is it possible to buy stamps? ____________

7. Airmail ? ____________

8. Where is it possible to send a package? ____________

9. At counter seven. ____________

10. Where is counter seven ? ____________

הִנֵּה are more verbs.

give me = תֵּן לִי *(lee) (ten)* to write = לִכְתּוֹב *(liH-tohv)* to pay (for) = לְשַׁלֵּם *(luh-shah-lem)* my name is = שְׁמִי *(shmee)*

____________ ____________ ____________ ____________

תֵּן לִי *(lee) (ten)* — me give

סֵפֶר, בְּבַקָּשָׁה. *(sef-er) (buh-vah-kuh-shah)* ____ תֵּן לִי

כַּרְטִיס, בְּבַקָּשָׁה. *(kar-tis)* ticket ____ תֵּן לִי

גְּלוּיָה, בְּבַקָּשָׁה. *(gloo-yah)* ____ תֵּן לִי

בּוּלִים, בְּבַקָּשָׁה. *(boo-lim)* ____ תֵּן לִי

לִכְתּוֹב *(liH-tohv)* — write to

אֲנִי ____ כּוֹתֵב ____ מִכְתָּב. *(miH-tahv)* letter

הוּא / אַתָּה ____ כּוֹתֵב ____ סֵפֶר. *(sef-er)*

הִיא / אַתְּ ____ כּוֹתֶבֶת ____ גְּלוּיָה. *(gloo-yah)*

אֲנַחְנוּ / הֵם ____ כּוֹתְבִים ____ מִבְרָק *(miv-rahk)* telegram

לְשַׁלֵּם *(luh-shah-lem)* — (for) pay to

אֲנִי ____ מְשַׁלֵּם ____ הַחֶדֶר. *(hah-Hed-er)* room the

הוּא / אַתָּה ____ מְשַׁלֵּם ____ הַטַּקְסִי. *(hah-tahk-see)* taxi the

הִיא / אַתְּ ____ מְשַׁלֶּמֶת ____ הָאוֹטוֹבּוּס. *(hah-oh-toh-boos)* bus the

אֲנַחְנוּ / הֵם ____ מְשַׁלְּמִים ____ הַכַּרְטִיסִים. *(hah-kar-tih-sim)* tickets the

שְׁמִי . . . *(shmee)* — is name my

שְׁמִי ____________ . *(shmee)*

שְׁמוֹ ____________ . *(shmoh)* is name his

שְׁמָהּ ____________ . *(shmah)* is name her

שִׁמְךָ ____________ . *(shim-Hah)* is name your

הַתְּשׁוּבוֹת

1. אֵיפֹה טֶלֶפוֹן צִבּוּרִי?
2. אֵיפֹה אֶפְשָׁר לִקְנוֹת בּוּלִים?
3. אֵיפֹה אֶפְשָׁר לִשְׁלוֹחַ מִבְרָק?
4. אֵיפֹה אֶפְשָׁר לִשְׁלוֹחַ גְּלוּיוֹת?
5. אֵיפֹה מִשְׂרַד הַדּוֹאַר?
6. אֵיפֹה אֶפְשָׁר לִקְנוֹת בּוּלִים?
7. בְּדוֹאַר אֲוִיר?
8. אֵיפֹה אֶפְשָׁר לִשְׁלוֹחַ חֲבִילָה?
9. בְּאֶשְׁנָב שֶׁבַע.
10. אֵיפֹה אֶשְׁנָב שֶׁבַע?

Step 16

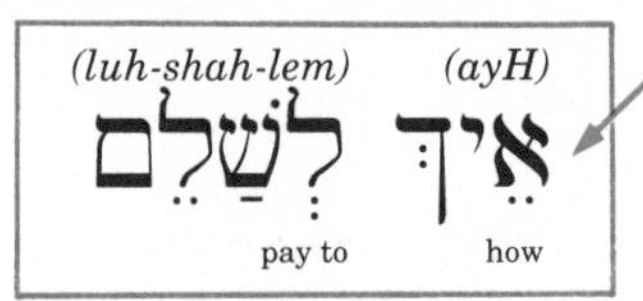

(ken) כֵּן, there are also (Hesh-boh-noht) חֶשְׁבּוֹנוֹת (bills) to pay בְּיִשְׂרָאֵל. You have just finished your delicious meal וְ you would like (hah-Hesh-bon) הַחֶשְׁבּוֹן (bill the). (ayH) אֵיךְ do you do this? אַתָּה call for the (mel-tsar) מֶלְצָר (waiter), or the (mel-tsah-rit) מֶלְצָרִית (waitress):

(buh-vah-kah-shah) (hah-Hesh-bon) (mel-tsar)
מֶלְצָר, הַחֶשְׁבּוֹן בְּבַקָּשָׁה.

(mel-tsah-rit)
מֶלְצָרִית, הַחֶשְׁבּוֹן בְּבַקָּשָׁה.

(hah-mel-tsar) הַמֶּלְצָר will normally reel off what אַתָּה have eaten, while writing rapidly. (hoo) הוּא will then place a piece of paper on (hah-shool-Hahn) הַשּׁוּלְחָן that looks like the one (bah-tmoo-nah) בַּתְּמוּנָה (picture the in), while saying something like:

(shkah-lim) (Hah-mish-im) (oh-leh) (zeh)
"זֶה עוֹלֶה חֲמִשִּׁים שְׁקָלִים."

אַתָּה will pay (hah-mel-tsar) הַמֶּלְצָר or perhaps אַתָּה will pay the (koo-pah-ee) קוּפַּאי (cashier). Remember, the service is generally included in (hah-Hesh-bon) הַחֶשְׁבּוֹן.

If אַתָּה are planning to dine out בְּיִשְׂרָאֵל, you should make reservations. It can be very difficult to get into a popular (mis-ah-dah) מִסְעָדָה. Nevertheless, the experience is well worth the trouble אַתָּה will go to to obtain a reservation. וְ remember, אַתָּה know enough עִבְרִית to make a reservation!

פּ	Passover	(pes-aH)	פֶּסַח
	statue	(pes-el)	פֶּסֶל
	project	(proh-yekt)	פְּרוֹיֶקְט
	permanent	(pair-mah-nent)	פֶּרְמָנֶנְט
	park	(park)	פַּרְק

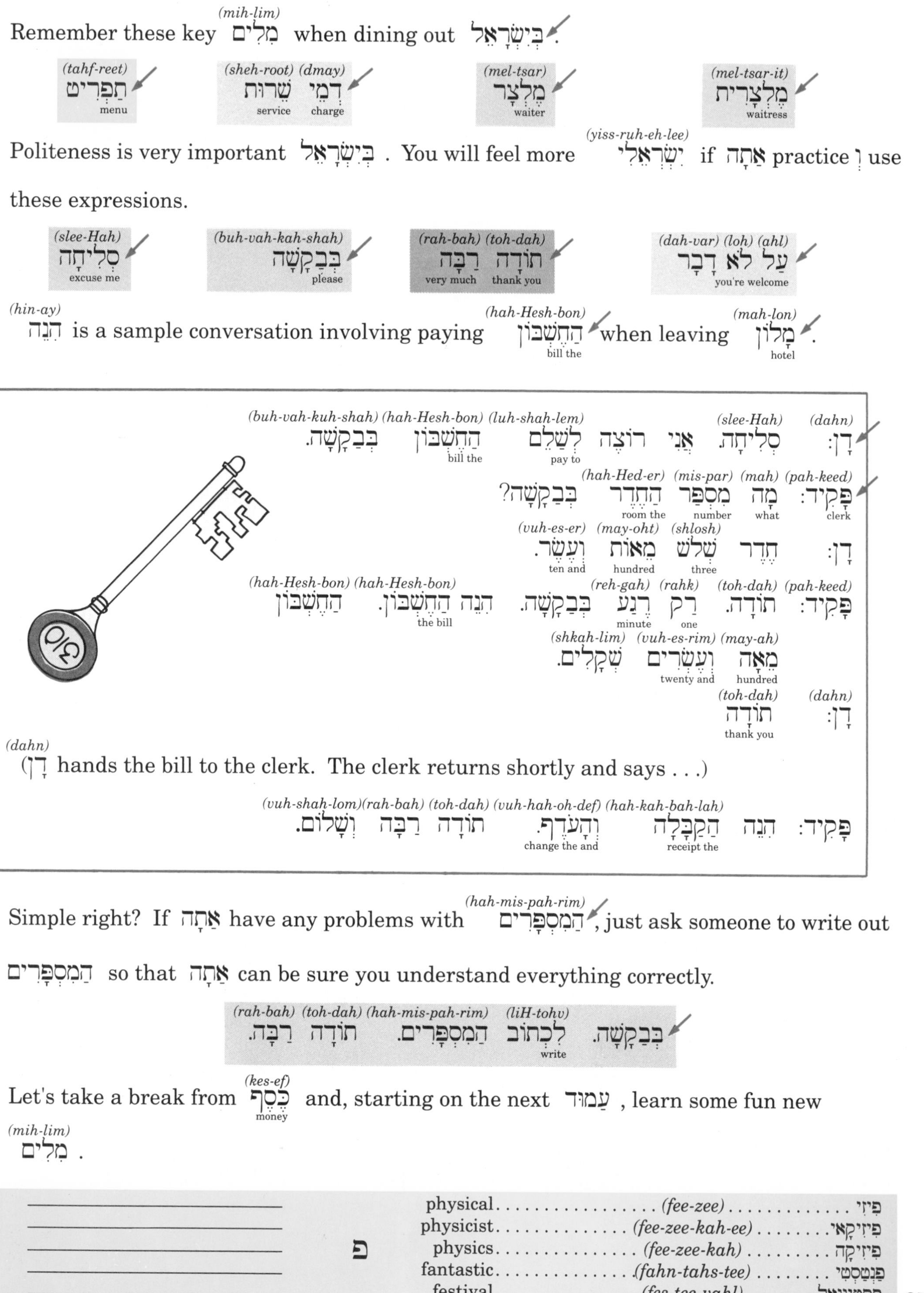

Remember these key (mih-lim) מִלִּים when dining out בְּיִשְׂרָאֵל.

(tahf-reet) תַּפְרִיט menu	(sheh-root) (dmay) שֵׁרוּת דְּמֵי service charge	(mel-tsar) מֶלְצַר waiter	(mel-tsar-it) מֶלְצָרִית waitress

Politeness is very important בְּיִשְׂרָאֵל . You will feel more (yiss-ruh-eh-lee) יִשְׂרְאֵלִי if אַתָּה practice וְ use these expressions.

(slee-Hah) סְלִיחָה excuse me	(buh-vah-kah-shah) בְּבַקָּשָׁה please	(rah-bah) (toh-dah) תּוֹדָה רַבָּה thank you very much	(dah-var) (loh) (ahl) עַל לֹא דָבָר you're welcome

(hin-ay) הִנֵּה is a sample conversation involving paying (hah-Hesh-bon) הַחֶשְׁבּוֹן (the bill) when leaving (mah-lon) מָלוֹן (hotel).

דָּן: (dahn) סְלִיחָה. (slee-Hah) אֲנִי רוֹצֶה לְשַׁלֵּם (luh-shah-lem, to pay) הַחֶשְׁבּוֹן (hah-Hesh-bon, the bill) בְּבַקָּשָׁה. (buh-vah-kuh-shah)

פָּקִיד: (pah-keed, clerk) מָה (mah, what) מִסְפַּר (mis-par, number) הַחֶדֶר (hah-Hed-er, the room) בְּבַקָּשָׁה?

דָּן: חֶדֶר שְׁלֹשׁ (shlosh, three) מֵאוֹת (may-oht, hundred) וָעֶשֶׂר. (vuh-es-er, and ten)

פָּקִיד: (pah-keed) תּוֹדָה. (toh-dah) רַק (rahk, one) רֶגַע (reh-gah, minute) בְּבַקָּשָׁה. הִנֵּה הַחֶשְׁבּוֹן. (hah-Hesh-bon, the bill) הַחֶשְׁבּוֹן (hah-Hesh-bon)
מֵאָה (may-ah, hundred) וְעֶשְׂרִים (vuh-es-rim, and twenty) שְׁקָלִים. (shkah-lim)

דָּן: (dahn) תּוֹדָה (toh-dah, thank you)

((dahn) דָּן hands the bill to the clerk. The clerk returns shortly and says . . .)

פָּקִיד: הִנֵּה הַקַּבָּלָה (hah-kah-bah-lah, the receipt) וְהָעֹדֶף. (vuh-hah-oh-def, and the change) תּוֹדָה (toh-dah) רַבָּה (rah-bah) וְשָׁלוֹם. (vuh-shah-lom)

Simple right? If אַתָּה have any problems with (hah-mis-pah-rim) הַמִּסְפָּרִים, just ask someone to write out הַמִּסְפָּרִים so that אַתָּה can be sure you understand everything correctly.

בְּבַקָּשָׁה. לִכְתּוֹב (liH-tohv, write) הַמִּסְפָּרִים. (hah-mis-pah-rim) תּוֹדָה (toh-dah) רַבָּה. (rah-bah)

Let's take a break from (kes-ef) כֶּסֶף (money) and, starting on the next עַמּוּד , learn some fun new (mih-lim) מִלִּים .

פ

physical	(fee-zee)	פִיזִי
physicist	(fee-zee-kah-ee)	פִיזִיקַאי
physics	(fee-zee-kah)	פִיזִיקָה
fantastic	(fahn-tahs-tee)	פַנְטַסְטִי
festival	(fes-tee-vahl)	פֶסְטִיבָל

(bah-ree) (hoo)
הוּא בָּרִיא.
healthy
(Hoh-leh) (hoo)
הוּא חוֹלֶה.
sick
(tohv) (zeh)
זֶה טוֹב.
it
(tohv) (loh) (zeh)
זֶה לֹא טוֹב.
not it
(rah)
זֶה רַע.
bad
בְּקוֹל רָם
(rahm) (buh-kohl) (muh-dah-bair)
אַתָּה מְדַבֵּר בְּקוֹל רָם.
voice loud a in speak
(buh-shek-et)(muh-dah-bair) (hoo)
הוּא מְדַבֵּר בְּשֶׁקֶט.
softly speaks
בְּשֶׁקֶט
(Hah-mim) (hah-mah-yim)
הַמַּיִם חַמִּים
hot water the
(mah-ah-loht)(vuh-Hah-mesh) (shloh-shim)
שְׁלֹשִׁים וְחָמֵשׁ מַעֲלוֹת
degrees
35°
(kar-im) (hah-mah-yim)
הַמַּיִם קָרִים.
cold
(mah-ah-loht) (Hah-mesh)
חָמֵשׁ מַעֲלוֹת.
5°
(kah-tsar)(hah-ah-dohm)(hah-kahv)
הַקַּו הָאָדוֹם קָצָר.
short red line the
(ah-roH)(hah-kah-Hohl)(hah-kahv)
הַקַּו הַכָּחוֹל אָרוֹךְ.
long blue
(gvoh-hah) (hah-ish-ah)
הָאִשָּׁה גְּבוֹהָה.
tall woman the
(nah-mooH) (hah-yel-ed)
הַיֶּלֶד נָמוּךְ.
short child the
(may-ahl)
מֵעַל
(lah)
לַ
(smohl)
שְׂמֹאל
(yah-meen)
יָמִין
(mee-tah-Haht)
מִתַּחַת
(lah)
לַ
(ah-veh) (hah-ah-dohm) (hah-sef-er)
הַסֵּפֶר הָאָדוֹם עָבֶה.
thick red book the
(dahk)(hah-yah-rok)
הַסֵּפֶר הַיָּרוֹק דַּק.
thin green
(luh-shah-ah) (kee-loh-met-er) (Hah-mish-ah)
חֲמִשָּׁה קִילוֹמֶטֶר לְשָׁעָה
five
(luh-shah-ah) (kee-loh-met-er) (may-ah)
מֵאָה קִילוֹמֶטֶר לְשָׁעָה
hour (per) kilometers hundred
(luh-aht)
לְאַט
slow
(mah-hair)
מַהֵר
fast
צ
painter. . . . . (tsah-bah) . . . . צַבָּע
paint. . . . . (tseh-vah) . . . . צֶבַע
diver. . . . . (tsoh-luh-lahn) . . . . צוֹלְלָן
civilization. . . . .(tsee-vee-lee-zah-tsee-yah) . . . . . . צִיוִילִיזַאצְיָה
painting. . . . .(tsee-oor) . . . . ציּוּר

(met-er) (eh-lah-fim) (shloh-shet) (gvoh-him) (hem) (gvoh-him) (heh-hah-rim)
הֶהָרִים גְּבוֹהִים. הֵם גְּבוֹהִים שְׁלֹשֶׁת אֲלָפִים מֶטֶר.
meters thousand three they high mountains the

(met-er) (may-oht) (shmoh-neh) (rahk) (nim-ooH-im)
הֶהָרִים נְמוּכִים. הֵם גְּבוֹהִים רַק שְׁמוֹנֶה מֵאוֹת מֶטֶר.
hundred eight only low

(shiv-im) (ben) (hoo) (zah-ken)(hah-sah-bah)
הַסַּבָּא זָקֵן. הוּא בֶּן שִׁבְעִים.
seventy he old grandfather the

(es-er) (ben) (rahk) (hoo)(kah-tahn)(hah-yel-ed)
הַיֶּלֶד קָטָן. הוּא רַק בֶּן עֶשֶׂר.
ten only young child the

(shkah-lim)(vuh-shih-shim)(may-ah) (oh-leh) (hoo) (yah-kar)(bah-mah-lon)(hah-Hed-er)
הַחֶדֶר בְּמָלוֹן יָקָר. הוּא עוֹלֶה מֵאָה וְשִׁשִּׁים שְׁקָלִים.
sixty and hundred costs expensive

(ar-bah-im) (oh-leh) (hoo) (zohl) (noh-ar) (buh-aH-sahn-yaht)
הַחֶדֶר בְּאַכְסַנְיַת נוֹעַר זוֹל. הוּא עוֹלֶה אַרְבָּעִים שְׁקָלִים.
forty cheap youth hostel

(kes-ef) (har-bay) (zeh) (ah-sheer) (el-ef) (lee) (yesh)
יֵשׁ לִי אֶלֶף שְׁקָלִים. אֲנִי עָשִׁיר. זֶה הַרְבֵּה כֶּסֶף.
money lot (is) it rich have I

(kes-ef) (muh-aht) (zeh)(ah-nee) (hoo) (may-ah) (rahk) (loh) (yesh)
יֵשׁ לוֹ רַק מֵאָה שְׁקָלִים. הוּא עָנִי. זֶה מְעַט כֶּסֶף.
little poor only has he

to know (how) = (lah-dah-aht) לָדַעַת   to read = (lik-roh) לִקְרֹא   I can = (yah-Hohl) יָכוֹל   I must = (tsah-reeH) צָרִיךְ

________________ ________________ ________________ ________________

Use the flash cards at the back of הַסֵּפֶר to drill these ן other verbs. You will see the (☺) and (☻) "I" form of each verb, so choose the appropriate one and drill yourself.

The verbs (yah-Hohl) יָכוֹל can and (tsah-reeH) צָרִיךְ must can be joined with another verb:

(iv-rit) (lik-roh)(yah-Hohl)
אֲנִי יָכוֹל לִקְרֹא עִבְרִית.

(luh-hah-veen)(yah-Hohl)
אֲנִי יָכוֹל לְהָבִין עִבְרִית.
understand

(luh-dah-bair)
אֲנִי יָכוֹל לְדַבֵּר עִבְרִית.
speak

(iv-rit) (lil-mohd)(tsah-reeH)
אֲנִי צָרִיךְ לִלְמוֹד עִבְרִית.
learn

(gloo-yah) (lik-noht)(tsah-reeH)
אֲנִי צָרִיךְ לִקְנוֹת גְּלוּיָה.
buy

(luh-yiss-rah-el)(lin-soh-ah)
אֲנִי צָרִיךְ לִנְסוֹעַ לְיִשְׂרָאֵל.
travel

צ

cynical. . . . .(tsee-nee) . . . . צִינִי
plant. . . . .(tseh-maH) . . . . צֶמַח
bird. . . . .(tsih-pohr) . . . . צִפּוֹר
France. . . . .(tsar-faht) . . . . צָרְפַת
French. . . . .(tsar-fah-tee) . . . . צָרְפָתִי

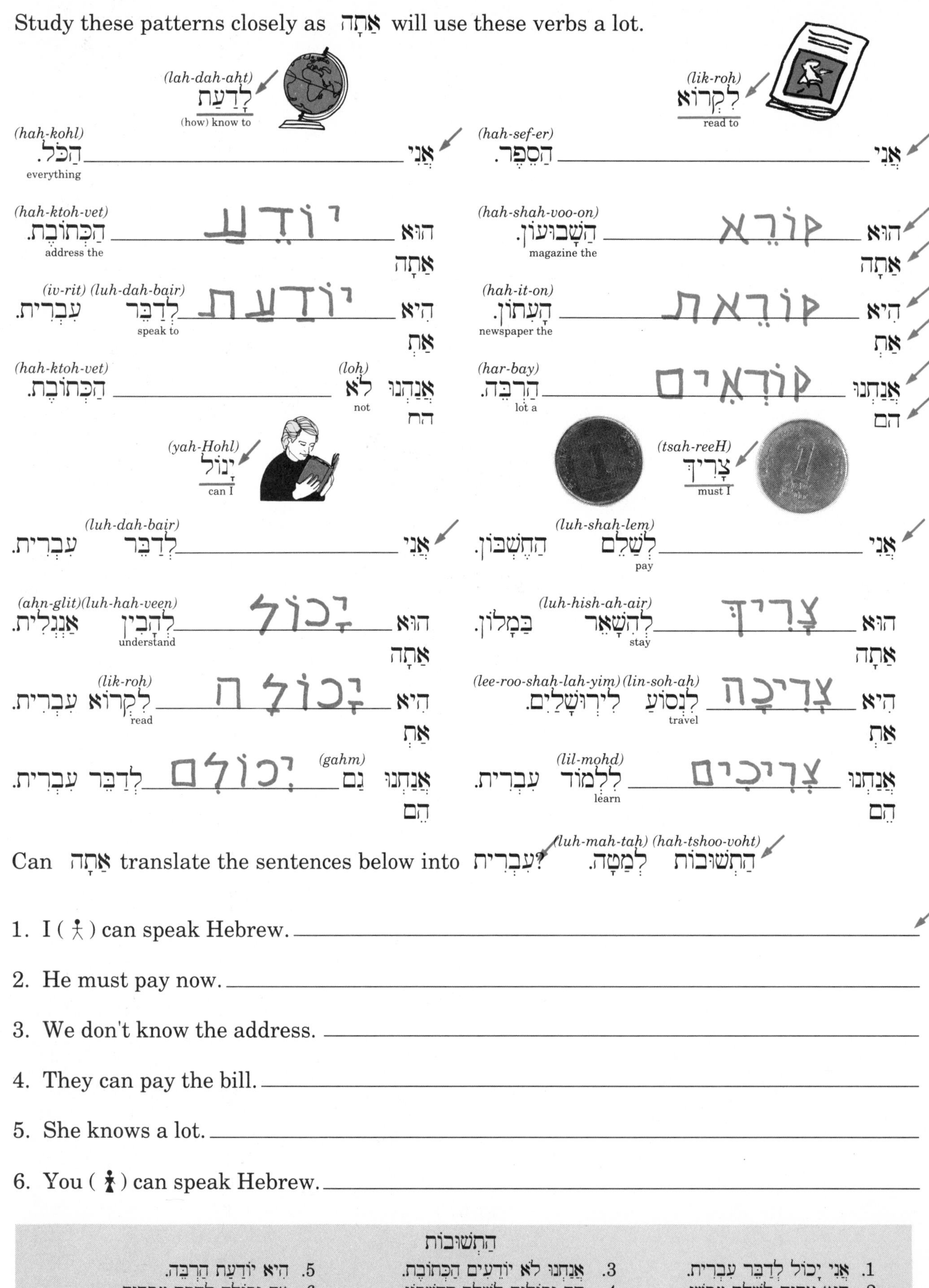

Study these patterns closely as אַתָּה will use these verbs a lot.

(lik-roh) לִקְרוֹא — read to

אֲנִי ______ הַסֵּפֶר. (hah-sef-er)

הוּא / אַתָּה ___קוֹרֵא___ הַשָּׁבוּעוֹן. (hah-shah-voo-on) magazine the

הִיא / אַתְּ ___קוֹרֵאת___ הָעִתּוֹן. (hah-it-on) newspaper the

אֲנַחְנוּ / הֵם ___קוֹרְאִים___ הַרְבֵּה. (har-bay) lot a

(lah-dah-aht) לָדַעַת — (how) know to

אֲנִי ______ הַכֹּל. (hah-kohl) everything

הוּא / אַתָּה ___יוֹדֵעַ___ הַכְּתוֹבֶת. (hah-ktoh-vet) address the

הִיא / אַתְּ ___יוֹדַעַת___ לְדַבֵּר (luh-dah-bair) speak to עִבְרִית. (iv-rit)

אֲנַחְנוּ / הֵם לֹא (loh) not ______ הַכְּתוֹבֶת. (hah-ktoh-vet)

(tsah-reeH) צָרִיךְ — must I

אֲנִי ______ לְשַׁלֵּם (luh-shah-lem) pay הַחֶשְׁבּוֹן.

הוּא / אַתָּה ___צָרִיךְ___ לְהִשָּׁאֵר (luh-hish-ah-air) stay בַּמָּלוֹן.

הִיא / אַתְּ ___צְרִיכָה___ לִנְסוֹעַ (lin-soh-ah) travel לִירוּשָׁלַיִם. (lee-roo-shah-lah-yim)

אֲנַחְנוּ / הֵם ___צְרִיכִים___ לִלְמוֹד (lil-mohd) learn עִבְרִית.

(yah-Hohl) יָכוֹל — can I

אֲנִי ______ לְדַבֵּר (luh-dah-bair) עִבְרִית.

הוּא / אַתָּה ___יָכוֹל___ לְהָבִין (luh-hah-veen) understand אַנְגְּלִית. (ahn-glit)

הִיא / אַתְּ ___יְכוֹלָה___ לִקְרוֹא (lik-roh) read עִבְרִית.

אֲנַחְנוּ / הֵם גַּם (gahm) ___יְכוֹלִים___ לְדַבֵּר עִבְרִית.

Can אַתָּה translate the sentences below into עִבְרִית? הַתְּשׁוּבוֹת (hah-tshoo-voht) לְמַטָּה. (luh-mah-tah)

1. I (🚹) can speak Hebrew. ______
2. He must pay now. ______
3. We don't know the address. ______
4. They can pay the bill. ______
5. She knows a lot. ______
6. You (🚺) can speak Hebrew. ______

הַתְּשׁוּבוֹת

1. אֲנִי יָכוֹל לְדַבֵּר עִבְרִית.
2. הוּא צָרִיךְ לְשַׁלֵּם עַכְשָׁו.
3. אֲנַחְנוּ לֹא יוֹדְעִים הַכְּתוֹבֶת.
4. הֵם יְכוֹלִים לְשַׁלֵּם הַחֶשְׁבּוֹן.
5. הִיא יוֹדַעַת הַרְבֵּה.
6. אַתְּ יְכוֹלָה לְדַבֵּר עִבְרִית.

(aH-shahv) עַכְשָׁו draw lines *(bane)* בֵּין (between) the opposites *(luh-mah-tah)* לְמַטָּה. Don't forget to say them out loud. Use these מִלִּים everyday to describe *(hah-dvah-rim)* הַדְּבָרִים in your *(bah-yit)* בַּיִת, in your *(hah-sef-er)* הַסֵּפֶר *(bait)* בֵּית (school), at work, etc.

אַתָּה will probably want to try swimming in *(hah-mel-aH) (yahm)* הַמֶּלַח יָם (Dead Sea) — it is very *(nah-mooH)* נָמוּךְ (low). In fact it is the lowest place on earth! Not far away is the fortress of *(muh-tsah-dah)* מְצָדָה (Masada) — it is *(gvoh-hah)* גְבוֹהָה (high). In your travels, you should also include *(kin-eh-ret) (yahm)* כִּנֶּרֶת יָם (Sea of Galilee) plus *(hah-mah-ah-rah-vee) (hah-koh-tel)* הַמַּעֲרָבִי הַכֹּתֶל and of course *(hah-ah-tee-kah) (hah-eer)* הָעַתִּיקָה הָעִיר (Old City the) on your list of places to visit בְּיִשְׂרָאֵל.

______________________	ק	kibbutz	*(kih-boots)*	קִבּוּץ
______________________		comedy	*(koh-meh-dee-ah)*	קוֹמֶדְיָה
______________________		congress	*(kohn-gres)*	קוֹנְגְרֶס
______________________		conflict	*(kohn-fleekt)*	קוֹנְפְלִיקְט
______________________		cocktail	*(kohk-tail)*	קוֹקְטֵיל

Step 17

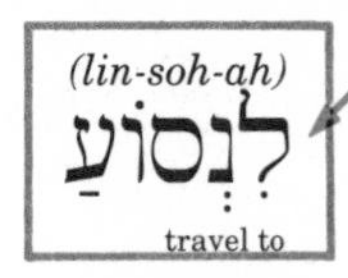

(lin-soh-ah) לִנְסוֹעַ travel to

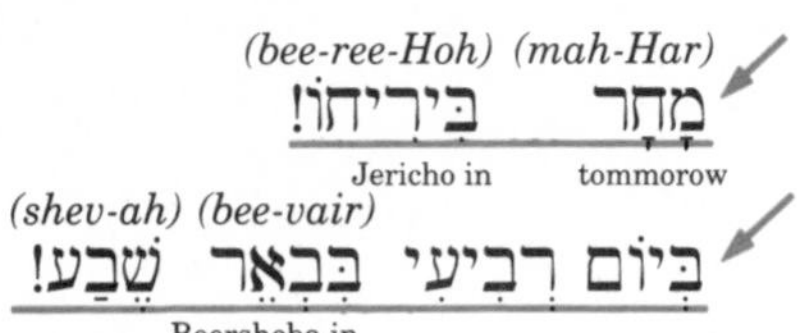

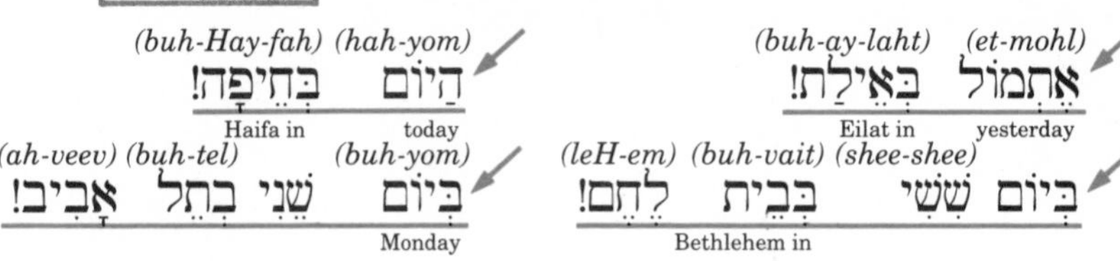

(et-mohl) (buh-ay-laht) אֶתְמוֹל בְּאֵילַת! yesterday Eilat in

(hah-yom) (buh-Hay-fah) הַיּוֹם בְּחֵיפָה! today Haifa in

(mah-Har) (bee-ree-Hoh) מָחָר בִּירִיחוֹ! tommorow Jericho in

(shee-shee) (buh-vait) (leH-em) בְּיוֹם שִׁשִּׁי בְּבֵית לֶחֶם! Bethlehem in

(buh-yom) (buh-tel) (ah-veev) בְּיוֹם שֵׁנִי בְּתֵל אָבִיב! Monday

(bee-vair) (shev-ah) בְּיוֹם רְבִיעִי בִּבְאֵר שֶׁבַע! Beersheba in

אַתָּה will find it easy to travel around בְּיִשְׂרָאֵל, as it is a very small country. אַתָּה will also be surprised at the variety of scenery בְּיִשְׂרָאֵל.

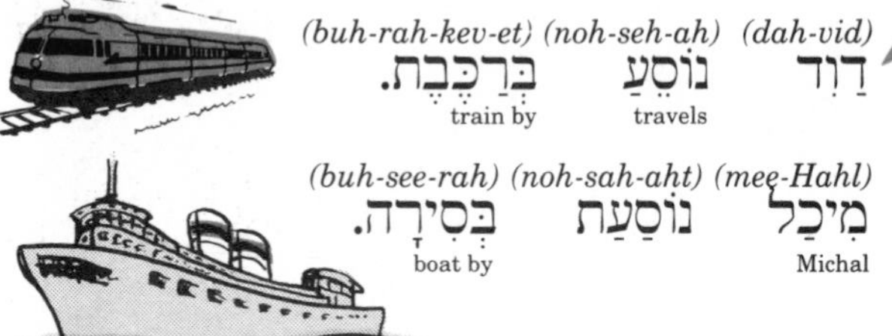

(dah-vid) (noh-seh-ah) (buh-rah-kev-et) דָּוִד נוֹסֵעַ בְּרַכֶּבֶת. travels train by

(Hah-nah) (noh-sah-aht) (bee-muh-Hoh-nit) חַנָּה נוֹסַעַת בִּמְכוֹנִית.

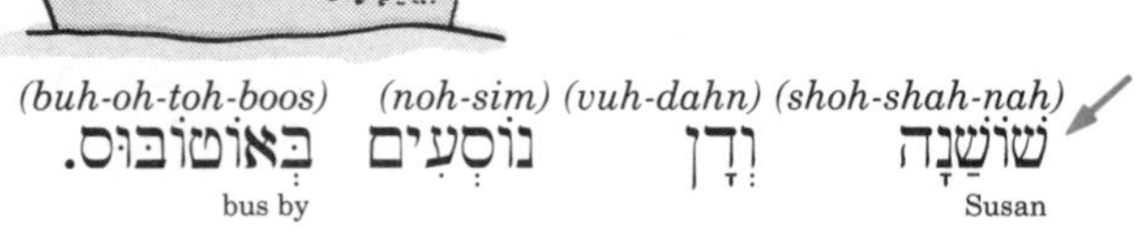

(mee-Hahl) (noh-sah-aht) (buh-see-rah) מִיכַל נוֹסַעַת בְּסִירָה. Michal boat by

(boh-ahz) (noh-seh-ah) (buh-mah-tohs) בּוֹעַז נוֹסֵעַ בְּמָטוֹס. airplane by

(shoh-shah-nah) (vuh-dahn) (noh-sim) (buh-oh-toh-boos) שׁוֹשַׁנָּה וְדָן נוֹסְעִים בְּאוֹטוֹבּוּס. Susan bus by

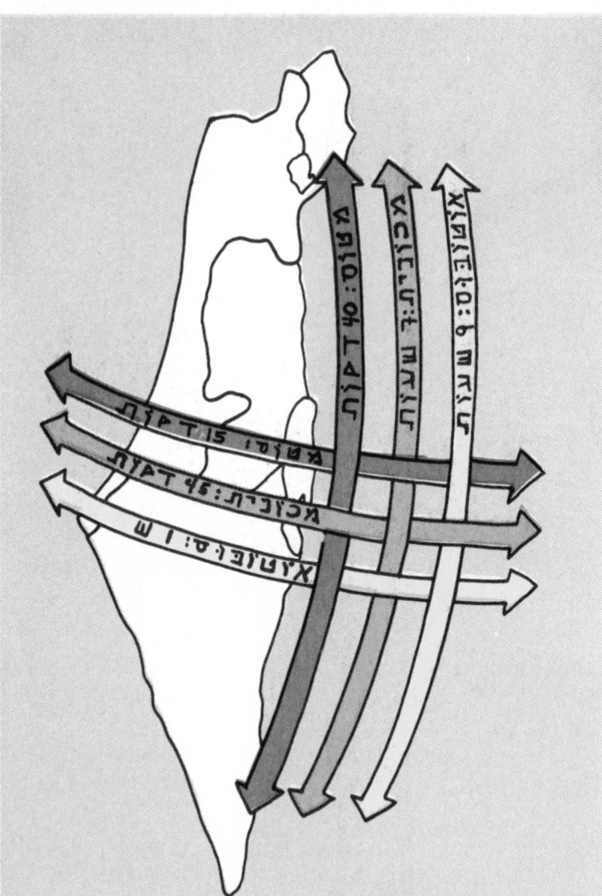

(hah-im) (roh-eh) הַאִם אַתָּה רוֹאֶה do see

(hah-mah-pah) (mee-smohl) (zoht) הַמַּפָּה מִשְּׂמֹאל? זֹאת map the left on is it

(mee-tsah-fon) יִשְׂרָאֵל. מִצָּפוֹן north from

(luh-dar-om) (noh-seh-ah) לְדָרוֹם אַתָּה נוֹסֵעַ south to travel

(ar-bah-im) (dah-koht) (buh-mah-tohs) אַרְבָּעִים דַּקּוֹת בְּמָטוֹס, minutes plane by

(bee-muh-Hoh-nit) (sheh-vah) (shah-oht) בִּמְכוֹנִית שֶׁבַע שָׁעוֹת, car by hours

(tay-shah) (shah-oht) וּבְאוֹטוֹבּוּס תֵּשַׁע שָׁעוֹת. bus by and nine

(loh) (rah) (nah-Hon) לֹא רָע, נָכוֹן? not bad it is

kiosk	(kee-ohsk)	קִיוֹסְק	ק
easy	(kahl)	קַל	
client	(klee-ent)	קְלִיאֶנְט	
campus	(kahm-poos)	קַמְפּוּס	
Canada	(kah-nah-dah)	קָנָדָה	

(hah-yiss-ruh-el-im) הַיִשְׂרְאֵלִים (Israelis the) love *(lin-soh-ah)* לִנְסוֹעַ (travel to) so *(loh)(zeh)* זֶה לֹא (no (is) it) wonder to find many מִלִים revolving around the concept of travel which is exactly what אַתָּה want to do. Practice saying the following מִלִים many times. אַתָּה will see them often.

(nuh-see-ah) נְסִיעָה — trip/journey

(lin-soh-ah) לִנְסוֹעַ — travel to

(noh-say-ah) נוֹסֵעַ — traveler

(lin-soh-ah) (buh-mah-tohs) לִנְסוֹעַ בְּמָטוֹס — airplane by

(buh-see-rah) לִנְסוֹעַ בְּסִירָה — boat by

(bee-muh-Hoh-nit) לִנְסוֹעַ בִּמְכוֹנִית

(buh-rah-kev-et) לִנְסוֹעַ בְּרַכֶּבֶת — train by

(buh-oh-toh-boos) לִנְסוֹעַ בְּאוֹטוֹבּוּס

(buh-oh-fah-nah-yim) לִנְסוֹעַ בְּאוֹפַנַּיִם — bicycle by

(nuh-see-ah) (toh-vah) נְסִיעָה טוֹבָה! — journey good

(soH-noot) (nuh-see-oht) סוֹכְנוּת נְסִיעוֹת — agency travel

(lah-leH-et) (bah-reg-el) לָלֶכֶת בָּרֶגֶל — go to foot (on)

(luh-mah-tah) לְמַטָּה are some basic signs which אַתָּה should learn to recognize quickly. Most of these מִלִים come from the verbs *(luh-hih-kah-ness)* לְהִכָּנֵס (enter to) and *(lah-tset)* לָצֵאת (exit to).

(kuh-nee-sah) כְּנִיסָה — entrance ______________________

(yuh-tsee-ah) יְצִיאָה — exit ______________________

(ayn) (yuh-tsee-ah) אֵין יְצִיאָה — no ______________________

(ayn) (kuh-nee-sah) אֵין כְּנִיסָה — no ______________________

(duh-Hohf) דְּחוֹף — push ______________________

(muh-shoH) מְשׁוֹךְ — pull ______________________

כניסה

יציאה

משוך

דחוף

ק

______________	motor home	*(kah-rah-vahn)*	קָרָאוָן
______________	carp	*(kar-pee-ohn)*	קַרְפִּיוֹן
______________	circus	*(keer-kahs)*	קִרְקָס
______________	butcher	*(kah-tsahv)*	קַצָּב
______________	difficult	*(kah-sheh)*	קָשֶׁה

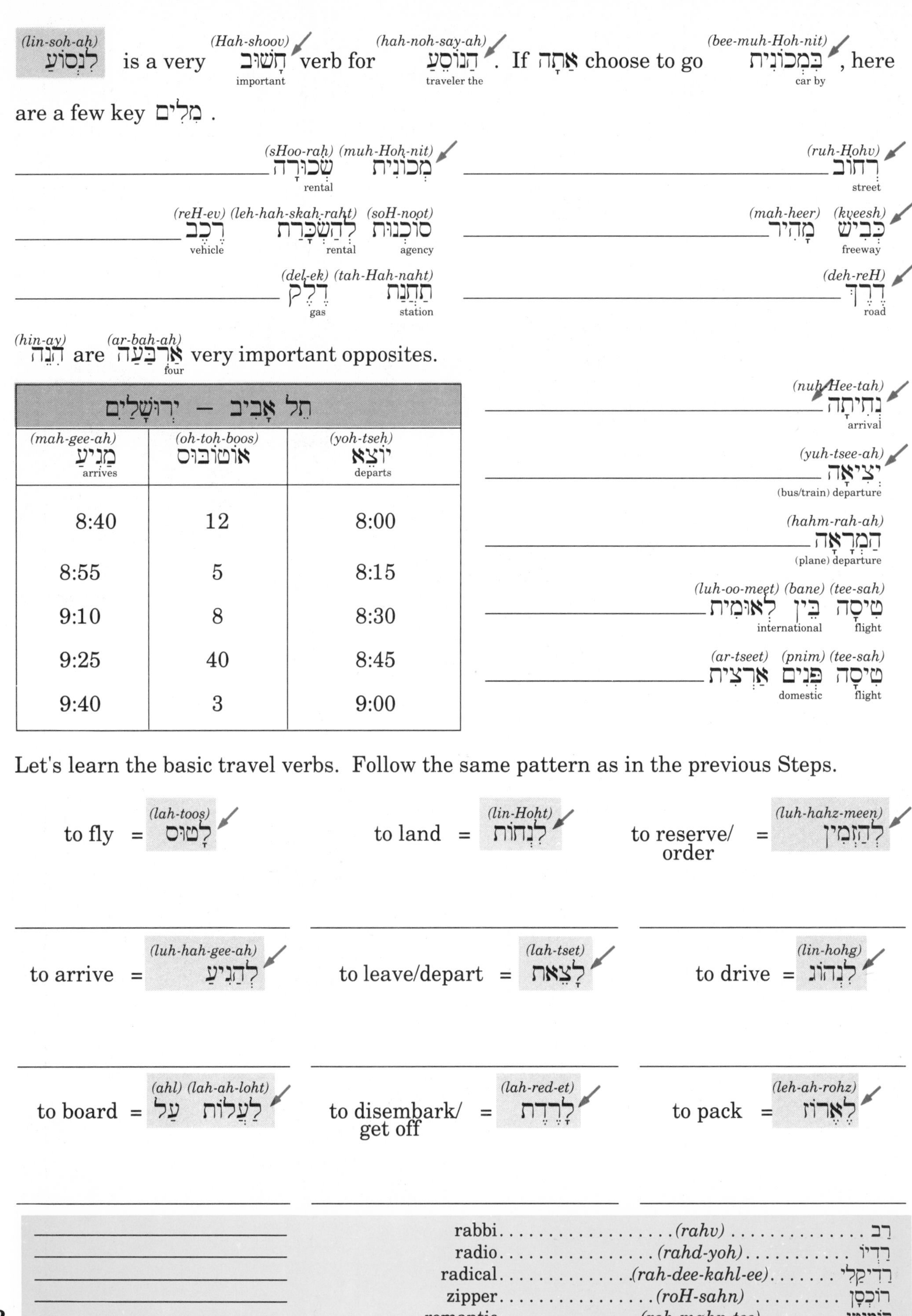

(lin-soh-ah) לִנְסוֹעַ is a very (Hah-shoov) חָשׁוּב (important) verb for (hah-noh-say-ah) הַנּוֹסֵעַ (traveler the). If אַתָּה choose to go (bee-muh-Hoh-nit) בִּמְכוֹנִית (car by), here are a few key מִלִּים .

(ruh-Hohv) רְחוֹב (street) ______________________ (sHoo-rah) (muh-Hoh-nit) שְׂכוּרָה מְכוֹנִית (rental) ______________________

(mah-heer) (kveesh) מָהִיר כְּבִישׁ (freeway) ______________________ (reH-ev) (leh-hah-skah-raht) (soH-noot) רֶכֶב לְהַשְׂכָּרַת סוֹכְנוּת (vehicle, rental, agency) ______________________

(deh-reH) דֶּרֶךְ (road) ______________________ (del-ek) (tah-Hah-naht) דֶּלֶק תַּחֲנַת (gas, station) ______________________

(hin-ay) הִנֵּה are (ar-bah-ah) אַרְבַּעָה (four) very important opposites.

תֵּל אָבִיב — יְרוּשָׁלַיִם		
(mah-gee-ah) מַגִּיעַ arrives	(oh-toh-boos) אוֹטוֹבּוּס	(yoh-tseh) יוֹצֵא departs
8:40	12	8:00
8:55	5	8:15
9:10	8	8:30
9:25	40	8:45
9:40	3	9:00

(nuh-Hee-tah) נְחִיתָה (arrival) ______________________

(yuh-tsee-ah) יְצִיאָה ((bus/train) departure) ______________________

(hahm-rah-ah) הַמְרָאָה ((plane) departure) ______________________

(luh-oo-meet) (bane) (tee-sah) לְאוּמִית בֵּין טִיסָה (international, flight) ______________________

(ar-tseet) (pnim) (tee-sah) אַרְצִית פְּנִים טִיסָה (domestic, flight) ______________________

Let's learn the basic travel verbs. Follow the same pattern as in the previous Steps.

to fly = (lah-toos) לָטוּס

to land = (lin-Hoht) לִנְחוֹת

to reserve/order = (luh-hahz-meen) לְהַזְמִין

____

to arrive = (luh-hah-gee-ah) לְהַגִּיעַ

to leave/depart = (lah-tset) לָצֵאת

to drive = (lin-hohg) לִנְהוֹג

____

to board = (ahl) (lah-ah-loht) עַל לַעֲלוֹת

to disembark/get off = (lah-red-et) לָרֶדֶת

to pack = (leh-ah-rohz) לֶאֱרוֹז

____

rabbi . . . . (rahv) . . . . רַב
radio . . . . (rahd-yoh) . . . . רַדְיוֹ
radical . . . . (rah-dee-kahl-ee) . . . . רַדִיקָלִי
zipper . . . . (roH-sahn) . . . . רוֹכְסָן
romantic . . . . (roh-mahn-tee) . . . . רוֹמַנְטִי

עִם (im) [with] these verbs אַתָּה are ready for any נְסִיעָה (nuh-see-ah) [journey] anywhere. אַתָּה should have no problem עִם these verbs, just remember the basic "plug-in" formula אֲנַחְנוּ (ah-naH-noo) learned already. Use that knowledge to translate the following thoughts into עִבְרִית (iv-rit). הַתְּשׁוּבוֹת (hah-tshoo-voht) [answers the] לְמַטָּה. [below]

1. I (♂) reserve a car. ______________________________
2. He boards the bus to Bethlehem. ______________________________
3. The bus leaves at 9:30. ______________________________
4. We arrive tomorrow in Israel. ______________________________
5. You (♀) get off in Haifa. ______________________________
6. They travel to Tel Aviv. ______________________________
7. Where is the bus to Jerusalem? ______________________________
8. How do we fly to Israel? With KLM or EL AL? ______________________________

____

הִנֵּה (hin-ay) are some new מִלִּים for your נְסִיעָה (nuh-see-ah). As always, write out הַמִּלִּים and practice the sample sentences out loud.

תַּחֲנַת רַכֶּבֶת (tah-Hah-naht) (rah-kev-et) — station, train

תַּחֲנַת אוֹטוֹבּוּס (tah-Hah-naht) (oh-toh-boos) — station, bus

שְׂדֵה הַתְּעוּפָה (sday) (hah-too-fah) — airport

______________ ______________ ______________

סְלִיחָה. אֵיפֹּה תַּחֲנַת רַכֶּבֶת? (rah-kev-et)

סְלִיחָה. אֵיפֹּה תַּחֲנַת אוֹטוֹבּוּס? (slee-Hah) (tah-Hah-naht)

סְלִיחָה. אֵיפֹּה שְׂדֵה הַתְּעוּפָה? (slee-Hah) (ay-foh) [excuse me] (sday) (hah-too-fah)

הַתְּשׁוּבוֹת

1. אֲנִי מַזְמִין מְכוֹנִית.
2. הוּא עוֹלֶה עַל הָאוֹטוֹבּוּס לְבֵית לֶחֶם.
3. הָאוֹטוֹבּוּס יוֹצֵא בְּתֵשַׁע וָחֵצִי.
4. אֲנַחְנוּ מַגִּיעִים מָחָר לְיִשְׂרָאֵל.
5. אַתְּ יוֹרֶדֶת בְּחֵיפָה.
6. הֵם נוֹסְעִים לְתֵל אָבִיב.
7. אֵיפֹה הָאוֹטוֹבּוּס לִירוּשָׁלַיִם ?
8. אֵיךְ טָסִים לְיִשְׂרָאֵל ? בְּק.ל.ם. אוֹ בְּאֶל עַל ?

(bahnk) בַּנְק
bank

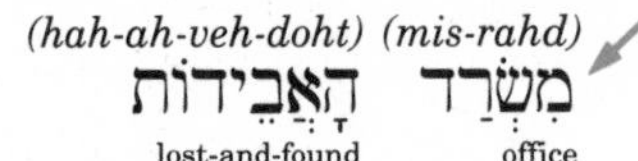

(hah-ah-veh-doht) (mis-rahd)
מִשְׂרַד הָאֲבֵידוֹת
lost-and-found office

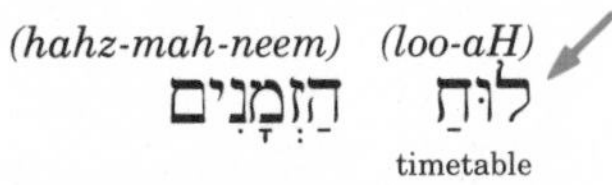

(hahz-mah-neem) (loo-aH)
לוּחַ הַזְּמַנִּים
timetable

תל אביב		
מגיע	#	יוצא
0:41	50	12:41
7:40	19	19:40
12:15	10	0:15
14:32	4	2:32
21:40	22	9:40

______ ______ ______

(slee-Hah)
סְלִיחָה. אֵיפֹה
(hahz-mah-neem) (loo-aH)
לוּחַ הַזְּמַנִּים?

(slee-Hah)
סְלִיחָה. אֵיפֹה
(hah-ah-veh-doht) (mis-rahd)
מִשְׂרַד הָאֲבֵידוֹת?

סְלִיחָה. אֵיפֹה
יֵשׁ בַּנְק?

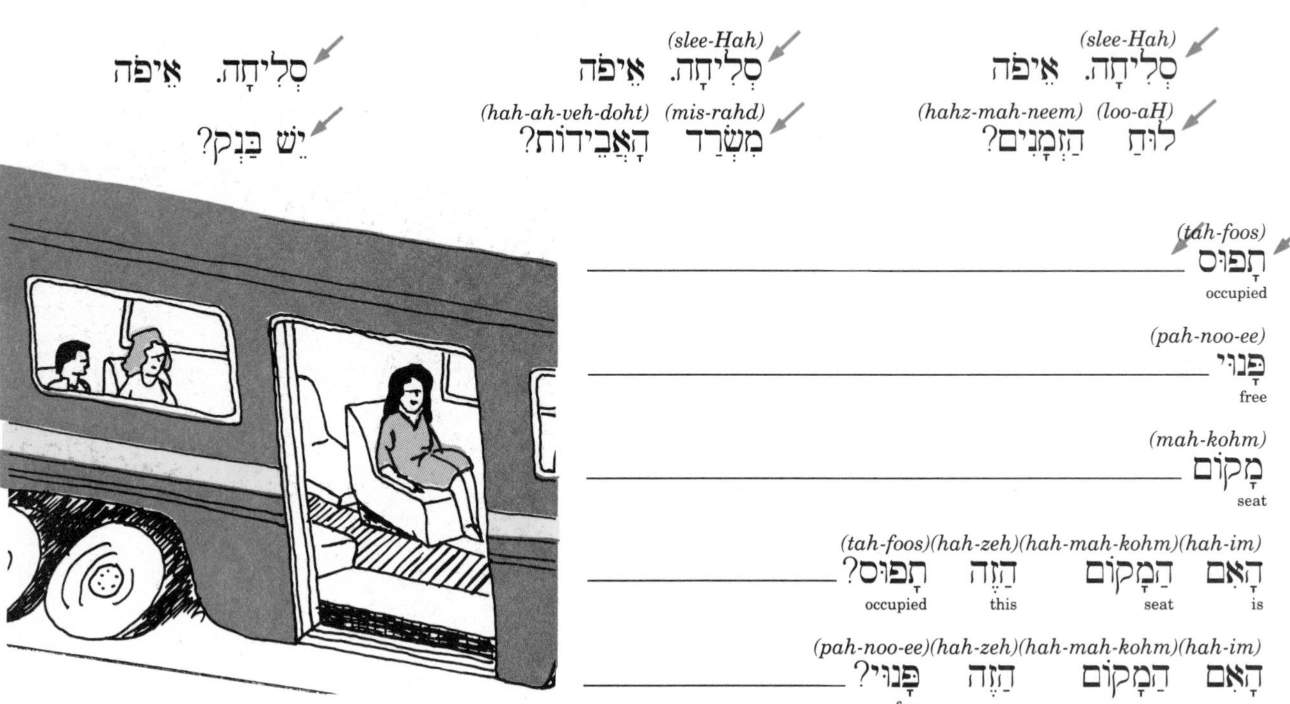

(tah-foos) תָּפוּס occupied ______

(pah-noo-ee) פָּנוּי free ______

(mah-kohm) מָקוֹם seat ______

(tah-foos)(hah-zeh)(hah-mah-kohm)(hah-im)
הַאִם הַמָּקוֹם הַזֶּה תָּפוּס?
is seat this occupied ______

(pah-noo-ee)(hah-zeh)(hah-mah-kohm)(hah-im)
הַאִם הַמָּקוֹם הַזֶּה פָּנוּי?
is seat this free ______

Practice writing out the following (shuh-eh-loht) שְׁאֵלוֹת. It will help you later.

(hah-sheh-roo-tim) (slee-Hah)
סְלִיחָה. אֵיפֹה הַשֵּׁרוּתִים?
toilets the ______

(shmoh-neh) (esh-nahv)
סְלִיחָה. אֵיפֹה אֶשְׁנָב שְׁמוֹנֶה?
counter eight ______

(hah-moh-dee-een)
סְלִיחָה. אֵיפֹה הַמּוֹדִיעִין?
counter information the ______

(luh-ah-shane)(moo-tar)
מוּתָר לְעַשֵּׁן?
allowed smoking ______

(luh-ah-shane) (loh)
לֹא לְעַשֵּׁן!
no smoking ______

______	ר	doctor	(roh-feh)	רוֹפֵא
______		dentist	(roh-feh-shih-nah-yim)	רוֹפֵא שִׁנַּיִם
______		Russian	(roo-see)	רוּסִי
______		Russia	(roos-yah)	רוּסְיָה
______		wet	(rah-tohv)	רָטוֹב

Increase your travel מִלִּים by writing out (luh-mah-tah)(hah-mih-lim) הַמִּלִּים לְמַטָּה and practicing the sample sentences below.

(may) מֵ from ______________________
אֵיפֹה הָאוֹטוֹבּוּס מֵאֵילַת?

(luh) לְ to ______________________
אֵיפֹה הָאוֹטוֹבּוּס לִטְבֶרְיָה?

(hah-moh-dee-een) הַמּוֹדִיעִין information ______________________
אֵיפֹה הַמּוֹדִיעִין?

(kar-tis) כַּרְטִיס ticket ______________________
כַּמָּה עוֹלֶה כַּרְטִיס לְתֵל אָבִיב?

(Hah-fah-tseem)(shmee-raht) שְׁמִירַת חֲפָצִים left-luggage office ______________________
אֵיפֹה שְׁמִירַת הַחֲפָצִים?

(ah-gah-lah) עֲגָלָה cart ______________________
אֵיפֹה יֵשׁ עֲגָלָה?

Practice these מִלִּים every (yom) יוֹם (day). You will be surprised (ayH) אֵיךְ (how) often אַתָּה will use them.

Can אַתָּה read the following paragraph?

> אַתָּה (bah-mah-tohs) בְּמָטוֹס לְיִשְׂרָאֵל. יֵשׁ לְךָ (luh-Hah)(have you) כֶּסֶף (kes-ef), הַכַּרְטִיס (hah-kar-tis), הַדַּרְכּוֹן (hah-dar-kon)(passport) וְהַמִּזְוָדוֹת (vuh-hah-miz-vah-doht)(suitcases the and).
>
> אַתָּה תַּיָּר (tah-yar)(tourist) עַכְשָׁו. אַתָּה מַגִּיעַ (mah-gee-ah)(arrive) מָחָר (mah-Har) בְּעֶשֶׂר (buh-es-er)(ten at) בַּבֹּקֶר (bah-boh-ker) לְיִשְׂרָאֵל. נְסִיעָה (nuh-see-ah) טוֹבָה (toh-vah)!

בְּיִשְׂרָאֵל the bus is the most common form of transport. There are buses in the large towns and cities, as well as three kinds of inter-city buses: (yah-sheer) יָשִׁיר (fastest), (ex-press) אֶקְסְפְּרֶס (fast) and (muh-ah-sef) מְאַסֵּף (slow). A (rah-kev-et) רַכֶּבֶת runs along the coast from (nah-hah-ree-yah) נַהֲרִיָּה (Nahariya) to (ah-veev)(tel) תֵּל אָבִיב, and from (ah-veev)(tel) תֵּל אָבִיב to (yah-roo-shah-lah-yim) יְרוּשָׁלַיִם.

> Note that on (bah-eh-rev) בָּעֶרֶב שִׁשִּׁי (yom) יוֹם and אוֹטוֹבּוּסִים (oh-toh-boos-im) אוֹ (rah-kah-voht) רַכָּבוֹת (trains) (ayn) אֵין (no) (shah-baht) שַׁבָּת (yom) יוֹם.

But don't worry, you will not be stranded. You can always take a (sheh-root) שֵׁרוּת (taxi shared) which runs in and between towns וְ cities. It is an interesting way to meet יִשְׂרְאֵלִים. If אַתָּה travel (buh-rah-kev-et) בְּרַכֶּבֶת, remember that distances are short. There may be a snack bar on the (rah-kev-et) רַכֶּבֶת. Remember, אַתָּה know אֵיךְ to ask things like this. Practice your possible (shuh-eh-loht) שְׁאֵלוֹת by writing out the following samples.

אֵיפֹה (hah-miz-non) הַמִּזְנוֹן? (buffet/snack bar) ______________________

מָתַי (yoh-tseh)(mah-tie) יוֹצֵא הָאוֹטוֹבּוּס (lee-nuh-tahn-yah) לִנְתַנְיָה? ______________________

______________	ר	empty . . . . (rake)	רֵיק
______________		Ramadan . . . . (rah-mah-dahn)	רָמָדָאן
______________		traffic lights . . . . (rahm-zoh-reem)	רַמְזוֹרִים
______________		dancer . . . . (rahk-dahn)	רַקְדָן
______________		rational . . . . (rah-tsee-oh-nah-lee)	רַצְיוֹנָאלִי

What about inquiring about the price of כַּרְטִיסִים? Remember, אַתָּה מְדַבֵּר (muh-dah-bair) speak עִבְרִית and אַתָּה can ask שְׁאֵלוֹת (shuh-eh-loht).

כַּמָּה (kah-mah) עוֹלֶה (oh-leh) כַּרְטִיס (kar-tis) לִירוּשָׁלַיִם? ____________________

הָלוֹךְ (hah-loH) וָשׁוֹב (vah-shohv) round trip? ____ הָלוֹךְ וָשׁוֹב? ____

כַּמָּה עוֹלֶה כַּרְטִיס לִבְאֵר (lee-veer) Beersheba to שֶׁבַע (sheh-vah)? ____________________

מָה (mah) what about times of הַמְּרָאוֹת (hahm-rah-oht) departures and נְחִיתוֹת (nuh-Hit-oht) arrivals? אַתָּה can also ask these שְׁאֵלוֹת (shuh-eh-loht).

מָתַי (mah-tie) when יוֹצֵאת (yoh-tset) leaves הָרַכֶּבֶת (hah-rah-kev-et) train the לְתֵל (luh-tel) אָבִיב (ah-veev)? ____________________

מָתַי (mah-tie) יוֹצֵא (yoh-tseh) הָאוֹטוֹבּוּס לִנְתַנְיָה (lee-nah-tahn-yah) Netanya to? ____________________

מָתַי מַגִּיעַ (mah-gee-ah) arrives הָאוֹטוֹבּוּס מִבְּאֵר (mee-bair) Beersheba from שֶׁבַע (sheh-vah)? ____________________

מָתַי מַגִּיעַ (mah-gee-ah) הַמָּטוֹס (hah-mah-tohs) plane the מִנְיוּ (mee-new) New from יוֹרְק (york) York? ____________________

אַתָּה have arrived in יִשְׂרָאֵל. אַתָּה are עַכְשָׁו at הָאוֹטוֹבּוּס תַּחֲנַת (tah-Hah-naht) station.

אַתָּה רוֹצֶה (roh-tseh) לִנְסוֹעַ (lin-soh-ah) travel to לְחֵיפָה (luh-Hay-fah) Haifa to? Well, tell that to the person at הָאֶשְׁנָב (hah-esh-nahv) counter the selling כַּרְטִיסִים (kar-tih-sim).

אֲנִי רוֹצֶה (roh-tseh) לִנְסוֹעַ (lin-soh-ah) לְחֵיפָה (luh-Hay-fah) Haifa to. ____________________

אֲנִי רוֹצֶה לִנְסוֹעַ (lin-soh-ah) לְתֵל (luh-tel) אָבִיב (ah-veev). ____________________

אֲנַחְנוּ (ah-naH-noo) רוֹצִים (roh-tsim) want לִנְסוֹעַ לִירוּשָׁלַיִם (lee-roo-shah-lah-yim). ____________________

מָתַי (mah-tie) יוֹצֵא (yoh-tseh) leaves הָאוֹטוֹבּוּס לִטְבֶרְיָה (lee-tveh-ree-yah) Tiberias to? ____________________

כַּמָּה (kah-mah) עוֹלֶה (oh-leh) costs כַּרְטִיס (kar-tis) ticket לְחֵיפָה (luh-Hay-fah)? ____________________

אֲנִי רוֹצֶה כַּרְטִיס לְתֵל (luh-tel) אָבִיב (ah-veev). ____________________

הָלוֹךְ (hah-loH) וָשׁוֹב (vah-shohv) round trip? ____________________ תּוֹדָה (toh-dah) thank you. ____________________

עִם this practice, אַתָּה are off וְ running. These travel מִלִּים will make your holiday twice as enjoyable וְ at least three times as easy. Review these new מִלִּים by doing the crossword puzzle on page 77. Practice drilling yourself on this step by selecting other locations ָ asking your own שְׁאֵלוֹת about רַכָּבוֹת, אוֹטוֹבּוּסִים and מְטוֹסִים that go there. Select new מִלִּים from your מִלּוֹן *(mih-lon)* dictionary and practice asking שְׁאֵלוֹת that begin with

אֵיפֹה	מָתַי	כַּמָּה	כַּמָּה עוֹלֶה

or making statements like:

אֲנִי רוֹצֶה לִנְסוֹעַ לְחֵיפָה.
אֲנִי רוֹצֶה לִקְנוֹת כַּרְטִיס.

ACROSS

1. to eat
3. mosque
5. to send
8. bread
10. I, you (☨) arrive
11. men
15. toilets
16. pleasant
18. ladies
19. stamp
20. we
22. west
24. September
26. street
27. north
28. closed
29. right
31. you (☨)
32. shower

DOWN

2. I, you (☨) learn
3. salt
4. eyeglasses
6. hot wind
7. hungry
9. towels
12. tomorrow
13. autumn
14. winter
17. kitchen
18. postcard
19. in Bethlehem
21. I, you (☨) travel
22. refrigerator
23. a quarter
24. knife
25. Eastern
27. I, you (☨) need
28. grandmother
30. fork

ACROSS

1. לֶאֱכֹל
3. מִסְגָּד
5. לִשְׁלוֹחַ
8. לֶחֶם
10. מַגִּיעַ
11. גְּבָרִים
15. שֵׁרוּתִים
16. נְעִימִים
18. גְּבָרוֹת
19. בּוּל
20. אֲנַחְנוּ
22. מַעֲרָב
24. סֶפְּטֶמְבֶּר
26. רְחוֹב
27. צָפוֹן
28. סָגוּר
29. יָמִין
31. אַתָּה
32. מִקְלַחַת

DOWN

2. לוֹמֵד
3. מֶלַח
4. מִשְׁקָפַיִם
6. חַמְסִין
7. רָעֵב
9. מַגָּבוֹת
12. מָחָר
13. סְתָו
14. חֹרֶף
17. מִטְבָּח
18. גְּלוּיָה
19. בְּבֵית לֶחֶם
21. נוֹסֵעַ
22. מְקָרֵר
23. רֶבַע
24. סַכִּין
25. מִזְרָחִי
27. צָרִיךְ
28. סַבְתָּא
30. מַזְלֵג

Step 18

עַכְשָׁו אַתָּה בְּיִשְׂרָאֵל. אַתָּה בְּחֶדֶר (buh-Hed-er) room in בְּמָלוֹן (buh-mah-lon). וְעַכְשָׁו (vuh-aH-shahv) now and? אַתָּה רָעֵב (rah-ev) hungry.

אַתָּה רוֹצֶה (roh-tseh) לֶאֱכֹל (leh-eh-Hohl) eat to. אֵיפֹה יֵשׁ מִסְעָדָה (mis-ah-dah) restaurant טוֹבָה (toh-vah)?

First of all, there are different types of places to eat. Let's learn them.

(mis-ah-dah) מִסְעָדָה	=	restaurant. Many different national cuisines are represented, so אַתָּה have plenty of interesting choices.
(miz-rah-Heet) (mis-ah-dah) מִסְעָדָה מִזְרָחִית	=	serves Middle Eastern food
(steak-ee-yah) סְטֵיקִיָּה	=	serves a variety of beef dishes: steaks, kebabs, shashlik
(fah-lah-fel) פָלָפֶל	=	Israeli "fast-food." There you can try פָלָפֶל (fried chick pea balls with lettuce in pita bread) which you can garnish with a variety of pickles and sauces.
(kah-feh) (bait) בֵּית קָפֶה	=	coffee shop, serves beverages and light snacks

מִסְעָדוֹת (mis-ah-doht) restaurants בְּיִשְׂרָאֵל (buh-yiss-rah-el) are generally כָּשֵׁר (kah-shair) kosher. They follow the dietary law of כַּשְׁרוּת (kash-root) purity, which forbids eating certain foods such as pork and shellfish. Milk וְ meat dishes are not served together. Most מִסְעָדוֹת (mis-ah-doht) – except מִסְעָדוֹת (mis-ah-doht) עַרְבִיּוֹת (ah-rah-vee-yoht) Arab – close for שַׁבָּת (shah-baht) (from Friday evening to Saturday evening). Try a variety of מִסְעָדוֹת (mis-ah-doht). Experiment! עַכְשָׁו you have found a מִסְעָדָה (mis-ah-dah) טוֹבָה (toh-vah) good. אַתָּה enter הַמִּסְעָדָה (hah-mis-ah-dah) and find a שׁוּלְחָן (shool-Hahn) table. אַתָּה call הַמֶּלְצַר (hah-mel-tsar) waiter the and say

"מֶלְצַר (mel-tsar), הַתַּפְרִיט (hah-tah-freet) menu the בְּבַקָּשָׁה."

______________	ש	path	(shveel)	שְׁבִיל
______________		Swedish	(shveh-dee)	שְׁוֵדִי
______________		Sweden	(shved-yah)	שְׁוֵדְיָה
______________		Switzerland	(shvites)	שְׁוַייץ
______________		policeman	(shoh-tair)	שׁוֹטֵר

בְּיִשְׂרָאֵל there are (shah-losh) שָׁלֹשׁ (three) main meals to enjoy every (yom) יוֹם, plus (kah-feh) קָפֶה and perhaps (oo-gah) עוּגָה (cake) for (hah-tah-yar) הַתַּיָּר (tourist the) (aH-ah-ray) אַחֲרֵי (hah-tsoh-hoh-rah-yim) הַצָּהֳרַיִם (afternoon the in).

(ah-roo-Haht) (boh-ker) אֲרוּחַת בֹּקֶר	=	breakfast . . . an Israeli breakfast may include yoghurt, cheese, herring, as well as לֶחֶם and קָפֶה or תֵּה.
(ah-roo-Haht) (tsoh-hoh-rah-yim) אֲרוּחַת צָהֳרַיִם	=	lunch . . . . . . the main meal of the day. Usually served between 12:00 and 14:00, but you will find felafel stands open all day.
(eh-rev) אֲרוּחַת עֶרֶב	=	dinner . . . . . Israelis eat a light meal in the evening. Dinner is usually served from 18:00 until the late evening.

When אַתָּה eat בְּמִסְעָדָה, you may want to begin your meal with a plate of (Hoo-moos) חוּמוּס (thick sauce of ground chick peas) or (tuh-Hee-nah) טְחִינָה (sauce of ground sesame seeds). Use your (pee-tah) פִּיתָה to scoop up your (Hoo-moos) חוּמוּס or (tuh-Hee-nah) טְחִינָה. Before beginning your (ah-roo-Hah) אֲרוּחָה (meal), be sure to wish those sharing your table (buh-tay-ah-von) בְּתֵאָבוֹן (enjoy you meal). If your מֶלְצַר asks if אַתָּה enjoyed your (ah-roo-Hah) אֲרוּחָה, a smile וְ a (ken) (toh-dah) (rah-bah) כֵּן, תּוֹדָה רַבָּה will tell him that אַתָּה did.

עַכְשָׁו, it may be breakfast time at home, but אַתָּה are בְּיִשְׂרָאֵל and it is 20:00. Some (mis-ah-doht) מִסְעָדוֹת post (hah-tah-freet) הַתַּפְרִיט (menu the) outside. Always read it before entering so אַתָּה know what type of meals וְ prices אַתָּה will encounter inside.

Did you notice that the words פָלָפֶל (felafel) and פִּלְפֵּל (pepper) are very similar once the vowels are removed? Keep an eye out for those slight differences.

אַתָּה will see the following main catagories on (hah-tah-freet) הַתַּפְרִיט.

______________	ש	table. . . . .(shool-Hahn) . . . . שׁוּלְחָן
______________		tablecloth. . . . . (mah-paht-shool-Hahn) . . . שׁוּלְחָן—
______________		table tennis. . . . . (teh-nis-shool-Hahn) שׁוּלְחָן טֶנִיס—
______________		judge. . . . . (shoh-fet) . . . . שׁוֹפֵט
______________		market. . . . . (shook) . . . . שׁוּק

appetizers	(ree-shoh-noht)(mah-noht)	מָנוֹת רִאשׁוֹנוֹת
soups	(muh-rah-kim)	מְרָקִים
fish dishes	(dah-gim)	דָגִים
main dishes	(ee-kah-ree-oht)(mah-noht)	מָנוֹת עִיקָרִיּוֹת
vegetables	(yuh-rah-koht)	יְרָקוֹת
salads	(sah-lah-tim)	סָלָטִים
dessert	(kin-oo-aH)	קִנּוּחַ
fruit	(peh-roht)	פֵּרוֹת
ice creams	(glee-doht)	גְלִידוֹת
pastries/cakes	(oo-goht)	עוּגוֹת
beverages	(mash-kah-oht)	מַשְׁקָאוֹת

Perhaps אַתָּה would like to try יַיִן (yah-yin) wine כּוֹס (kohs) glass with your אֲרוּחָה (ah-roo-Hah) meal. Ask about the local wine. עַכְשָׁו a preview of delights to come . . . At the back of this סֵפֶר you will find a sample תַּפְרִיט (tah-freet) יִשְׂרְאֵלִי (yiss-ruh-eh-lee). Read הַתַּפְרִיט (hah-tah-freet) today וְ learn the new מִלִּים ! When אַתָּה are ready to leave for יִשְׂרָאֵל , cut out הַתַּפְרִיט (hah-tah-freet), fold it וְ carry it in your pocket, wallet אוֹ purse. אַתָּה will be well prepared to go into a מִסְעָדָה (mis-ah-dah). Study הַתַּפְרִיט (hah-tah-freet) after אַתָּה have eaten אוֹ you will be רָעֵב (rah-ev) hungry.

ש

wristwatch	(shuh-on-yahd)	שְׁעוֹן יָד
gate	(shah-ar)	שַׁעַר
Jaffa Gate	(shah-ar-yah-foh)	שַׁעַר יָפוֹ
Damascus Gate	(shah-ar-shuh-Hem)	שַׁעַר שְׁכֶם
sun	(sheh-mesh)	שֶׁמֶשׁ

In addition, learning the following should help you identify what kind of meat אוֹ poultry אַתָּה can order and אֵיךְ it will be prepared.

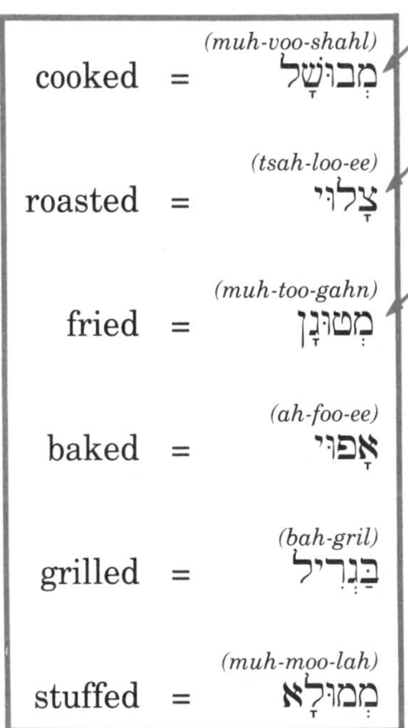

אַתָּה will also get יְרָקוֹת (yuh-rah-koht) vegetables with your אֲרוּחָה (ah-roo-Hah) and perhaps a סָלָט (sah-laht). One day at a שׁוּק (shook) market will teach you הַשֵּׁמוֹת (hah-sheh-moht) names the for all the different kinds of יְרָקוֹת (yuh-rah-koht) vegetables and פֵּרוֹת (peh-roht) fruit, plus it will be a delightful experience for you. אַתָּה can always consult your menu guide at the back of this סֵפֶר if אַתָּה forget the correct שֵׁם (shem) name. עַכְשָׁו you know what אַתָּה רוֹצָה לֶאֱכוֹל (leh-eh-Hohl) eat to and הַמֶּלְצָר מַגִּיעַ (mah-gee-ah) (hah-mel-tsar) arrives.

		ש	
______	field	(sah-deh)	שָׂדֶה
______	strawberries, field berries	(toot-sah-deh)	תּוּת שָׂדֶה —
______	bush	(see-aH)	שִׂיחַ
______	language	(sah-fah)	שָׂפָה
______	seaside	(sfaht-hah-yahm)	שְׂפַת הַיָּם

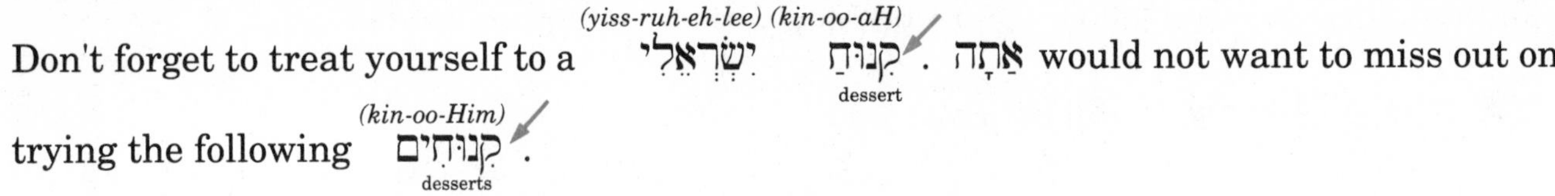

Don't forget to treat yourself to a *(yiss-ruh-eh-lee)* יִשְׂרְאֵלִי *(kin-oo-aH)* קִנּוּחַ (dessert). אַתָּה would not want to miss out on trying the following *(kin-oo-Him)* קִנּוּחִים (desserts).

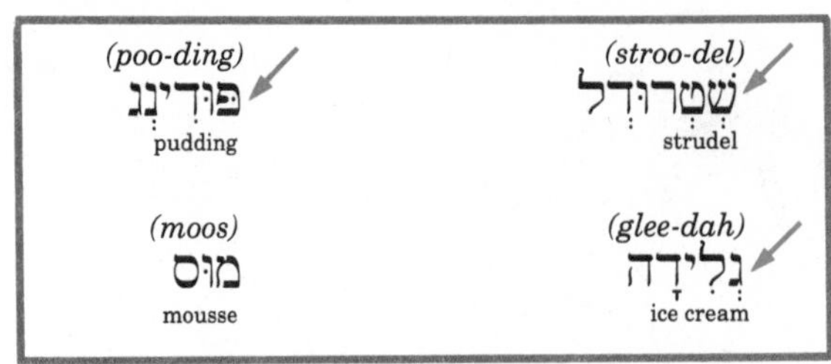

(poo-ding) פּוּדִינְג pudding	*(stroo-del)* שְׁטְרוּדֶל strudel
(moos) מוּס mousse	*(glee-dah)* גְלִידָה ice cream

After completing your *(ah-roo-Hah)* אֲרוּחָה (meal), call *(hah-mel-tsar)* הַמֶּלְצַר (waiter the) and pay just as אַתָּה have already learned in Step 16.

(hah-Hesh-bon)
מֶלְצַר, הַחֶשְׁבּוֹן בְּבַקָּשָׁה.

(luh-mah-tah) לְמַטָּה is a sample *(tah-freet)* תַּפְרִיט to help you prepare for your holiday.

(hah-pil) מִסְעָדָה "הַפִּיל"

תַּפְרִיט

מָנוֹת רִאשׁוֹנוֹת

	NIS
חוּמוּס (humus)	2,00
טְחִינָה (tehina)	2,00
זֵיתִים (olives)	1,00
כָּבֵד עוֹף (chicken livers)	1,50

מְרָקִים

מְרַק יְרָקוֹת (vegetable soup)	1,25
מְרַק עוֹף (chicken soup)	1,50
מְרַק עֲדָשִׁים (lentil soup)	1,25
מְרַק פִּטְרִיּוֹת (mushroom soup)	1,25

סָלָטִים

סָלָט מְלָפְפוֹנִים (cucumber salad)	2,50
סָלָט יְרָקוֹת (green salad)	2,00
סָלָט עַגְבָנִיּוֹת (tomato salad)	2,50

יְרָקוֹת

	NIS
בְּרוֹקוֹלִי בְּתַחְמִיץ (marinated broccoli)	3,00
שְׁעוּעִית יְרוּקָה (green beans)	2,50
גֶּזֶר מְזוּגָּג (glazed carrots)	2,50
כְּרוּבִית (cauliflower)	3,00
אֲפוּנָה בְּרוֹטֶב נַעְנַע (green peas in mint sauce)	3,00

קִנּוּחַ

מוּס מוֹקָה (mocha mousse)	2,75
מוּס שׁוֹקוֹלָד (chocolate mousse)	3,00
קְרֶם קָארָמֶל (creme caramel)	2,50
תּוּת שָׂדֶה בְּקַצֶּפֶת (strawberries & cream)	2,25

מַשְׁקָאוֹת

מִינֶרָלִיִּים (mineral water)	1,00
מִיץ תַּפּוּזִים (orange juice)	1,50
קָפֶה (coffee)	1,75
תֵּה (tea)	1,50
בִּירָה (beer)	2,50
יַיִן (wine)	3,00

מָנוֹת עִיקָּרִיּוֹת

	NIS
שַׁשְׁלִיק עִם אוֹרֶז (shashlik with rice)	4,50
דָּג אָפוּי בְּיַיִן וְתַפּוּחַ אֲדָמָה אָפוּי (fish with potatoes)	5,50
עוֹף בְּמִיץ תַּפּוּז וְצִמּוּקִים (chicken with oranges and raisins)	5,00
פְּרִיקָסֶה עוֹף עִם כּוּפְתָּאוֹת (chicken fricassee with dumplings)	5,00

ת

____________	theater	*(tay-ah-tron)* תֵּאַטְרוֹן
____________	Torah	*(toh-rah)* תּוֹרָה
____________	Turkish	*(toor-kee)* תּוּרְכִּי
____________	Turkey	*(toor-kee-yah)* תּוּרְכִּיָּה
____________	date, palm tree	*(tah-mar)* תָּמָר

(boh-ker) (ah-roo-Haht)(buh-yiss-rah-el) אֲרוּחַת בֹּקֶר בְּיִשְׂרָאֵל (breakfast) is delicious. A typical Israeli (boh-ker) (ah-roo-Haht) אֲרוּחַת בֹּקֶר (breakfast) includes yoghurt, cheese, eggs אוֹ herring, fruit וְ bread אוֹ rolls. (luh-mah-tah) לְמַטָּה is a sample of what אַתָּה can expect to greet you (bah-boh-ker) בַּבֹּקֶר (in the morning).

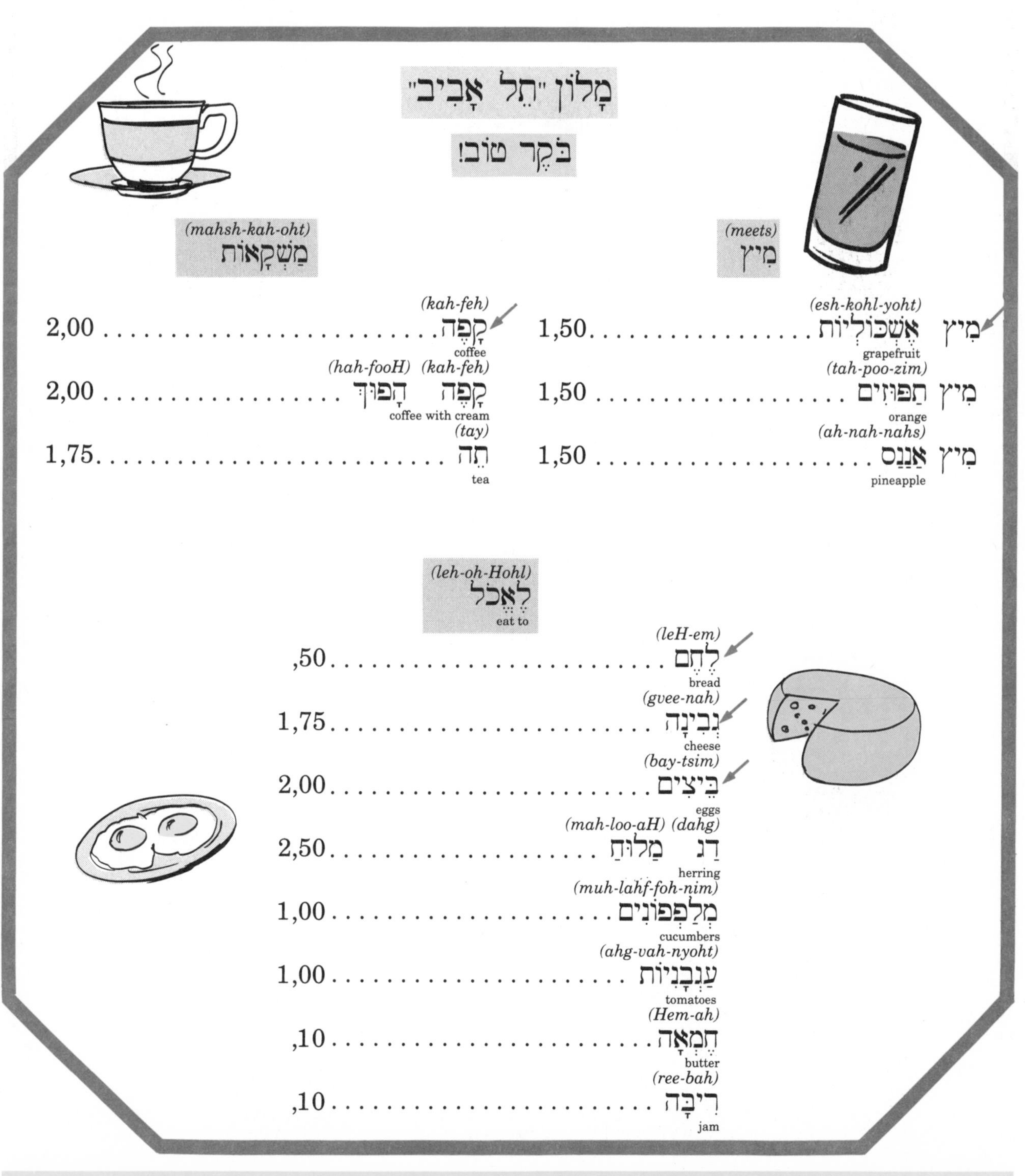

מָלוֹן "תֵּל אָבִיב"

בֹּקֶר טוֹב!

(meets) מִיץ

מִיץ אֶשְׁכּוֹלִיוֹת (esh-kohl-yoht) grapefruit	1,50
מִיץ תַּפּוּזִים (tah-poo-zim) orange	1,50
מִיץ אֲנָנָס (ah-nah-nahs) pineapple	1,50

(mahsh-kah-oht) מַשְׁקָאוֹת

קָפֶה (kah-feh) coffee	2,00
קָפֶה הָפוּךְ (kah-feh) (hah-fooH) coffee with cream	2,00
תֵּה (tay) tea	1,75

(leh-oh-Hohl) לֶאֱכֹל (to eat)

לֶחֶם (leH-em) bread	,50
גְּבִינָה (gvee-nah) cheese	1,75
בֵּיצִים (bay-tsim) eggs	2,00
דָּג מָלוּחַ (dahg) (mah-loo-aH) herring	2,50
מְלָפְפוֹנִים (muh-lahf-foh-nim) cucumbers	1,00
עַגְבָנִיּוֹת (ahg-vah-nyoht) tomatoes	1,00
חֶמְאָה (Hem-ah) butter	,10
רִיבָּה (ree-bah) jam	,10

ת

תְּמוּנָה	(tmoo-nah)	picture	____________
— אַלְבּוֹם תְּמוּנוֹת	(ahl-boom-tmoo-noht)	photo album	____________
תַּמְרוּר	(tahm-roor)	signpost	____________
תַּצְלוּם	(tahts-loom)	photograph	____________
תְּרוּפָה	(troo-fah)	medicine	____________

Step 15

מָה is different about בְּיִשְׂרָאֵל הַטֶלֶפוֹן *(hah-teh-leh-fohn)* telephone the? Well, אַתָּה never notice such things until אַתָּה רוֹצֶה *(roh-tseh)* to use them. Be warned עַכְשָׁו that בְּיִשְׂרָאֵל טֶלֶפוֹנִים *(teh-leh-foh-nim)* telephones are much less numerous than בְּאָמֶרִיקָה *(bah-meh-ree-kah)*. הַטֶלֶפוֹן allows you to reserve a חֶדֶר *(Hed-er)* room בְּמָלוֹן *(buh-mah-lon)* in another city, call חֲבֵרִים *(Hah-ver-im)* friends, reserve קוֹנְצֶרְט *(kohn-tsairt)* concert tickets, make emergency calls, check on הַשָּׁעוֹת *(hah-shah-oht)* hours the of a מוּזֵיאוֹן *(moo-zay-on)*, rent a מְכוֹנִית *(muh-Hoh-nit)* and all those other דְּבָרִים *(dvah-rim)* which אֲנַחְנוּ *(ah-naH-noo)* do on a daily basis. It also gives you a certain amount of freedom when אַתָּה can phone on your own. Having a טֶלֶפוֹן *(teh-leh-fohn)* in your מָלוֹן is not as common בְּיִשְׂרָאֵל as בְּאָמֶרִיקָה *(bah-meh-ree-kah)*. That means that אַתָּה must know אֵיפֹה to find טֶלֶפוֹנִים *(teh-leh-foh-nim)*.

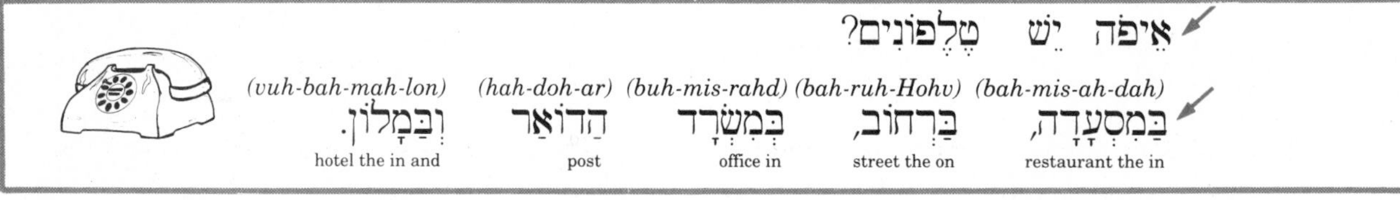

אַתָּה must לִקְנוֹת *(lik-noht)* buy a token, called אֲסִימוֹן *(ah-see-mon)*, before אַתָּה can use a טֶלֶפוֹן *(teh-leh-fohn)* צִבּוּרִי *(tsih-boo-ree)* public. You can buy אֲסִימוֹנִים *(ah-see-moh-nim)* at the post office.

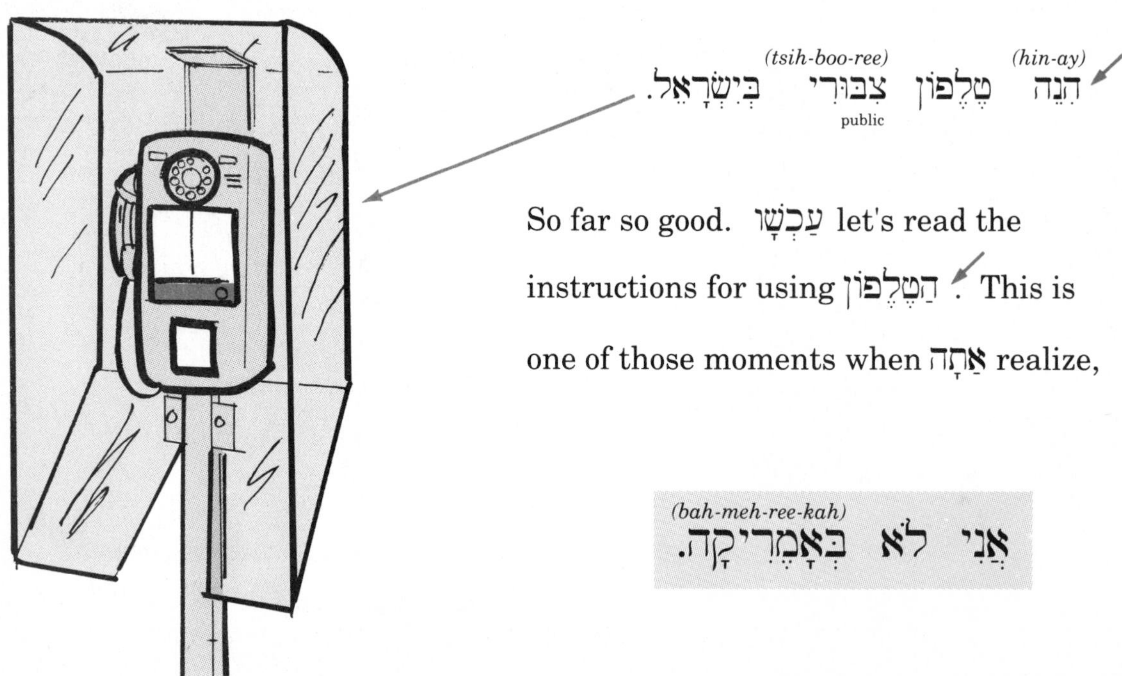

הִנֵה *(hin-ay)* טֶלֶפוֹן צִבּוּרִי *(tsih-boo-ree)* public בְּיִשְׂרָאֵל.

So far so good. עַכְשָׁו let's read the instructions for using הַטֶלֶפוֹן. This is one of those moments when אַתָּה realize,

אֲנִי לֹא בְּאָמֶרִיקָה. *(bah-meh-ree-kah)*

So let's learn how to operate הַטֶלֶפוֹן.

The instructions look complicated but actually are not — אַתָּה should be able to recognize some of these מִלִּים already. Let's learn the others. Here's how the instructions go.

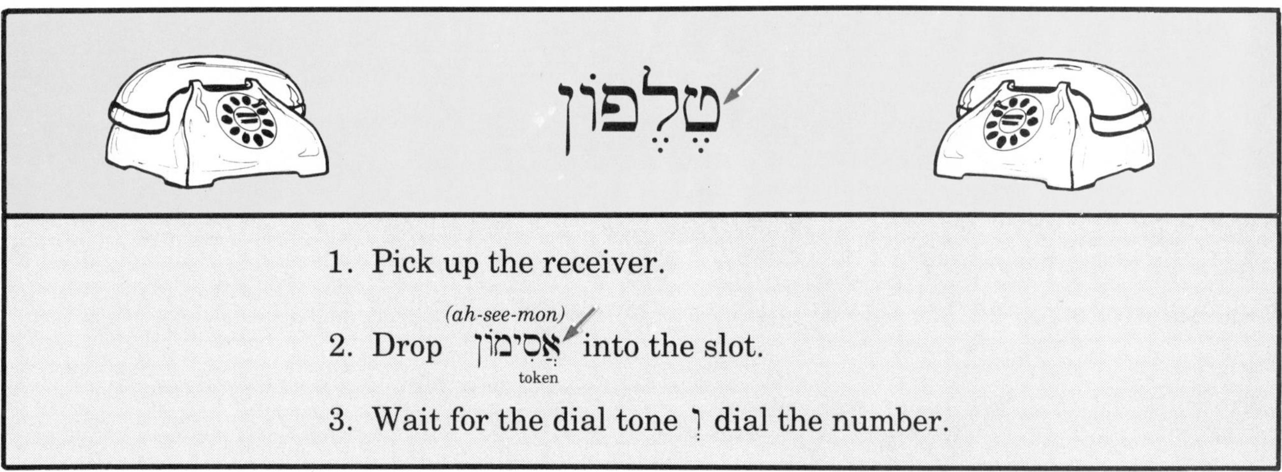

These are free telephone calls:

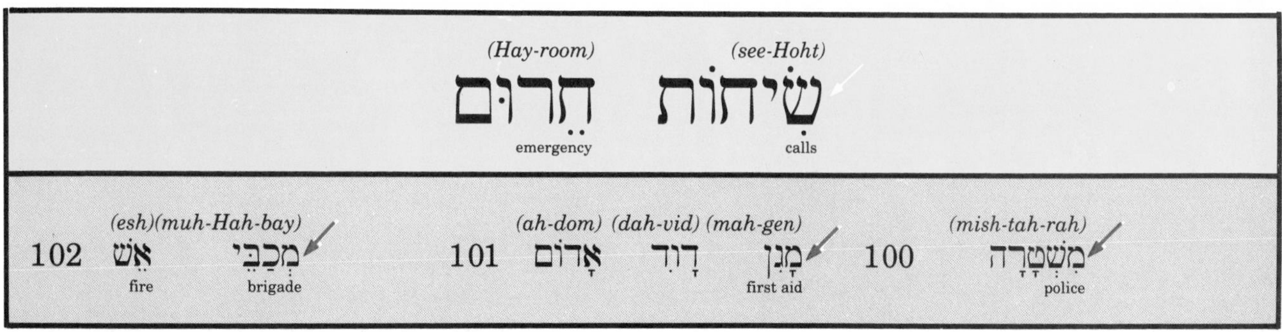

(iv-rit) עִבְרִית		(ahn-glit) אַנְגְּלִית	עִבְרִית		אַנְגְּלִית
(teh-leh-fohn) טֶלֶפוֹן	=	telephone	טֶלֶפוֹן צִבּוּרִי	=	public telephone
(luh-tahl-fane) לְטַלְפֵּן	=	to telephone	סֵפֶר טֶלֶפוֹן	=	telephone book
(mair-kah-zah-nit) מֶרְכָּזָנִית	=	operator	(see-Haht) שִׂיחַת טֶלֶפוֹן	=	telephone conversation
(ah-see-mon) אֲסִימוֹן	=	token			

So (yah-Hohl) יָכוֹל can אַתָּה now use (hah-teh-leh-fohn) הַטֶלֶפוֹן to make a call (buh-yiss-rah-el) בְּיִשְׂרָאֵל . אַתָּה will find that the majority of מִסְפָּרִים in יִשְׂרָאֵל have שֵׁשׁ digits, such as 38 37 04. (yesh) יֵשׁ also area codes called (kee-doh-met) קִדוֹמֶת, and these are listed in the סֵפֶר הַטֶלֶפוֹן.

When answering הַטֶלֶפוֹן , אַתָּה pick up the receiver וְ say:

"(poh) פֹּה here ______________."

When saying goodbye, אַתָּה say "(shah-lom) שָׁלוֹם!"

הִנֵה are some sample טֶלֶפוֹן (see-Hoht) שִׂיחוֹת. Write them in the blanks (luh-mah-tah) לְמַטָה.

אֲנִי (ah-nee) רוֹצֶה (roh-tseh) לְדַבֵּר (luh-dah-bair) speak to עִם הַמוֹדִיעִין (hah-moh-dee-een) information. ______________

אֲנִי רוֹצֶה לְטַלְפֵן (luh-tahl-fane) telephone to לְשִׁיקָגוֹ (luh-shik-ah-goh) Chicago to. ______________

אֲנִי רוֹצֶה לְדַבֵּר (luh-dah-bair) עִם יוֹחָנָן (yoh-Hah-nahn) John שְׁמוּאֵלִי (shmoo-eh-lee) Shmueli בְּחֵיפָה (buh-Hay-fah) Haifa in. ______________

אֲנִי רוֹצֶה לְדַבֵּר (luh-dah-bair) עִם רָחֵל (rah-Hel) Rachel לֵוִי (lah-vee) Levi בְּאֵילַת (buh-ay-laht) Eilat in. ______________

אֲנִי רוֹצֶה לְדַבֵּר עִם "אֵל (el)—עַל (ahl)" El Al בִּשְׂדֵה (buh-sday) airport in הַתְעוּפָה (hah-too-fah). ______________

אֲנִי רוֹצֶה לְטַלְפֵן (luh-tahl-fane) קוֹלֶקְט (koh-lekt) collect. ______________

אֵיפֹה (ay-foh) יֵשׁ טֶלֶפוֹן (teh-leh-fohn) צִבּוּרִי (tsih-boo-ree) public? ______________

אֵיפֹה סֵפֶר הַטֶלֶפוֹן? ______________

מָה what מִסְפָּר (mis-par) number הַטֶלֶפוֹן (hah-teh-leh-fohn) telephone שֶׁלְךָ (shel-Hah) your? ______________

הַמִסְפָּר (hah-mis-par) number שֶׁלִי (sheh-lee) (is) my 24 16 74. ______________

מָה מִסְפָּר (mis-par) הַמָלוֹן (hah-mah-lon) hotel the? ______________

מָה מִסְפָּר הַמִסְעָדָה (hah-mis-ah-dah)? ______________

הִנֵה is another possible (see-Hah) שִׂיחָה conversation. Pay close attention to (hah-mih-lim) הַמִלִים and (ayH) אֵיךְ they are used.

(gveh-ret) (luh-dah-bair) (lah-vee) (boh-ahz) (poh) (shah-lom) (boh-ahz)

בּוֹעַז: שָׁלוֹם. פֹּה בּוֹעַז לָבִיא. אֲנִי רוֹצֶה לְדַבֵּר עִם גְּבֶרֶת

Mrs. Levi here Boaz

(ah-lon)

אַלּוֹן, בְּבַקָּשָׁה.

Alon

(tah-foos)(hah-kahv) (ah-vahl) (mits-tah-eh-ret) (eh-Hahd)(reh-gah) (mahz-kee-rah)

מַזְכִּירָה: רֶגַע אֶחָד, בְּבַקָּשָׁה. אֲנִי מִצְטַעֶרֶת אֲבָל הַקַּו תָּפוּס.

busy line the but sorry (am) one moment secretary

(muh-aht) (rahk) (muh-dah-bair) (pahm) (ohd)

בּוֹעַז: עוֹד פַּעַם, בְּבַקָּשָׁה. אֲנִי מְדַבֵּר רַק מְעַט עִבְרִית.

little only more once

(yoh-tair) (luh-aht)

בְּבַקָּשָׁה לְאַט יוֹתֵר.

repeat slowly

(tah-foos)(hah-kahv) (ah-vahl)(mits-tah-eh-ret)

מַזְכִּירָה: אֲנִי מִצְטַעֶרֶת אֲבָל הַקַּו תָּפוּס.

but sorry (am)

(shah-lom) (rah-bah) (toh-dah)

בּוֹעַז: תּוֹדָה רַבָּה, שָׁלוֹם.

וְ still another possibility . . .

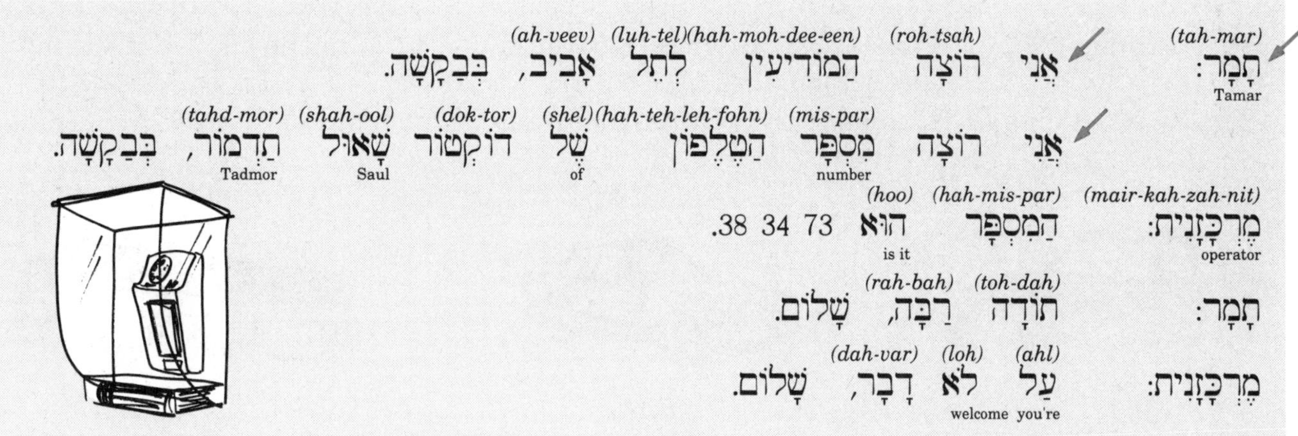

(ah-veev) (luh-tel)(hah-moh-dee-een) (roh-tsah) (tah-mar)

תָּמָר: אֲנִי רוֹצָה הַמּוֹדִיעִין לְתֵל אָבִיב, בְּבַקָּשָׁה.

Tamar

(tahd-mor) (shah-ool) (dok-tor) (shel)(hah-teh-leh-fohn) (mis-par)

אֲנִי רוֹצָה מִסְפַּר הַטֶּלֶפוֹן שֶׁל דוֹקְטוֹר שָׁאוּל תַּדְמוֹר, בְּבַקָּשָׁה.

Tadmor Saul of number

(hoo) (hah-mis-par) (mair-kah-zah-nit)

מֶרְכָּזָנִית: הַמִּסְפָּר הוּא 73 34 38.

is it operator

(rah-bah) (toh-dah)

תָּמָר: תּוֹדָה רַבָּה, שָׁלוֹם.

(dah-var) (loh) (ahl)

מֶרְכָּזָנִית: עַל לֹא דָבָר, שָׁלוֹם.

welcome you're

עַכְשָׁו, you are ready to use any טֶלֶפוֹן in יִשְׂרָאֵל *(yiss-rah-el)*. Just take it slowly וְ speak clearly.

Don't forget that *(yah-Hohl)* יָכוֹל (can) אַתָּה ask . . .

(muh-koh-mit) (see-Hah) (oh-lah)(kah-mah)

כַּמָּה עוֹלָה שִׂיחָה מְקוֹמִית?

local call costs

____

(luh-ay-laht) (Hoots) (oh-lah)

כַּמָּה עוֹלָה שִׂיחַת חוּץ לְאֵילַת?

Eilat to long-distance

____

(lah-meh-ree-kah)

כַּמָּה עוֹלָה שִׂיחָה לְאָמֶרִיקָה?

____

(ah-veev) (luh-tel) (Hoots)

כַּמָּה עוֹלָה שִׂיחַת חוּץ לְתֵל אָבִיב?

____

(lah-teh-leh-fohn)(ah-see-mon) (tsah-reeH)

Remember: אַתָּה צָרִיךְ אֲסִימוֹן לַטֶּלֶפוֹן!

token need

Step 20

יֵשׁ (yesh) [are there] several ways of getting around in cities בְּיִשְׂרָאֵל (buh-yiss-rah-el). Most יִשְׂרְאֵלִים (yiss-ruh-eh-lim) travel בְּאוֹטוֹבּוּס, but הֵם (hem) are often very crowded during rush hour. An alternative to הָאוֹטוֹבּוּס is **הַשֵּׁרוּת** (hah-sheh-root), or shared taxi. You can even take a שֵׁרוּת (sheh-root) from one town to another. The שֵׁרוּת (sheh-root) leaves from a specific place and follows fixed routes. Ask for the שֵׁרוּת (sheh-root) to your destination: "אֵיפֹה הַשֵּׁרוּת (hah-sheh-root) לְתֵל (luh-tel) אָבִיב (ah-veev)?" When אַתָּה נוֹסֵעַ (noh-seh-ah) [travel] בְּשֵׁרוּת (buh-sheh-root) each person pays for his own seat and הַשֵּׁרוּת (hah-sheh-root) יוֹצֵא (yoh-tseh) [leaves] when it is full — with שִׁבְעָה (shev-ah-ah) [seven] people. אַתָּה רוֹצֶה (roh-tseh) לִנְסוֹעַ (lin-soh-ah) [travel to] בְּטַקְסִי (buh-tahk-see)? In that case, hail a טַקְסִי on הָרְחוֹב (hah-ruh-Hohv) [street the] or have one called to your מָלוֹן. What מִלִּים are necessary for a נוֹסֵעַ (noh-seh-ah) [traveler] in the city? Let's learn them by practicing them aloud וְ then by writing them in the blanks לְמַטָּה (luh-mah-tah).

(sheh-root) שֵׁרוּת sherut | (tahk-see) טַקְסִי taxi | (oh-toh-boos) אוֹטוֹבּוּס bus

________________ ________________ ________________

________________________________ station/stop = תַּחֲנָה (tah-Hah-nah)

________________________________ line = קַו (kahv)

מִסְפָּר, מִסְפָּר ________________ number = מִסְפָּר (mis-par)

________________________________ driver = נֶהָג (nah-hahg)

Let's also review the "transportation" verbs at this point.

to arrive = **לְהַגִּיעַ** (luh-hah-gee-ah) | to leave = **לָצֵאת** (lah-tset)

________________ ________________

to travel = **לִנְסוֹעַ** (lin-soh-ah) | to board = **לַעֲלוֹת עַל** (lah-ah-loht) (ahl)

________________ ________________

At the הָאוֹטוֹבּוּס תַּחֲנַת *(tah-Hah-naht)* stop check הַשֵּׁם *(hah-shem)* name the of the last תַּחֲנָה *(tah-Hah-nah)* stop on הַקַּו *(hah-kahv)* line the that אַתָּה want to take וְ catch הָאוֹטוֹבּוּס traveling in that direction. If the stops are not posted, ask הַנֶּהָג *(hah-nah-hahg)* driver the of הָאוֹטוֹבּוּס if your destination is on his קַו *(kahv)* line. לְמַטָּה is a sample מַפָּה *(mah-pah)* map that shows several places to which אַתָּה may want לִנְסוֹעַ *(lin-soh-ah)*.

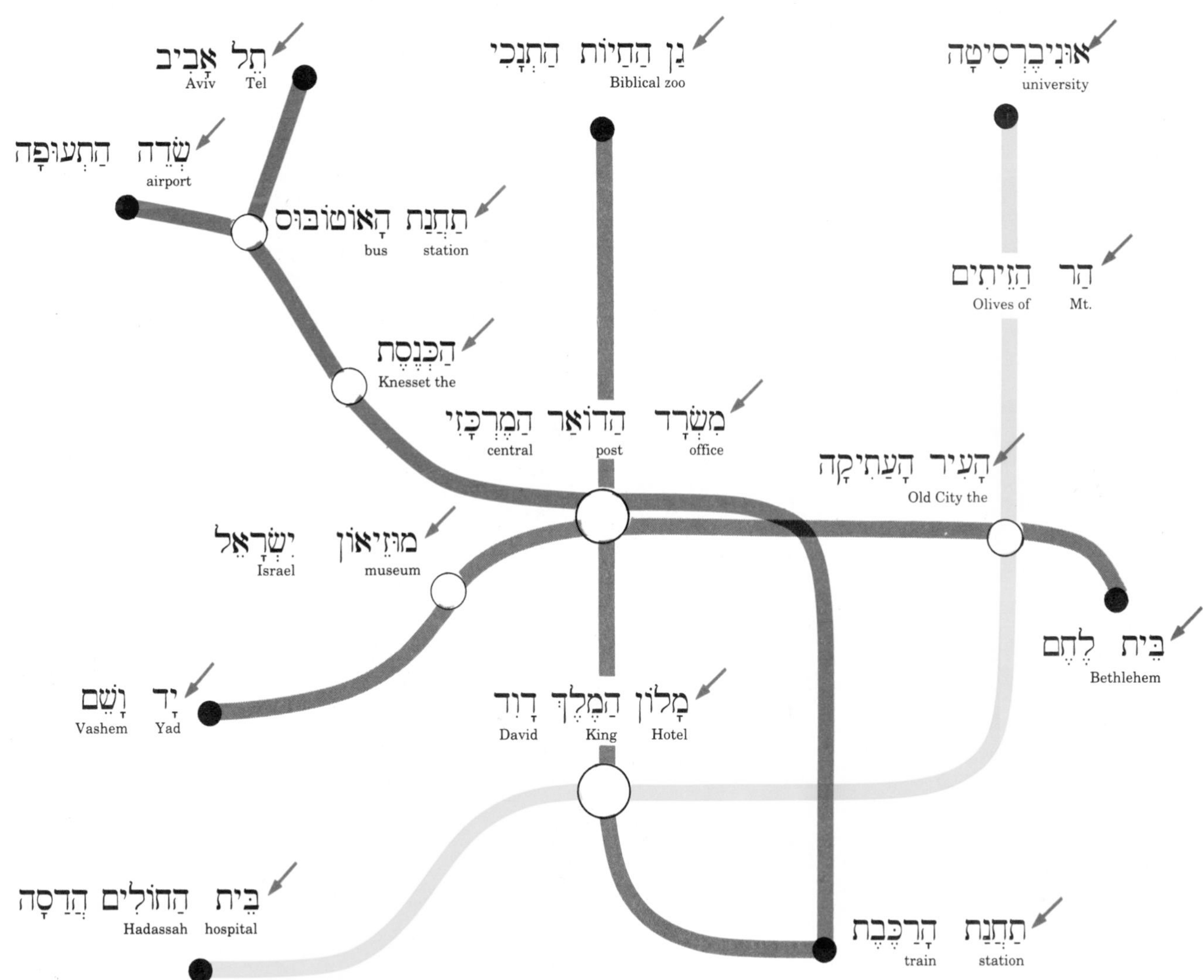

The same basic set of מִלִּים and שְׁאֵלוֹת will see you through traveling בְּאוֹטוֹבּוּס, בִּמְכוֹנִית *(buh-muh-Hoh-nit)* or even בְּרַכֶּבֶת *(buh-rah-kev-et)* train by.

Naturally, the first (shuh-eh-lah) שְׁאֵלָה is ?אֵיפֹה

(tah-Hah-naht)
אֵיפֹה תַּחֲנַת הָאוֹטוֹבּוּס?

אֵיפֹה הַטַּקְסִי?

(hah-sheh-root)
אֵיפֹה הַשֵּׁרוּת?

אֵיפֹה תַּחֲנַת הָרַכֶּבֶת?

Practice the following basic (shuh-eh-loht) שְׁאֵלוֹת out loud ְו then write them in the blank (mee-smohl) מִשְּׂמֹאל (left the to).

1. (tah-Hah-naht) אֵיפֹה תַּחֲנַת (stop) הָאוֹטוֹבּוּס? ____

(hah-sheh-root) אֵיפֹה תַּחֲנַת הַשֵּׁרוּת? ____

2. (kohl) (kah-mah) כֹּל כַּמָּה (how often) (zmahn) זְמַן (bah) בָּא (comes) הָאוֹטוֹבּוּס (luh-nah-tseh-ret) לְנָצֶרֶת? (Nazareth for) ____

(kohl) (kah-mah) כֹּל כַּמָּה (zmahn) זְמַן (bah) בָּא הָאוֹטוֹבּוּס (luh-ah-rahd) לַעֲרָד? (Arad for) ____

כֹּל כַּמָּה (zmahn) זְמַן בָּא הָאוֹטוֹבּוּס (luh-sday) לִשְׂדֵה (hah-too-fah) הַתְּעוּפָה? (airport the for) ____

3. (mah-tie) מָתַי (yoh-tset) יוֹצֵאת (leaves) הָרַכֶּבֶת? ____

מָתַי (yoh-tseh) יוֹצֵא (leaves) הָאוֹטוֹבּוּס? ____

מָתַי יוֹצֵא הַטַּקְסִי? ____

מָתַי יוֹצֵאת (hah-rah-kev-et) הָרַכֶּבֶת (luh-Hay-fah) לְחֵיפָה? (Haifa for) ____

מָתַי יוֹצֵא הָאוֹטוֹבּוּס (luh-kar-mee-el) לְכַּרְמִיאֵל? (Carmiel for) ____

מָתַי יוֹצֵא (hah-sheh-root) הַשֵּׁרוּת (luh-ah-koh) לְעַכּוֹ? (Acre for) ____

4. (kah-mah) כַּמָּה (oh-leh) עוֹלֶה (kar-tis) כַּרְטִיס אוֹטוֹבּוּס? ____

כַּמָּה עוֹלֶה כַּרְטִיס (lah-ooh-nee-vair-see-tah) לָאוּנִיבֶרְסִיטָה? (university the for) ____

כַּמָּה עוֹלֶה כַּרְטִיס (lah-kness-et) לַכְּנֶסֶת? (Knesset the for) ____

כַּמָּה עוֹלֶה כַּרְטִיס (luh-tel) לְתֵל (ah-veev) אָבִיב? ____

עַכְשָׁו that אַתָּה are in the swing of things, practice the following patterns aloud, substituting "רַכֶּבֶת" for "אוֹטוֹבּוּס" and so on.

(koh-neh)
1. אֵיפֹה אֲנִי קוֹנֶה כַּרְטִיס אוֹטוֹבּוּס? לָרַכֶּבֶת?
buy

(luh-ay-laht) (lee-roo-shah-lah-yim) (ah-veev) (luh-tel) (luh-Hay-fah) (yoh-tseh)
2. מָתַי יוֹצֵא הָאוֹטוֹבּוּס לְחֵיפָה? לְתֵל אָבִיב? לִירוּשָׁלַיִם? לְאֵילַת?

(lah-shook) (lah-ooh-nee-vair-see-tah) (lee-kness-et) (lee-muh-tsah-dah) (hah-too-fah) (lee-sday)
לִשְׂדֵה הַתְּעוּפָה? לִמְצָדָה? לַכְּנֶסֶת? לָאוּנִיבֶרְסִיטָה? לַשּׁוּק?
market the to — Masada to — airport the for

(lah-kness-et)
3. אֵיפֹה הָאוֹטוֹבּוּס לַכְּנֶסֶת?
Knesset the to

(hah-eer) (luh-mair-kahz)
אֵיפֹה הָאוֹטוֹבּוּס לְמֶרְכַּז הָעִיר?
city — center the to

(hah-Hah-yoht) (luh-gahn)
אֵיפֹה הָאוֹטוֹבּוּס לְגַן הַחַיּוֹת?
zoo the to

(hah-tfoo-tsoht) (bait) (luh-moo-zay-on)
אֵיפֹה הָאוֹטוֹבּוּס לְמוּזֵיאוֹן בֵּית הַתְּפוּצוֹת?
Diaspora Museum

(yiss-rah-el)(luh-moo-zay-on)
אֵיפֹה הָאוֹטוֹבּוּס לְמוּזֵיאוֹן יִשְׂרָאֵל?

(lah-ooh-nee-vair-see-tah)
אֵיפֹה הָאוֹטוֹבּוּס לָאוּנִיבֶרְסִיטָה?

(lah-shook)
אֵיפֹה הָאוֹטוֹבּוּס לַשּׁוּק?
market the to

אֵיפֹה הָאוֹטוֹבּוּס לְתֵל אָבִיב?

כנסת
מוזיאון ישראל
אוניברסיטה
יד ושם
שדה התעופה
שוק

Read the following very typical conversation וְ write it in the blanks מִשְּׂמֹאל. (mee-smohl)
left the to

(hah-mair-kah-zit) (lah-tah-Hah-nah)(noh-seh-ah) (mis-par) (ay-zeh)
אֵיזֶה מִסְפָּר אוֹטוֹבּוּס נוֹסֵעַ לַתַּחֲנָה הַמֶּרְכָּזִית? ______________________
central — station the to — travels — which

אוֹטוֹבּוּס מִסְפָּר 10. ______________________

(zmahn) (kah-mah) (kohl)
כֹּל כַּמָּה זְמַן? ___כֹּל כַּמָּה זְמַן?___
often how

(dah-koht) (Hah-mesh) (kohl)
כֹּל חָמֵשׁ דַּקּוֹת. ______________________
minutes — five — every

(hah-mair-kah-zit)(hah-tah-Hah-nah) (ahd) (mee-poh) (tsah-reeH) (zmahn)
כַּמָּה זְמַן אֲנִי צָרִיךְ מִפֹּה עַד הַתַּחֲנָה הַמֶּרְכָּזִית? ______________________
central — to — here from — need — time

(dah-koht) (es-rim) (loh-kay-aH) (zeh)
זֶה לוֹקֵחַ עֶשְׂרִים דַּקּוֹת. ______________________
minutes — takes

(lee-roo-shah-lah-yim) (oh-leh)
כַּמָּה עוֹלֶה כַּרְטִיס לִירוּשָׁלַיִם? ______________________

(shloh-shah)
שְׁלֹשָׁה שְׁקָלִים. ______________________
three

Can אַתָּה translate the following thoughts into עִבְרִית ? הַתְּשׁוּבוֹת (hah-tshoo-voht) לְמַטָּה.

1. Where is the train station? ______________________

2. What does a ticket cost to the Old City? ______________________

3. How often does the bus go to the airport? ______________________

4. Where do I (🚹) buy a ticket? ______________________

5. Where is the bus stop? ______________________

6. I (🚹) want to get off please. ______________________

7. Where must I (🚺) get off? ______________________

8. When does the bus leave for Tel Aviv? ______________________

הִנֵּה (hin-ay) are two more verbs.

כּוּתֹנֶת

to wash (clothes) = לְכַבֵּס (luh-Hah-bes)

it takes = זֶה לוֹקֵחַ (zeh) (loh-kay-aH)

______________________ ______________________

You know the basic formula, so try to translate these sentences into עִבְרִית . Give it your best shot. הַתְּשׁוּבוֹת לְמַטָּה.

1. I (🚹) wash the shirt. ______________________

2. It takes 20 minutes to travel to Acre. ______________________

3. It takes one hour by car. ______________________

4. It takes one hour by bus from Tel Aviv to Jerusalem. ______________________

הַתְּשׁוּבוֹת

1. אֵיפֹה תַּחֲנַת הָרַכֶּבֶת?
2. כַּמָּה עוֹלֶה כַּרְטִיס לָעִיר הָעַתִּיקָה?
3. כֹּל כַּמָּה זְמַן נוֹסֵעַ הָאוֹטוֹבּוּס לִשְׂדֵה הַתְּעוּפָה?
4. אֵיפֹה אֲנִי קוֹנֶה כַּרְטִיס?
5. אֵיפֹה תַּחֲנַת הָאוֹטוֹבּוּס?
6. אֲנִי רוֹצֶה לָרֶדֶת בְּבַקָּשָׁה.
7. אֵיפֹה אֲנִי צְרִיכָה לָרֶדֶת?
8. מָתַי יוֹצֵא הָאוֹטוֹבּוּס לְתֵל אָבִיב?

---

1. אֲנִי מְכַבֵּס הַכּוּתֹנֶת.
2. זֶה לוֹקֵחַ עֶשְׂרִים דַּקּוֹת לִנְסוֹעַ לְעַכּוֹ.
3. זֶה לוֹקֵחַ שָׁעָה בִּמְכוֹנִית.
4. זֶה לוֹקֵחַ שָׁעָה בָּאוֹטוֹבּוּס מִתֵּל אָבִיב לִירוּשָׁלַיִם.

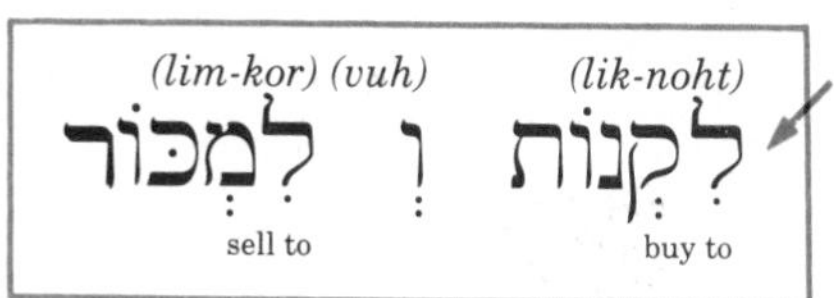

Step 21

לִקְנוֹת (lik-noht) buy to **וְ** (vuh) **לִמְכּוֹר** (lim-kor) sell to

Shopping abroad is exciting. The simple everyday task of buying a לִיטֶר (lit-air) liter חָלָב (Hah-lahv) milk or a תַּפּוּחַ (tah-poo-aH) apple becomes a challenge that אַתָּה should עַכְשָׁו be able to meet quickly וְ easily. Of course, אַתָּה will purchase גְלוּיוֹת (gloo-yoht), בּוּלִים (boo-lim) וּמַזְכָּרוֹת (vuh-mahz-kah-roht) souvenirs but don't forget those many other דְבָרִים ranging from shoelaces to אַסְפִּירִין (ahs-pee-reen) aspirin that אַתָּה might need unexpectedly. Do you know the difference between מַסְפֵּרָה (mahs-peh-rah) hairdresser and מַאֲפִיָּה (mah-ah-fee-yah) bakery? לֹא. Let's learn about the different חֲנוּיוֹת (Hah-noo-yoht) stores/shops in יִשְׂרָאֵל. לְמַטָּה is a מַפָּה of a section of יְרוּשָׁלַיִם.

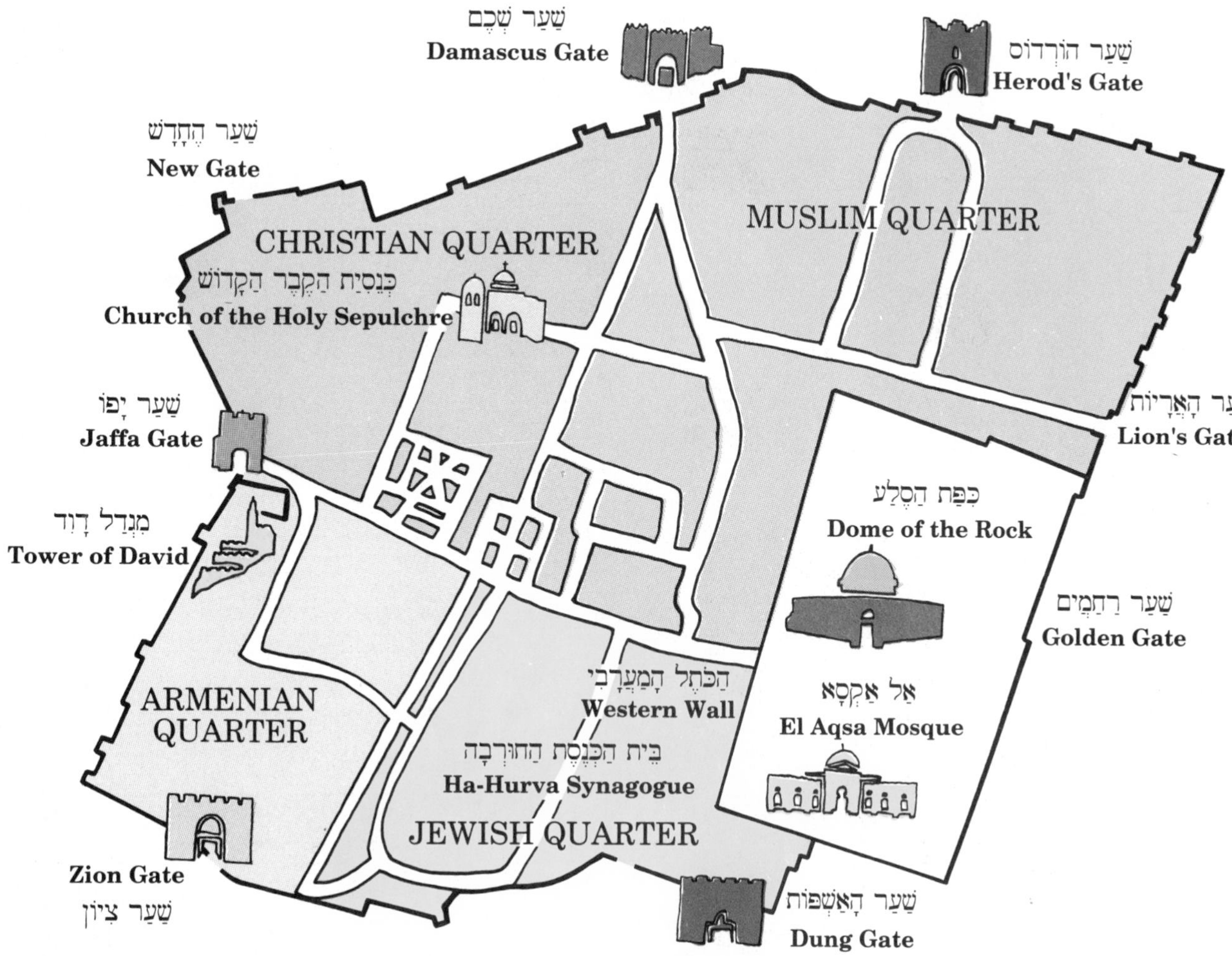

שַׁעַר שְׁכֶם
Damascus Gate
שַׁעַר הוֹרְדוֹס
Herod's Gate
שַׁעַר הֶחָדָשׁ
New Gate
MUSLIM QUARTER
CHRISTIAN QUARTER
כְּנֵסִיַּת הַקֶּבֶר הַקָּדוֹשׁ
Church of the Holy Sepulchre
שַׁעַר יָפוֹ
Jaffa Gate
שַׁעַר הָאֲרָיוֹת
Lion's Gate
כִּפַּת הַסֶּלַע
Dome of the Rock
מִגְדַּל דָּוִד
Tower of David
שַׁעַר רַחֲמִים
Golden Gate
הַכֹּתֶל הַמַּעֲרָבִי
Western Wall
אֶל אַקְצָא
El Aqsa Mosque
ARMENIAN QUARTER
בֵּית הַכְּנֶסֶת הַחוּרְבָה
Ha-Hurva Synagogue
JEWISH QUARTER
Zion Gate
שַׁעַר צִיּוֹן
שַׁעַר הָאַשְׁפּוֹת
Dung Gate

On the following עַמּוּדִים there are all types of חֲנוּיוֹת (Hah-noo-yoht) stores/shops in יִשְׂרָאֵל. Be sure to fill in the blanks מִתַּחַת (mee-tah-Haht) under לַתְּמוּנוֹת (lah-tmoo-noht) with the names of הַחֲנוּיוֹת (heh-Hah-noo-yoht) stores the.

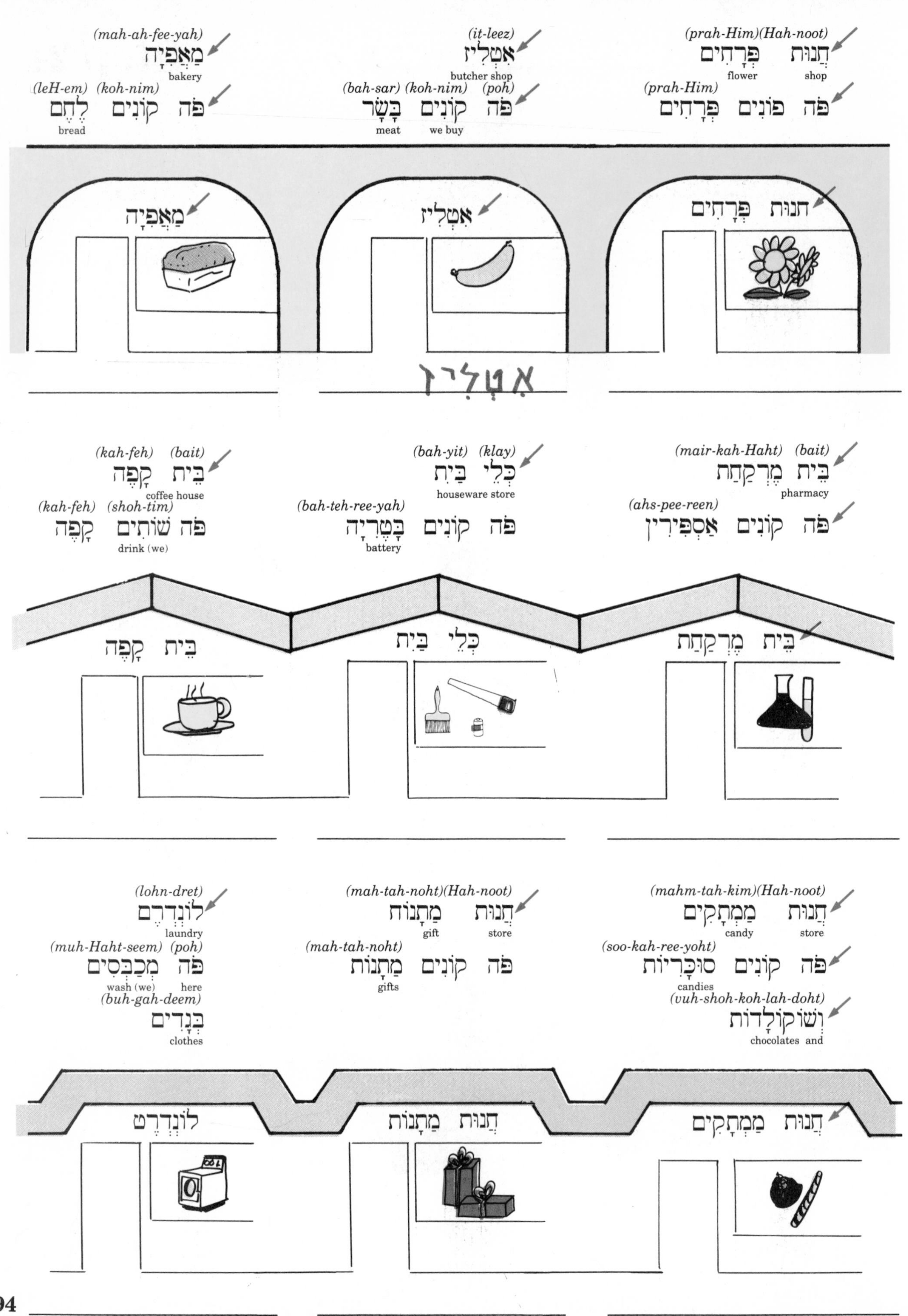
(prah-Him)(Hah-noot)
חֲנוּת פְּרָחִים
flower shop
(prah-Him)
פֹּה פּוֹנִים פְּרָחִים
(it-leez)
אִטְלִיז
butcher shop
(bah-sar) (koh-nim) (poh)
פֹּה קוֹנִים בָּשָׂר
meat we buy
(mah-ah-fee-yah)
מַאֲפִיָּה
bakery
(leH-em) (koh-nim)
פֹּה קוֹנִים לֶחֶם
bread
חנות פְּרָחִים
אִטְלִיז
מַאֲפִיָּה
אטליז
(mair-kah-Haht) (bait)
בֵּית מֶרְקַחַת
pharmacy
(ahs-pee-reen)
פֹּה קוֹנִים אַסְפִּירִין
(bah-yit) (klay)
כְּלֵי בַּיִת
houseware store
(bah-teh-ree-yah)
פֹּה קוֹנִים בָּטֶרְיָה
battery
(kah-feh) (bait)
בֵּית קָפֶה
coffee house
(kah-feh) (shoh-tim)
פֹּה שׁוֹתִים קָפֶה
drink (we)
בֵּית מֶרְקַחַת
כְּלֵי בַּיִת
בֵּית קָפֶה
(mahm-tah-kim)(Hah-noot)
חֲנוּת מַמְתַּקִים
candy store
(soo-kah-ree-yoht)
פֹּה קוֹנִים סוּכָּרִיּוֹת
candies
(vuh-shoh-koh-lah-doht)
וְשׁוֹקוֹלָדוֹת
chocolates and
(mah-tah-noht)(Hah-noot)
חֲנוּת מַתָּנוֹת
gift store
(mah-tah-noht)
פֹּה קוֹנִים מַתָּנוֹת
gifts
(lohn-dret)
לוֹנְדְּרֶט
laundry
(muh-Haht-seem) (poh)
פֹּה מְכַבְּסִים
wash (we) here
(buh-gah-deem)
בְּגָדִים
clothes
חֲנוּת מַמְתַּקִים
חֲנוּת מַתָּנוֹת
לוֹנְדְּרֶט

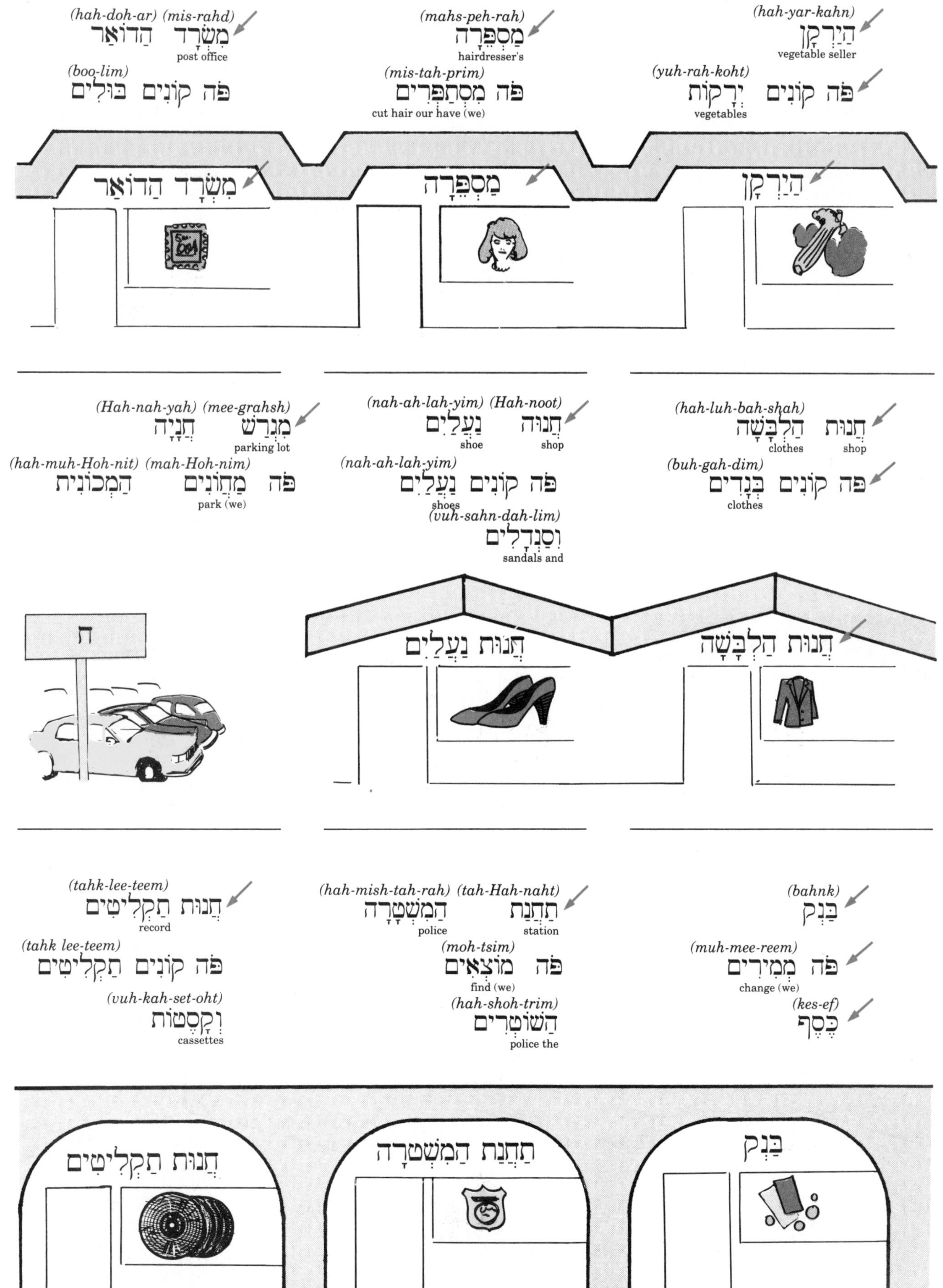

(hah-yar-kahn)
הַיַּרְקָן
vegetable seller
(yuh-rah-koht)
פֹּה קוֹנִים יְרָקוֹת
vegetables
(mahs-peh-rah)
מַסְפֵּרָה
hairdresser's
(mis-tah-prim)
פֹּה מִסְתַּפְּרִים
cut hair our have (we)
(hah-doh-ar) (mis-rahd)
מִשְׂרַד הַדּוֹאַר
post office
(boo-lim)
פֹּה קוֹנִים בּוּלִים
הַיַּרְקָן
מַסְפֵּרָה
מִשְׂרַד הַדּוֹאַר
(hah-luh-bah-shah)
חֲנוּת הַלְבָּשָׁה
clothes
shop
(buh-gah-dim)
פֹּה קוֹנִים בְּגָדִים
clothes
(nah-ah-lah-yim) (Hah-noot)
חֲנוּת נַעֲלַיִם
shoe
shop
(nah-ah-lah-yim)
פֹּה קוֹנִים נַעֲלַיִם
shoes
(vuh-sahn-dah-lim)
וְסַנְדָּלִים
sandals and
(Hah-nah-yah) (mee-grahsh)
מִגְרַשׁ חֲנָיָה
parking lot
(hah-muh-Hoh-nit) (mah-Hoh-nim)
פֹּה מַחֲנִים הַמְּכוֹנִית
park (we)
חֲנוּת הַלְבָּשָׁה
חֲנוּת נַעֲלַיִם
ח
(bahnk)
בַּנְק
(muh-mee-reem)
פֹּה מְמִירִים
change (we)
(kes-ef)
כֶּסֶף
(hah-mish-tah-rah) (tah-Hah-naht)
תַּחֲנַת הַמִּשְׁטָרָה
police
station
(moh-tsim)
פֹּה מוֹצְאִים
find (we)
(hah-shoh-trim)
הַשּׁוֹטְרִים
police the
(tahk-lee-teem)
חֲנוּת תַּקְלִיטִים
record
(tahk lee-teem)
פֹּה קוֹנִים תַּקְלִיטִים
(vuh-kah-set-oht)
וְקָסֶטוֹת
cassettes
בַּנְק
תַּחֲנַת הַמִּשְׁטָרָה
חֲנוּת תַּקְלִיטִים

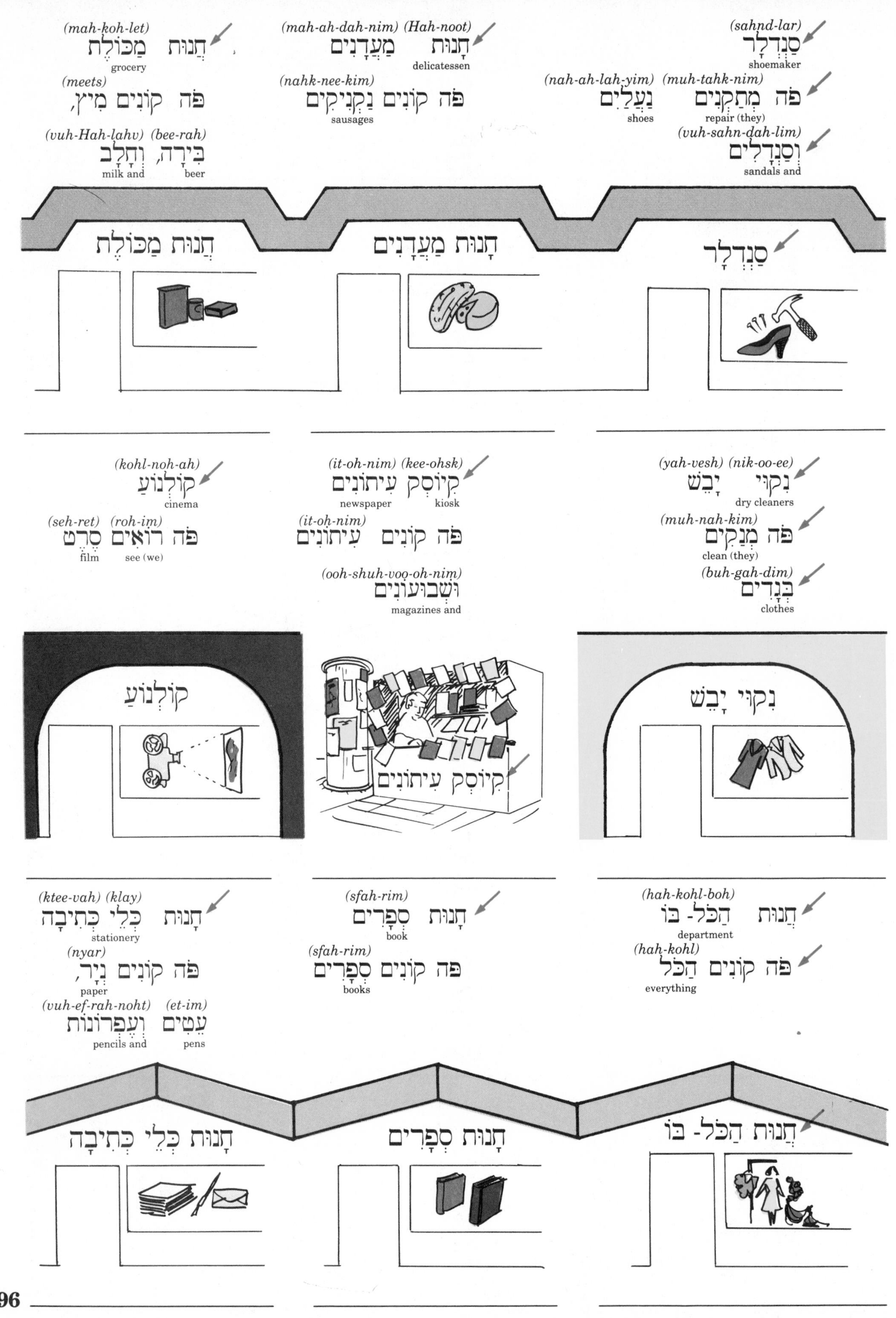

(sahnd-lar)
סַנְדְּלָר
shoemaker
(muh-tahk-nim) (nah-ah-lah-yim)
פֹּה מְתַקְּנִים נַעֲלַיִם
repair (they) shoes
(vuh-sahn-dah-lim)
וְסַנְדָּלִים
sandals and
(Hah-noot) (mah-ah-dah-nim)
חֲנוּת מַעֲדָנִים
delicatessen
(nahk-nee-kim)
פֹּה קוֹנִים נַקְנִיקִים
sausages
(mah-koh-let)
חֲנוּת מַכּוֹלֶת
grocery
(meets)
פֹּה קוֹנִים מִיץ,
(bee-rah) (vuh-Hah-lahv)
בִּירָה, וְחָלָב
beer milk and
סַנְדְּלָר
חֲנוּת מַעֲדָנִים
חֲנוּת מַכּוֹלֶת
(nik-oo-ee) (yah-vesh)
נִקּוּי יָבֵשׁ
dry cleaners
(muh-nah-kim)
פֹּה מְנַקִּים
clean (they)
(buh-gah-dim)
בְּגָדִים
clothes
(kee-ohsk) (it-oh-nim)
קִיוֹסְק עִיתוֹנִים
kiosk newspaper
(it-oh-nim)
פֹּה קוֹנִים עִיתוֹנִים
(ooh-shuh-voo-oh-nim)
וּשְׁבוּעוֹנִים
magazines and
(kohl-noh-ah)
קוֹלְנוֹעַ
cinema
(roh-im) (seh-ret)
פֹּה רוֹאִים סֶרֶט
see (we) film
נִקּוּי יָבֵשׁ
קִיוֹסְק עִיתוֹנִים
קוֹלְנוֹעַ
(hah-kohl-boh)
חֲנוּת הַכֹּל-בּוֹ
department
(hah-kohl)
פֹּה קוֹנִים הַכֹּל
everything
(sfah-rim)
חֲנוּת סְפָרִים
book
(sfah-rim)
פֹּה קוֹנִים סְפָרִים
books
(klay) (ktee-vah)
חֲנוּת כְּלֵי כְּתִיבָה
stationery
(nyar)
פֹּה קוֹנִים נְיָר,
paper
(et-im) (vuh-ef-rah-noht)
עֵטִים וְעֶפְרוֹנוֹת
pens pencils and
חֲנוּת הַכֹּל-בּוֹ
חֲנוּת סְפָרִים
חֲנוּת כְּלֵי כְּתִיבָה

(shook) שׁוּק — market

(peh-roht) (vuh-yuh-rah-koht) פֹּה קוֹנִים פֵּרוֹת וִירָקוֹת — fruit, vegetables and

(tsil-oom) חֲנוּת צִילּוּם — photo

(film) פֹּה קוֹנִים פִילְם

(del-ek)(tah-Hah-naht) תַּחֲנַת דֶלֶק — gas station

(del-ek) פֹּה קוֹנִים דֶלֶק

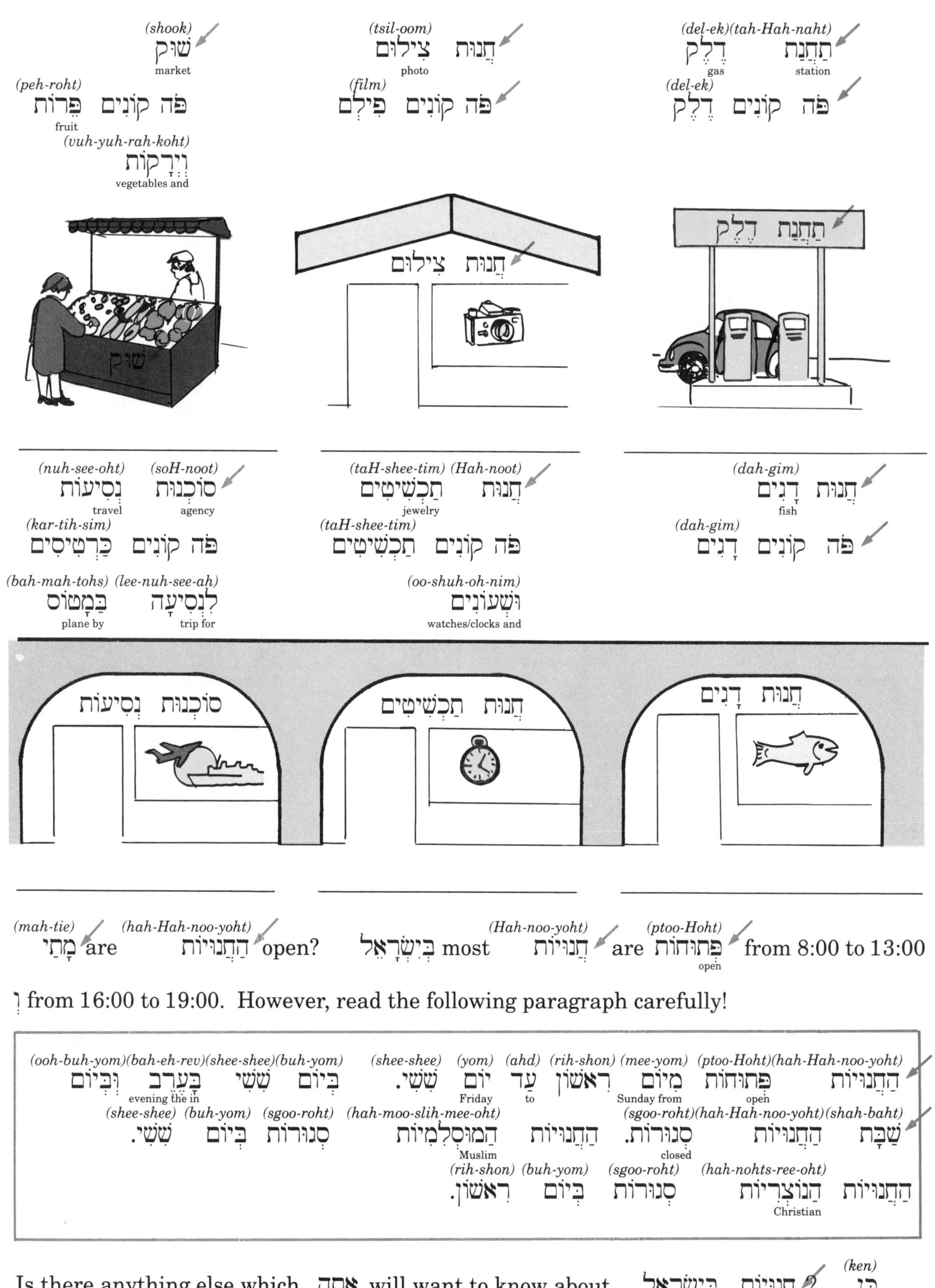

(nuh-see-oht) (soH-noot) סוֹכְנוּת נְסִיעוֹת — agency, travel

(kar-tih-sim) פֹּה קוֹנִים כַּרְטִיסִים

(bah-mah-tohs) (lee-nuh-see-ah) לִנְסִיעָה בַּמָּטוֹס — trip for, plane by

(taH-shee-tim) (Hah-noot) חֲנוּת תַכְשִׁיטִים — jewelry

(taH-shee-tim) פֹּה קוֹנִים תַכְשִׁיטִים

(oo-shuh-oh-nim) וּשְׁעוֹנִים — watches/clocks and

(dah-gim) חֲנוּת דָגִים — fish

(dah-gim) פֹּה קוֹנִים דָגִים

(mah-tie) מָתַי are (hah-Hah-noo-yoht) הַחֲנוּיוֹת open? בְּיִשְׂרָאֵל most (Hah-noo-yoht) חֲנוּיוֹת are (ptoo-Hoht) פְּתוּחוֹת (open) from 8:00 to 13:00 וְ from 16:00 to 19:00. However, read the following paragraph carefully!

> (hah-Hah-noo-yoht)(ptoo-Hoht)(mee-yom)(rih-shon)(ahd)(yom)(shee-shee) הַחֲנוּיוֹת פְּתוּחוֹת מִיּוֹם רִאשׁוֹן עַד יוֹם שִׁשִּׁי. (open, Sunday from, to, Friday) (buh-yom)(shee-shee)(bah-eh-rev)(ooh-buh-yom) בְּיוֹם שִׁשִּׁי בָּעֶרֶב וּבְיוֹם (evening the in)
>
> (shah-baht)(hah-Hah-noo-yoht)(sgoo-roht) שַׁבָּת הַחֲנוּיוֹת סְגוּרוֹת. (closed) (hah-moo-slih-mee-oht) הַחֲנוּיוֹת הַמּוּסְלְמִיּוֹת (Muslim) (sgoo-roht)(buh-yom)(shee-shee) סְגוּרוֹת בְּיוֹם שִׁשִּׁי.
>
> (hah-nohts-ree-oht)(sgoo-roht)(buh-yom)(rih-shon) הַחֲנוּיוֹת הַנּוֹצְרִיּוֹת (Christian) סְגוּרוֹת בְּיוֹם רִאשׁוֹן.

Is there anything else which אַתָּה will want to know about חֲנוּיוֹת בְּיִשְׂרָאֵל ? (ken) כֵּן .

Look at הַתְּמוּנָה on the next עַמּוּד .

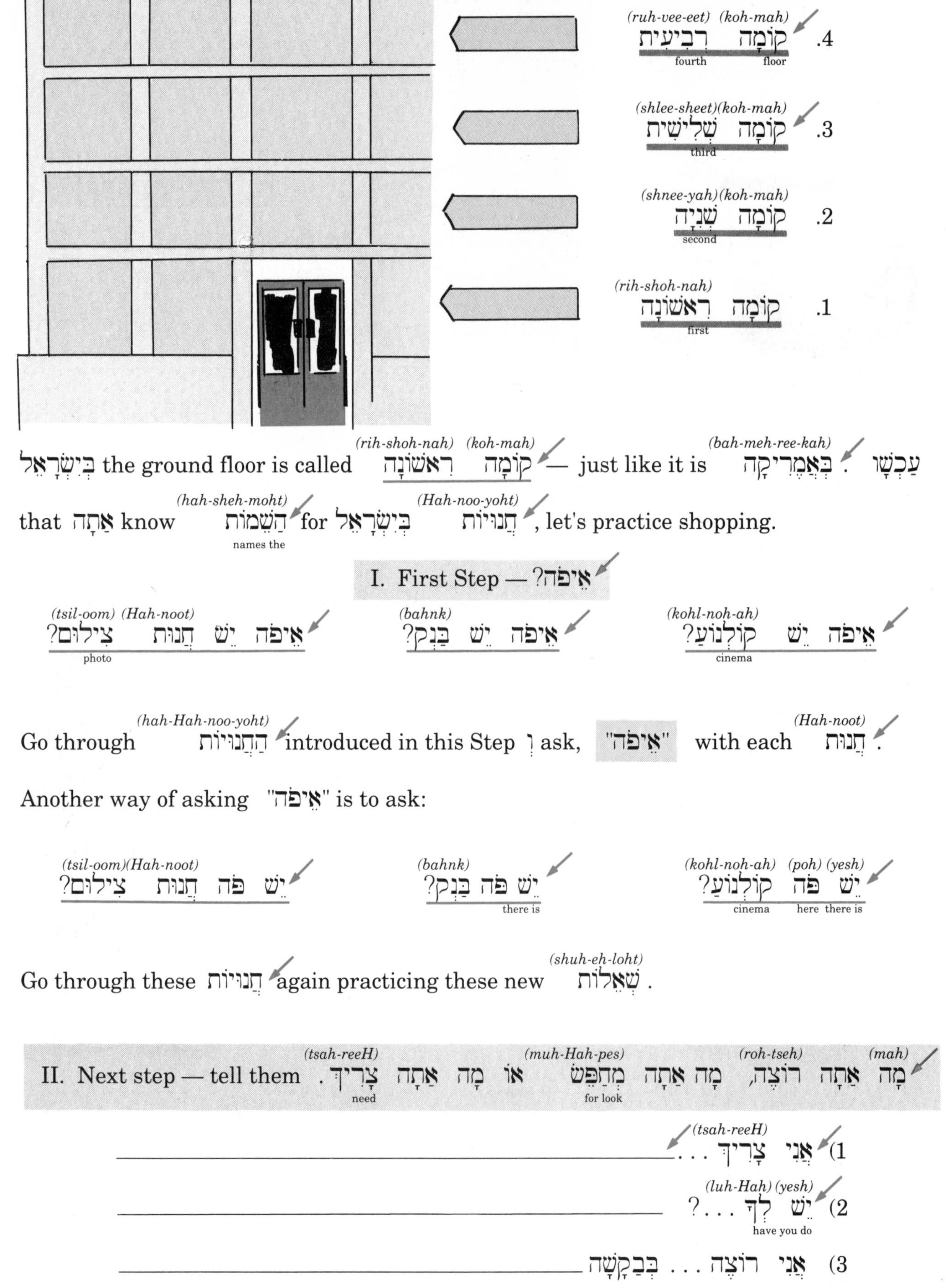

עַכְשָׁו . בְּאֲמֶרִיקָה (bah-meh-ree-kah) the ground floor is called קוֹמָה (koh-mah) רִאשׁוֹנָה (rih-shoh-nah) — just like it is בְּיִשְׂרָאֵל

that אַתָּה know הַשֵּׁמוֹת (hah-sheh-moht) names the for בְּיִשְׂרָאֵל חֲנוּיוֹת (Hah-noo-yoht), let's practice shopping.

I. First Step — אֵיפֹה?

אֵיפֹה יֵשׁ קוֹלְנוֹעַ? (kohl-noh-ah) cinema

אֵיפֹה יֵשׁ בַּנְק? (bahnk)

אֵיפֹה יֵשׁ חֲנוּת (Hah-noot) צִילוּם? (tsil-oom) photo

Go through הַחֲנוּיוֹת (hah-Hah-noo-yoht) introduced in this Step וְ ask, "אֵיפֹה" with each חֲנוּת (Hah-noot).

Another way of asking "אֵיפֹה" is to ask:

יֵשׁ (yesh) there is פֹּה (poh) here קוֹלְנוֹעַ? (kohl-noh-ah) cinema

יֵשׁ פֹּה בַּנְק? (bahnk) there is

יֵשׁ פֹּה חֲנוּת (Hah-noot) צִילוּם? (tsil-oom)

Go through these חֲנוּיוֹת again practicing these new שְׁאֵלוֹת (shuh-eh-loht).

II. Next step — tell them מָה (mah) אַתָּה רוֹצֶה (roh-tseh), מָה אַתָּה מְחַפֵּשׂ (muh-Hah-pes) for look אוֹ מָה אַתָּה צָרִיךְ (tsah-reeH) need.

1) אֲנִי צָרִיךְ (tsah-reeH) . . . ______________________

2) יֵשׁ (yesh) לְךָ (luh-Hah) have you do . . . ? ______________________

3) אֲנִי רוֹצֶה . . . בְּבַקָּשָׁה ______________________

4) אֲנִי מְחַפֵּשׂ . . . ______________________

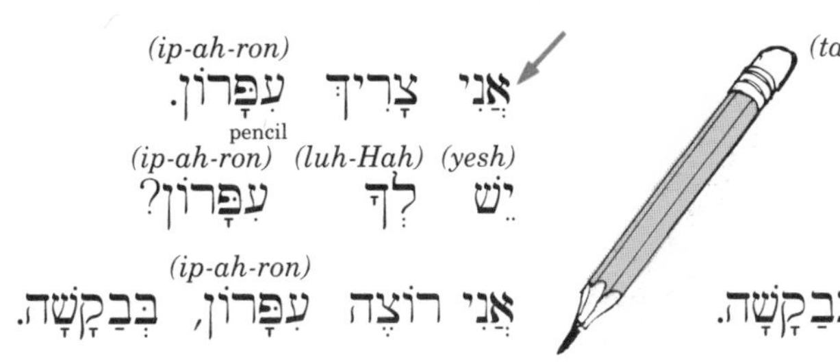

(ip-ah-ron)
אֲנִי צָרִיךְ עִפָּרוֹן.
pencil

(ip-ah-ron) (luh-Hah) (yesh)
יֵשׁ לְךָ עִפָּרוֹן?

(ip-ah-ron)
אֲנִי רוֹצֶה עִפָּרוֹן, בְּבַקָּשָׁה.

(tah-poo-Him) (kee-loh) (tsah-reeH)
אֲנִי צָרִיךְ קִילוֹ תַּפּוּחִים.
apples kilo

(tah-poo-Him)(kee-loh)(luh-Hah)(yesh)
יֵשׁ לְךָ קִילוֹ תַּפּוּחִים?
have you do

אֲנִי רוֹצֶה קִילוֹ תַּפּוּחִים, בְּבַקָּשָׁה.

Go through the glossary at the end of this סֵפֶר and select עֶשְׂרִים (es-rim) מִלִּים. Drill the above patterns עִם these עֶשְׂרִים מִלִּים. Don't cheat. Drill them הַיּוֹם (hah-yom). Now, take עֶשְׂרִים more מִלִּים from your glossary וְ do the same. מָחָר (mah-Har) take another עֶשְׂרִים מִלִּים and do the same again.

III. Next step — find out כַּמָּה (kah-mah) זֶה (zeh) עוֹלֶה (oh-leh)?

כַּמָּה זֶה עוֹלֶה?________________________________

(hah-ip-ah-ron)
כַּמָּה עוֹלֶה הָעִפָּרוֹן?

(hah-gloo-yah) (oh-lah)
כַּמָּה עוֹלָה הַגְּלוּיָה?

(hah-bool)
כַּמָּה עוֹלֶה הַבּוּל?

(tah-poo-Him) (kee-loh)
כַּמָּה עוֹלֶה קִילוֹ תַּפּוּחִים?
apples

(tah-poo-zim)
כַּמָּה עוֹלֶה קִילוֹ תַּפּוּזִים?
oranges

(bah-sar)
כַּמָּה עוֹלֶה קִילוֹ בָּשָׂר?
meat

Using these same מִלִּים that אַתָּה selected לְמַעְלָה (luh-mah-ah-lah) (above), drill these שְׁאֵלוֹת (shuh-eh-loht) also.

IV. If אַתָּה don't know אֵיפֹה to find something, ask

(mish-kah-fah-yim) (lik-noht) (ef-shar)
אֵיפֹה אֶפְשָׁר לִקְנוֹת מִשְׁקָפַיִם?
sunglasses buy to possible it is

(ahs-pee-reen) (lik-noht) (ef-shar)
אֵיפֹה אֶפְשָׁר לִקְנוֹת אַסְפִּירִין?

Once אַתָּה find what אַתָּה רוֹצֶה say,

(zeh) (et)
אֲנִי רוֹצֶה אֶת זֶה, בְּבַקָּשָׁה.
this

Or, if אַתָּה would not like it,

(toh-dah) (zeh) (et) (loh)
אֲנִי לֹא רוֹצֶה אֶת זֶה, תּוֹדָה.

עַכְשָׁו, אַתָּה are all set to shop for anything!

Step 22

At this point, אַתָּה should just about be ready for your נְסִיעָה (nuh-see-ah) (trip) to יִשְׂרָאֵל . אַתָּה have gone shopping for those last minute odds 'n ends. Most likely, the store directory at your local חֲנוּת הַכֹּל-בּוֹ (Hah-noot) (hah-kohl-boh) did not look like the one לְמַטָּה (luh-mah-tah). אַתָּה already know many מִלִּים and אַתָּה could guess at many others. אַתָּה יוֹדֵעַ (yoh-day-ah) (know) that "יֶלֶד" (yel-ed) is Hebrew for "child," so if אַתָּה צָרִיךְ (tsah-reeH) something for a יֶלֶד (yel-ed), you would probably look on הַקּוֹמָה הַשְּׁלִישִׁית (hah-koh-mah)(hah-shlee-sheet) wouldn't you?

קוֹמָה			
7 קוֹמָה	קָפֶטֶרְיָה מַעֲדָנִים יֵינוֹת	פֵּרוֹת יְרָקוֹת מַאֲפִיָּה	דָּג קָפוּא בָּשָׂר עוֹפוֹת
6 קוֹמָה	מִיטּוֹת כְּלֵי מִיטָּה מַרְאוֹת	רָהִיטִים מְנוֹרוֹת שְׁטִיחִים	תְּמוּנוֹת דִּבְרֵי חַשְׁמַל
5 קוֹמָה	חַרְסִינָה זְכוּכִית	סַכִּינִים כְּלֵי מִטְבָּח	מַפְתְּחוֹת קֶרָמִיקָה
4 קוֹמָה	סְפָרִים מַחְלֶקֶת צִילוּם צַעֲצוּעִים	מִסְעָדָה תַּקְלִיטִים כְּלֵי כְּתִיבָה	טַבָּק עִיתוֹנִים שְׁבוּעוֹנִים
3 קוֹמָה	מַחְלֶקֶת יְלָדִים נַעֲלֵי יְלָדִים רָהִיטֵי יְלָדִים	מַחְלֶקֶת גְּבָרִים בִּגְדֵי גְבָרִים נַעֲלֵי גְבָרִים	קוֹסְמֶטִיקָה עַתִּיקוֹת מִזְוָדוֹת
2 קוֹמָה	לִבְנֵי נָשִׁים נַעֲלֵי נָשִׁים	מַחְלֶקֶת נָשִׁים בִּגְדֵי נָשִׁים כּוֹבְעֵי נָשִׁים	דִּבְרֵי סְפּוֹרְט צִיּוּד קֶמְפִּינְג בִּגְדֵי יָם
1 קוֹמָה	מִטְרִיּוֹת מַפּוֹת כּוֹבָעִים תַּכְשִׁיטִים	כְּפָפוֹת דִּבְרֵי עוֹר גַּרְבַּיִם חֲגוֹרוֹת	שְׁעוֹנִים מִמְחָטוֹת בּוֹשֶׂם

Let's start a checklist for your נְסִיעָה (nuh-see-ah) (trip). Besides suitcases, מָה (mah) אַתָּה צָרִיךְ (tsah-reeH) בְּיִשְׂרָאֵל?

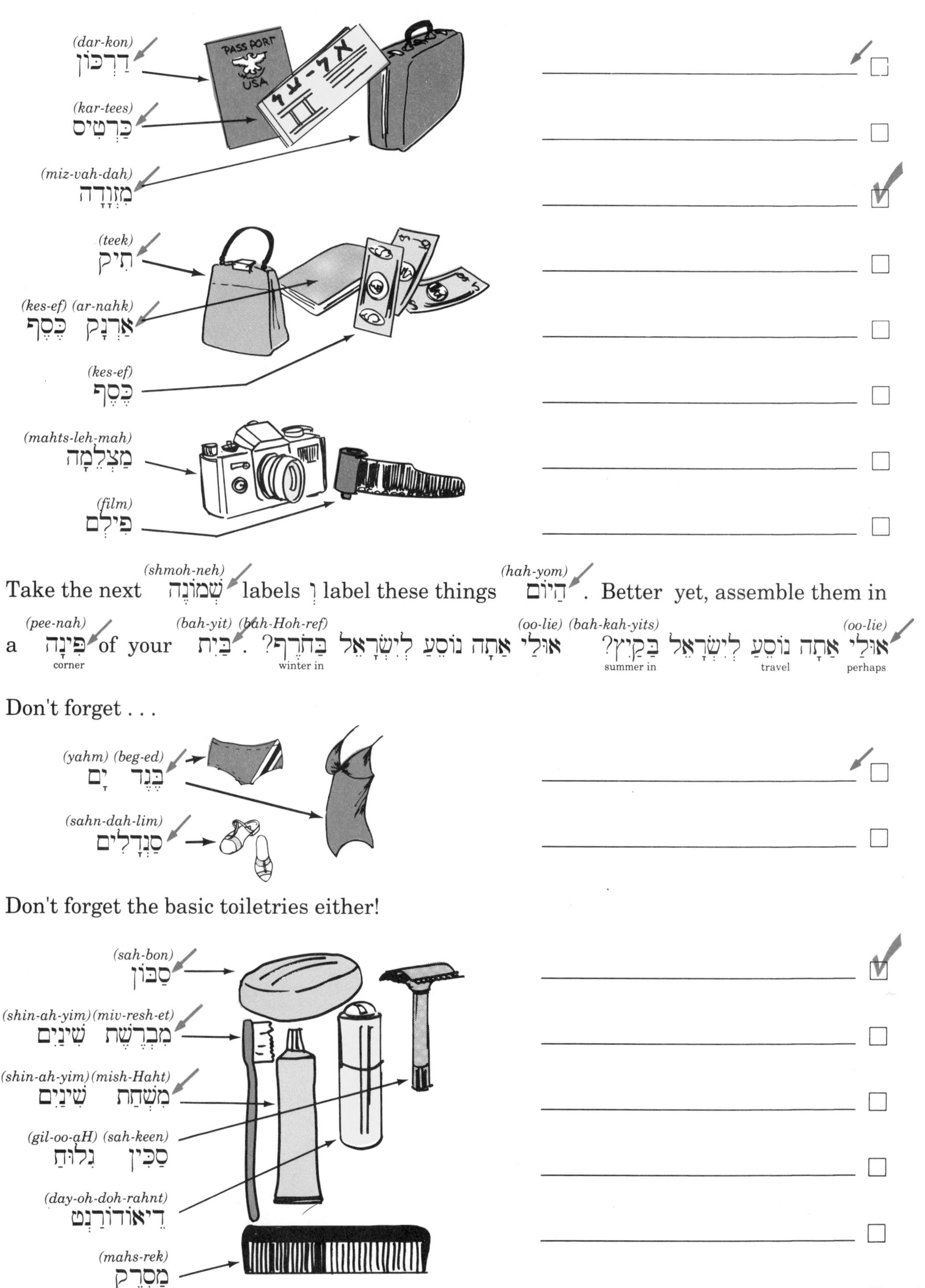

Take the next (shmoh-neh) שְׁמוֹנֶה labels וְ label these things (hah-yom) הַיּוֹם. Better yet, assemble them in a (pee-nah) פִּנָּה (corner) of your (bah-yit) בַּיִת. (oo-lie) אוּלַי (perhaps) אַתָּה נוֹסֵעַ (travel) לְיִשְׂרָאֵל (bah-kah-yits) בַּקַּיִץ (summer in)? (oo-lie) אוּלַי אַתָּה נוֹסֵעַ לְיִשְׂרָאֵל (bah-Hoh-ref) בַּחֹרֶף (winter in)?

Don't forget . . .

Don't forget the basic toiletries either!

For the rest of (hah-dvah-rim) הַדְבָרִים, let's start with the outside layers וְ work our way in.

(muh-eel) מְעִיל

(gesh-em) (muh-eel) מְעִיל גֶשֶׁם

(mit-ree-ah) מִטְרִיָה

(kfah-foht) כְּפָפוֹת

(koh-vah) כּוֹבַע

כּוֹבַע

(mah-gah-fah-yim) מַגָפַיִם

(nah-ah-lah-yim) נַעֲלַיִם

(gar-bah-yim) גַרְבַּיִם

(gar-bee-oh-nim) גַרְבִּיוֹנִים

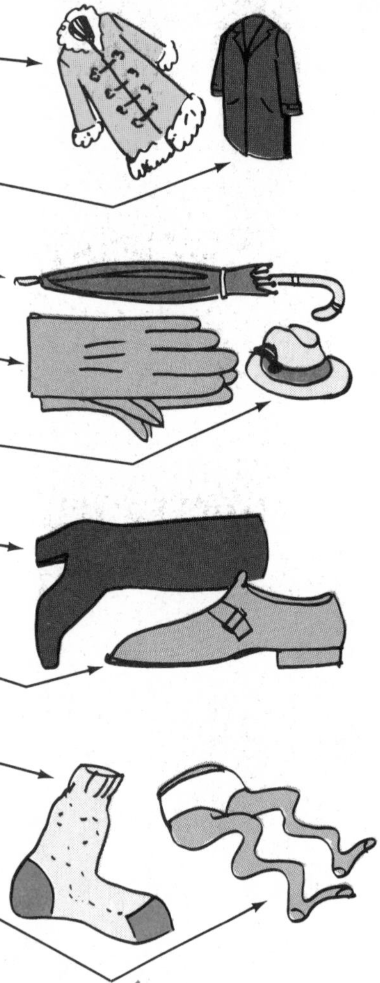

Take the next (es-reh) (Hah-mesh) עֶשְׂרֵה חֲמֵשׁ (fifteen) labels וְ label these דְבָרִים. Check וְ make sure that they are clean וְ ready for your (nuh-see-ah) נְסִיעָה (trip). Be sure to do the same עִם the rest of (hah-dvah-rim) הַדְבָרִים that אַתָה pack. Check them on this list as אַתָה organize them. From now on, אַתָה have

(shin-ah-yim) (mish-Haht) "מִשְׁחַת שִׁינַיִם" and not "toothpaste."

(pee-jah-mah) פִּיגָ'מָה

(lie-lah) (koo-toh-net) כּוּתֹנֶת לַיְלָה

(Hah-look) חָלוּק

(bah-yit) (nah-ah-lay) נַעֲלֵי בַּיִת

(hah-sahn-dah-lim) הַסַנְדָלִים can also double for you as (bah-yit) (nah-ah-lay) נַעֲלֵי בַּיִת.

Having assembled these (dvah-rim) דְבָרִים you are ready for your (nuh-see-ah) נְסִיעָה. However, being human means occasionally forgetting something. Look again at the (Hah-noot) חֲנוּת (hah-kohl-boh) הַכֹּל-בּוֹ (department) directory.

(buh-ay-zoh) בְּאֵיזוֹ (which on) (koh-mah) קוֹמָה (floor) (yesh) יֵשׁ (there is) . . .

(big-day) בִּגְדֵי (clothing) (gvah-rim) גְבָרִים (men)? (bah-koh-mah) בַּקוֹמָה (floor on) ______________________.

(nah-ah-lay) נַעֲלֵי (shoes) (nah-shim) נָשִׁים (women)? (bah-koh-mah) בַּקוֹמָה ______________________.

(sfah-rim) סְפָרִים (books)? (bah-koh-mah) בַּקוֹמָה ______________________.

(big-day) בִּגְדֵי (swimsuits) (yahm) יָם? בַּקוֹמָה ______________________.

(Har-see-nah) חַרְסִינָה? crystal — (bah-koh-mah) בַּקוֹמָה ________________.

(boh-sem) בּוֹשֶׂם? perfume — בַּקוֹמָה ________________.

(nah-shim) (big-day) בִּגְדֵי נָשִׁים? women clothing — בַּקוֹמָה ________________.

עַכְשָׁו, just remember your basic שְׁאֵלוֹת (questions). Repeat the typical conversation לְמַטָּה out loud.

Then practice the conversation by filling in the following blanks.

(nah-shim) (nah-ah-lay) (yesh) אֵיפֹה יֵשׁ נַעֲלֵי נָשִׁים? (shoes women) ________________

(hah-nah-shim) (buh-maH-lek-et) בְּמַחְלֶקֶת הַנָּשִׁים. (department in women) ________________

(hah-nah-shim) (maH-lek-et) אֵיפֹה מַחְלֶקֶת הַנָּשִׁים? ________________

(hah-shnee-yah) (bah-koh-mah) בַּקוֹמָה הַשְּׁנִיָּה. (second) ________________

(gar-bah-yim) (yesh) אֵיפֹה יֵשׁ גַּרְבַּיִם? ________________

(hah-rih-shoh-nah) (bah-koh-mah) בַּקוֹמָה הָרִאשׁוֹנָה. (first) ________________

Also, don't forget to ask . . .

(hah-mah-ah-lit) אֵיפֹה הַמַּעֲלִית? (elevator) ________________

(hah-mah-dreg-oht) אֵיפֹה הַמַּדְרֵגוֹת? (stairs the) ________________

(hah-nah-oht) (hah-mah-dreg-oht) אֵיפֹה הַמַּדְרֵגוֹת הַנָּעוֹת? (escalator the) ________________

Whether אַתָּה need (nah-shim) (nah-ah-lay) נַעֲלֵי נָשִׁים (shoes women) or a (luh-gev-air) (koo-toh-net) כּוּתוֹנֶת לְגֶבֶר (shirt man's) the necessary מִלִּים are the same.

(mee-dah) (ay-zoh)
אֵיזוֹ מִידָה?
size which

(nah-ah-lah-yim) (mis-par) (ay-zeh)
אֵיזֶה מִסְפַּר נַעֲלַיִם?
shoes size/number which

(mah-tim) (zeh)
זֶה מַתְאִים.
fits it

זֶה מַתְאִים.

(mah-tim) (loh) (zeh)
זֶה לֹא מַתְאִים.
fit doesn't it

(zeh) (et)
אֲנִי רוֹצֶה אֶת זֶה, בְּבַקָּשָׁה.
this

(kah-mah)
כַּמָּה זֶה עוֹלֶה?

(rah-bah) (toh-dah) (hah-kohl)
זֶה הַכֹּל. תּוֹדָה רַבָּה.
all it's

Clothing Sizes: (nah-shim) נָשִׁים

חוּלְצוֹת, סְוֶודֶרִים

American/British	32	34	36	38	40	42	44
Israeli	40	42	44	46	48	50	52

בְּגָדִים

American	8	10	12	14	16	18
British	10	12	14	16	18	20
Israeli	38	40	42	44	46	48

נַעֲלַיִם

American	5	5 1/2	6	6 1/2	7	7 1/2	8	8 1/2	9
Israeli	36	36 1/2	37	37 1/2	38	38 1/2	39	39 1/2	40

Clothing Sizes: (gvah-rim) גְּבָרִים

נַעֲלַיִם

American	7	7 1/2	8	8 1/2	9	9 1/2	10	10 1/2	11 1/2
Israeli	41	42	42	43	43	44	44	45	45

בְּגָדִים

American/British	34	36	38	40	42	44	46	48
Israeli	44	46	48	50	53	54	56	58

כּוּתֹנֶת

American/British	14	14 1/2	15	15 1/2	16	16 1/2	17	17 1/2
Israeli	36	37	38	39	40	41	42	43

עַכְשָׁו אַתָּה are ready for your (nuh-see-ah) נְסִיעָה (trip). You know everything that you need. The next Step will give you a quick review of international road signs וְ then אַתָּה are off to

(hah-too-fah) (sday) (toov) (kohl) (toh-vah) (nuh-see-ah)
שְׂדֵה הַתְּעוּפָה. נְסִיעָה טוֹבָה! כֹּל טוּב!

Step 23

= Caution!

אַתָּה will want to use caution when driving בְּיִשְׂרָאֵל . Here are some of the most important road signs. Remember, speed limits are in kilometers, not miles, per hour!

Caution

Curve

Intersection

Closed to all vehicles

Yield the right of way

Prohibited for motor vehicles

No entry

Stop

Stop sign ahead

Uneven road

Narrow bridge

Residential area, reduce speed

End of residential area

No passing

Traffic circle

No left turn

No U-turn

One way

Parking

Speed limit

Minimum speed

Speed limit on highway

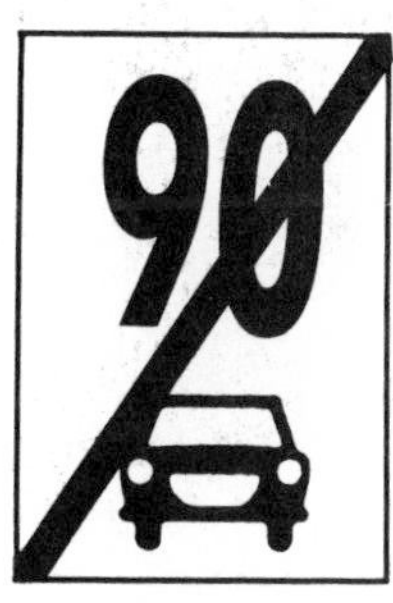

Highway ends, reduce speed

Motor vehicles only

Pedestrians only

Go straight

Right turn ahead

Youth hostel/UJA

GLOSSARY

א

father ... אָב
spring ... אָבִיב
but ... אֲבָל
agorot ... אוֹרוֹת
red ... אָדוֹם
sir ... אֲדוֹנִי
or ... אוֹ
August ... אוֹגוּסְט
bus ... אוֹטוֹבּוּס
autograph ... אוֹטוֹגְרָאף
perhaps ... אוּלַי
university ... אוּנִיבֶרְסִיטָה
bicycle ... אוֹפַנַּיִם
October ... אוֹקְטוֹבֶּר
light ... אוֹר
brother ... אַח
sister, nurse ... אָחוֹת
after ... אַחֲרֵת
afternoon ... אחרי הַצָּהֳרַיִם
one ... אַחַת
eleven ... אחת עֶשְׂרֵה
butcher shop ... אִטְלִיז
which ... אֵיזֶה
how ... אֵיךְ
no ... אֵין
where ... אֵיפֹה
man ... אִישׁ
woman ... אִשָּׁה
to ... אֶל
one thousand ... אֶלֶף
mother ... אֵם
American man ... אֲמֶרִיקָאִי
American woman ... אֲמֶרִיקָאִית
America ... אֲמֶרִיקָה
English man ... אַנְגְלִי
England, English woman ... אַנְגְלִיָה
English (language) ... אַנְגְלִית
I ... אֲנִי
we ... אֲנַחְנוּ
people ... אֲנָשִׁים
telephone token ... אֲסִימוֹן
aspirin ... אַסְפִּירִין
baked ... אָפוּי
gray ... אָפוֹר
April ... אַפְּרִיל
zero ... אֶפֶס
is it possible ... אֶפְשָׁר
four ... אַרְבַּע
fourteen ... אַרְבַּע עֶשְׂרֵה
forty ... אַרְבָּעִים
cupboard, wardrobe ... אָרוֹן
long ... אָרוֹךְ
meal ... אֲרוּחָה
breakfast ... אֲרוּחַת בֹּקֶר
dinner ... אֲרוּחַת עֶרֶב
lunch ... אֲרוּחַת צָהֳרַיִם
wallet ... אַרְנָק כֶּסֶף
counter ... אֶשְׁנָב
you (♀) ... אַתְּ
you (♂) ... אַתָּה
yesterday ... אֶתְמוֹל

בּ

in ... בְּ, בַּ
please ... בְּבַקָּשָׁה
swimsuit ... בֶּגֶד יָם
clothes ... בְּגָדִים
grilled ... בַּגְרִיל
by airmail ... בְּדוֹאַר אֲוִיר
good luck ... בְּהַצְלָחָה
stamp ... בּוּל
morning ... בֹּקֶר
good morning ... בֹּקֶר טוֹב
perfume ... בּוֹשֶׂם
battery ... בָּטֶרְיָה
between ... בֵּין
eggs ... בֵּיצִים
beer ... בִּירָה
house ... בַּיִת
synagogue ... בֵּית כְּנֶסֶת
pharmacy ... בֵּית מֶרְקַחַת
school ... בֵּית סֵפֶר
coffee shop ... בֵּית קָפֶה
toilet ... בֵּית שִׁמּוּשׁ
bottle ... בַּקְבּוּק
son ... בֵּן
ten (years old) ... בֶּן עֶשֶׂר
seventy (years old) ... בֶּן שִׁבְעִים
banana ... בָּנָנָה
bank ... בַּנְק
husband ... בַּעַל
on the corner ... בַּפִּינָה
healthy ... בָּרִיא
softly ... בְּשֶׁקֶט
meat ... בָּשָׂר
beef ... בְּשַׂר בָּקָר
mutton ... בְּשַׂר כֶּבֶשׂ
veal ... בְּשַׂר עֵגֶל
poultry ... בְּשַׂר עוֹף
daughter ... בַּת

ג

tall ... גְבוֹהָה
cheese ... גְבִינָה
ladies ... גְבָרוֹת
men ... גְבָרִים
Madam ... גְבֶרֶת
big ... גְדוֹלָה
underskirt ... גוּפִיָה
postcard ... גְלוּיָה
ice-cream ... גְלִידָה
also ... גַם
garden ... גַן
zoo ... גַן הַיּוֹת
stockings ... גַרְבּיוֹנִים
socks ... גַרְבַּיִם
rain ... גֶשֶׁם

ד

things ... דְבָרִים
herring ... דַג מָלוּחַ
fish dishes ... דָגִים
mail ... דֹאַר
uncle ... דוֹד
aunt ... דוֹדָה
push ... דְחוֹף
deodorant ... דֵיאוֹדוֹרַנְט
gas ... דֶלֶק
door ... דֶלֶת
service charge ... דְמֵי שֵׁרוּת
December ... דֶצֶמְבֶּר
thin ... דַק
minute ... דַקָה
south ... דָרוֹם
southern ... דְרוֹמִי
passport ... דַרְכּוֹן
road ... דֶרֶךְ
religion ... דָת

ה

he ... הוּא
parents ... הוֹרִים
she ... הִיא
today ... הַיּוֹם
vegetable seller ... הַיַּרְקָן
everything ... הַכֹּל
round trip ... הָלוֹךְ וָשׁוֹב
they ... הֵם
information counter ... הַמוֹדִיעִין
(plane) departure ... הַמְרָאָה
here (is) ... הִנֵה
a lot ... הַרְבֵּה
the police ... הַשׁוֹטְרִים
the hour/time ... הַשָּׁעָה

ו

and ... וְ
half past ... וָחֵצִי
curtain ... וִילוֹן
pink ... וָרֹד

ז

this, it is ... זֶה
cheap ... זוֹל
jacket ... זָ'קֶט
old ... זָקֵן

ח

package ... חֲבִילָה
friends ... חֲבֵרִים
room ... חֶדֶר
dining room ... חֲדַר אֹכֶל
bathroom ... חֲדַר אַמְבַּטְיָה
office, study ... חֲדַר עֲבוֹדָה
bedroom ... חֲדַר שֵׁינָה
new ... חֲדָשִׁים
month ... חֹדֶשׁ
sick ... חוֹלֶה
blouse ... חוּלְצָה
brown ... חוּם
winter ... חֹרֶף
brassière ... חֲזִיָּה
strong ... חֲזָקָה
milk ... חָלָב
window ... חַלּוֹן
bathrobe ... חָלוּק
suit ... חֲלִיפָה
hot ... חַם
butter ... חֶמְאָה
hot wind ... חַמְסִין
five ... חָמֵשׁ
fifteen ... חֲמֵשׁ עֶשְׂרֵה
fifty ... חֲמִישִּׁים
shop, store ... חֲנוּת
fish shop ... חֲנוּת דָּגִים
department store ... חֲנוּת הַכֹּל-בּוֹ
stationery store ... חֲנוּת כְּלֵי כְּתִיבָה
grocery store ... חֲנוּת מַכֹּלֶת
candy store ... חֲנוּת מַמְתַקִּים
gift store ... חֲנוּת מַתָּנוֹת
shoe shop ... חֲנוּת נַעֲלַיִם
bookstore ... חֲנוּת סְפָרִים
flower shop ... חֲנוּת פְּרָחִים
photo shop ... חֲנוּת צִילּוּם
jewelry shop ... חֲנוּת תַּכְשִׁיטִים
record store ... חֲנוּת תַּקְלִיטִים
skirt ... חֲצָאִית
half ... חֲצִי
bill ... חֶשְׁבּוֹן
important ... חָשׁוּב
cat ... חָתוּל

ט

good ... טוֹב
international flight ... טִיסָה בֵּין לְאוּמִית
domestic flight ... טִיסָה פְּנִים אַרְצִית
television ... טֶלֶוִיזְיָה
telephone ... טֶלֶפוֹן
public telephone ... טֶלֶפוֹן צִבּוּרִי
temperature ... טֶמְפֶּרָטוּרָה
taxi ... טַקְסִי

י

hand ... יָד
Jewish (man) ... יְהוּדִי
Jewish (woman) ... יְהוּדִיָּה
July ... יוּלִי
day ... יוֹם
Thursday ... יוֹם חֲמִישִׁי
Sunday ... יוֹם רִאשׁוֹן
Wednesday ... יוֹם רְבִיעִי
Saturday ... יוֹם שַׁבָּת
Tuesday ... יוֹם שְׁלִישִׁי
Monday ... יוֹם שֵׁנִי
Friday ... יוֹם שִׁשִּׁי
June ... יוּנִי
comes down ... יוֹרֵד
wine ... יַיִן
I can ... יָכוֹל
child ... יֶלֶד
sea ... יָם
days ... יָמִים
right ... יָמִין
to the right ... יָמִינָה
January ... יָנוּאָר
exit, departure (bus) ... יְצִיאָה
main exit ... יְצִיאָה רָאשִׁית
no exit ... אֵין יְצִיאָה
expensive ... יָקָר
green ... יָרוֹק
vegetables ... יְרָקוֹת
there is, there are ... יֵשׁ
I have ... יֵשׁ לִי
we have ... יֵשׁ לָנוּ
straight ahead ... יָשָׁר
Israel ... יִשְׂרָאֵל
Israelis ... יִשְׂרְאֵלִים

כּ

freeway ... כְּבִישׁ מָהִיר
ball ... כַּדּוּר
hat ... כּוֹבַע
glass ... כּוֹס
shirt ... כּוּתֹנֶת
nightshirt ... כּוּתֹנֶת לַיְלָה
blue ... כָּחוֹל
washstand ... כִּיּוֹר
dog ... כֶּלֶב
housewares store ... כְּלֵי בַּיִת
how many, how much ... כַּמָּה
yes ... כֵּן
entrance ... כְּנִיסָה
no entrance ... אֵין כְּנִיסָה
church ... כְּנֵסִיָּה
chair ... כִּסֵּא
spoon ... כַּפִּית
gloves ... כְּפָפוֹת
pillow ... כַּר
ticket ... כַּרְטִיס
kosher ... כָּשֵׁר
purity ... כַּשְׁרוּת
address ... כְּתֹבֶת
orange (color) ... כָּתֹם

ל

slowly ... לְאַט
to eat ... לֶאֱכֹל
to pack ... לֶאֱרֹז
to come ... לָבוֹא
white ... לָבָן
to order ... לְבַקֵּשׁ
to live, reside ... לָגוּר
to speak ... לְדַבֵּר
to know ... לָדַעַת
to understand ... לְהָבִין
to arrive ... לְהַגִּיעַ
to reserve, order ... לְהַזְמִין
to enter ... לְהִכָּנֵס
to stay ... לְהִשָּׁאֵר
no, not ... לֹא
timetable ... לוּחַ הַזְּמַנִּים
calendar ... לוּחַ שָׁנָה
to say ... לוֹמַר
laundry ... לוֹנְדְּרֶט
to repeat ... לַחֲזוֹר עַל
to wait for ... לְחַכּוֹת לְ
bread ... לֶחֶם
to look for ... לְחַפֵּשׂ
to fly ... לָטוּס
to phone ... לְטַלְפֵן לְ
night ... לַיְלָה
good night ... לַיְלָה טוֹב
to sleep ... לִישׁוֹן
to write ... לִכְתּוֹב
to go on foot ... לָלֶכֶת בָּרֶגֶל
to learn ... לִלְמוֹד
why ... לָמָּה
downstairs, below ... לְמַטָּה
to sell ... לִמְכּוֹר
upstairs, above ... לְמַעְלָה
to drive ... לִנְהוֹג
to land ... לִנְחוֹת
to travel ... לִנְסוֹעַ
to board ... לַעֲלוֹת עַל
smoking, to smoke ... לְעַשֵּׁן
in front of, before ... לִפְנֵי
to exit, depart ... לָצֵאת
to buy ... לִקְנוֹת
to read ... לִקְרוֹא
to see ... לִרְאוֹת
to disembark, get off ... לָרֶדֶת
to want ... לִרְצוֹת
to send ... לִשְׁלוֹחַ
to pay (for) ... לְשַׁלֵּם
(per) hour ... לְשָׁעָה
to drink ... לִשְׁתּוֹת

מ

from ... מִ, מֵ

hundred ... מֵאָה
very ... מְאֹד
behind ... מֵאֲחוֹרֵי
May ... מַאי
bakery ... מַאֲפִיָּה
cooked ... מְבוּשָּׁל
telegram ... מִבְרָק
toothbrush ... מִבְרֶשֶׁת שִׁינַּיִם
towels ... מַגָּבוֹת
towel ... מַגֶּבֶת
boots ... מַגָּפַיִם
parking lot ... מִגְרַשׁ חֲנָיָה
stairs ... מַדְרֵגוֹת
escalator ... מַדְרֵגוֹת הַנָּעוֹת
what ... מָה
How are you? ... מָה שְׁלוֹמְךָ?
fast ... מַהֵר
museum ... מוּזֵיאוֹן
mousse ... מוּס
garage ... מוּסָךְ
Muslim (man) ... מוּסְלְמִי
Muslim (woman) ... מוּסְלְמִית
allowed ... מוּתָּר
weather ... מֶזֶג הָאֲוִיר
suitcases ... מִזְוָדוֹת
secretary ... מַזְכִּירָה
souvenirs ... מַזְכָּרוֹת
fork ... מַזְלֵג
buffet/snack bar ... מִזְנוֹן
east ... מִזְרָח
eastern ... מִזְרָחִי
department ... מַחְלָקָה
tomorrow ... מָחָר
kitchen ... מִטְבָּח
coins ... מַטְבְּעוֹת
fried ... מְטוּגָּן
airplane ... מָטוֹס
umbrella ... מִטְרִיָּה
meters ... מֶטְרִים
who ... מִי
size ... מִידָּה
bed ... מִטָּה
juice ... מִיץ
pineapple juice ... מִיץ אֲנָנָס
grapefruit juice ... מִיץ אֶשְׁכּוֹלִיּוֹת
orange juice ... מִיץ תַּפּוּזִים
under ... מִתַּחַת לְ
car ... מְכוֹנִית
rental car ... מְכוֹנִית שְׂכוּרָה
trousers ... מִכְנָסַיִם
letter ... מִכְתָּב
word ... מִלָּה
dirty ... מְלוּכְלָךְ
hotel ... מָלוֹן
dictionary ... מִלּוֹן
salt ... מֶלַח
words ... מִלִּים
cucumbers ... מְלָפְפוֹנִים
waiter ... מֶלְצַר
waitress ... מֶלְצָרִית
stuffed ... מְמוּלָּא
handkerchief ... מִמְחָטָה
lamp ... מְנוֹרָה
main dishes ... מָנוֹת עִיקָּרוֹת
appetizers ... מָנוֹת רִאשׁוֹנוֹת

mosque ... מִסְגָּד
restaurant ... מִסְעָדָה
hairdresser ... מִסְפָּרָה
numbers ... מִסְפָּרִים
comb ... מַסְרֵק
coat ... מְעִיל
raincoat ... מְעִיל גֶּשֶׁם
over ... מֵעַל לְ
degrees ... מַעֲלוֹת
elevator ... מַעֲלִית
west ... מַעֲרָב
western ... מַעֲרָבִי
map ... מַפָּה
napkin ... מַפִּית
key ... מַפְתֵּחַ
sorry ... מִצְטַעֶרֶת
camera ... מַצְלֵמָה
seat ... מָקוֹם
shower ... מִקְלַחַת
maximum ... מַקְסִימוּם
refrigerator ... מְקָרֵר
Mr. ... מַר
operator ... מֶרְכָּזָנִית
March ... מֶרְץ
marzipan ... מַרְצִיפָּן
soup ... מָרָק
basement ... מַרְתֵּף
truck ... מַשָּׂאִית
pull ... מְשׁוֹךְ
toothpaste ... מִשְׁחַת שִׁינַּיִם
police ... מִשְׁטָרָה
family ... מִשְׁפָּחָה
beverages ... מַשְׁקָאוֹת
eyeglasses ... מִשְׁקָפַיִם
lost-and-found-office ... מִשְׂרַד הָאֲבֵידוֹת
when ... מָתַי
gift ... מַתָּנָה

נ

stream ... נַחַל
river ... נָהָר
November ... נוֹבֶמְבֶּר
traveler ... נוֹסֵעַ
Christian (man) ... נוֹצְרִי
Christian (woman) ... נוֹצְרִית
arrival ... נְחִיתָה
New Zealand ... נְיוּ-זִילַנְד
paper ... נְיָר
short ... נָמוּךְ
harbor ... נָמָל
trip, journey ... נְסִיעָה
pleasant ... נָעִים
slippers ... נַעֲלֵי בַּיִת
shoes ... נַעֲלַיִם
dry cleaners ... נִקּוּי יָבֵשׁ
sausages ... נַקְנִיקִים
candle ... נֵר

ס

grandfather ... סַבָּא
soap ... סַבּוֹן

grandmother ... סַבְתָּא
closed ... סָגוּר
soda water ... סוֹדָה
sweater ... סְוֶודֶר
sugar ... סוּכָּר
candies ... סוּכָּרִיּוֹת
travel agency ... סוֹכְנוּת נְסִיעוֹת
steak ... סְטֵייק
symphony ... סִימְפוֹנְיָה
boat ... סִירָה
knife ... סַכִּין
razor ... סַכִּין גִּלּוּחַ
wastepaper basket ... סַל נְיָרוֹת
living-room ... סָלוֹן
salad ... סָלָט
excuse me ... סְלִיחָה
salmon ... סַלְמוֹן
celery ... סֶלֶרִי
seminar ... סֶמִינָר
sandals ... סַנְדָּלִים
shoemaker ... סַנְדְּלָר
sofa ... סַפָּה
sport ... סְפּוֹרְט
September ... סֶפְּטֶמְבֶּר
cup ... סֵפֶל
book ... סֵפֶר
telephone book ... סֵפֶר טֶלֶפוֹן
ski ... סְקִי
sardines ... סַרְדִּינִים
movie, film ... סֶרֶט
autumn ... סְתָו

ע

thick ... עָבֶה
Hebrew ... עִבְרִית
tomatoes ... עַגְבָנִיּוֹת
cart ... עֲגָלָה
once more ... עוֹד פַּעַם
cake ... עוּגָה
change ... עוֹדֶף
costs ... עוֹלָה
pen ... עֵט
tired ... עָיֵף
now ... עַכְשָׁו
on ... עַל
next to ... עַל יַד
you're welcome ... עַל לֹא דָבָר
with ... עִם
page ... עַמּוּד
poor ... עָנִי
tie ... עֲנִיבָה
cloud ... עָנָן
pencil ... עִפָּרוֹן
tree ... עֵץ
evening ... עֶרֶב
good evening ... עֶרֶב טוֹב
Arab ... עֲרָבִי
Arabic ... עֲרָבִית
fog ... עֲרָפֶל
rich ... עָשִׁיר
grass ... עֵשֶׂב
ten ... עֶשֶׂר

twenty .... עֶשְׂרִים
newspaper .... עִתּוֹן
antique .... עַתִּיק

פּ

puzzle .... פָּאזֶל
pie .... פַּאי
pudding .... פּוּדִינְג
here .... פֹּה
pyjamas .... פִּיגָ׳מָה
elephant .... פִּיל
corner .... פִּינָה
picnic .... פִּיקְנִיק
pita bread .... פִּיתָה
pepper .... פִּלְפֵּל
turn .... פְּנֵה
free, vacant .... פָּנוּי
lantern .... פָּנָס
lamppost .... פָּנָס רְחוֹב
Passover .... פֶּסַח
statue .... פֶּסֶל
doorbell .... פַּעֲמוֹן
clerk .... פָּקִיד
project .... פְּרוֹיֶקְט
professor .... פְּרוֹפֶסוֹר
fruit .... פֵּרוֹת
permanent .... פֶּרְמָנֶנְט
park .... פַּרְק
open .... פָּתוּחַ

פ

Fahrenheit .... פַארֶנְהַייְט
February .... פֶבְּרוּאַר
film .... פִילְם
felafel .... פָלָפֶל
festival .... פֶסְטִיבָל

צ

colors .... צְבָעִים
yellow .... צָהֹב
diver .... צוֹלְלָן
roasted .... צָלוּי
centigrade .... צֶלְזְיוּס
plate .... צַלַּחַת
thirsty .... צָמֵא
plant .... צֶמַח
north .... צָפוֹן
northern .... צְפוֹנִי
I need .... צָרִיךְ

ק

kibbutz .... קִבּוּץ
receipt .... קַבָּלָה
area codes .... קִדּוֹמֶת
line .... קַו
cinema .... קוֹלְנוֹעַ
collect (call) .... קוֹלֶקְט
comedy .... קוֹמֶדְיָה
floor .... קוֹמָה
first floor .... קוֹמָה רִאשׁוֹנָה
fourth floor .... קוֹמָה רְבִיעִית
third floor .... קוֹמָה שְׁלִישִׁית
second floor .... קוֹמָה שְׁנִיָּה
concert .... קוֹנְצֶרְט
cashier .... קוּפַּאי
newspaper kiosk .... קִיוֹסְק עִתּוֹנִים
kilo .... קִילוֹ
kilometers .... קִילוֹמֶטֶר
summer .... קַיִץ
wall .... קִיר
Canada .... קָנָדָה
dessert .... קִנּוּחַ
cassettes .... קָסֶטוֹת
coffee .... קָפֶה
short .... קָצָר
little .... קְצָת
cold .... קַר
relatives .... קְרוֹבִים

ר

mirror .... רְאִי
a quarter .... רֶבַע
moment, minute .... רֶגַע
wind .... רוּחַ
doctor .... רוֹפֵא
I want .... רוֹצֶה
street .... רְחוֹב
jam .... רִיבָּה
bad .... רָע
hungry .... רָעֵב
only .... רַק

שׁ

question .... שְׁאֵלָה
week .... שָׁבוּעַ
magazine .... שָׁבוּעוֹן
seven .... שֶׁבַע
seventeen .... שְׁבַע עֶשְׂרֵה
Good Sabbath! .... שַׁבָּת שָׁלוֹם
market .... שׁוּק
chocolates .... שׁוֹקוֹלָדוֹת
table .... שׁוּלְחָן
desk .... שׁוּלְחָן כְּתִיבָה
black .... שָׁחוֹר
carpet .... שָׁטִיחַ
strudel .... שְׁטְרוּדֶל
bills .... שְׁטָרוֹת
snow .... שֶׁלֶג
hello/goodbye .... שָׁלוֹם
my .... שֶׁלִּי
your .... שֶׁלְּךָ
three .... שָׁלשׁ
thirteen .... שְׁלשׁ עֶשְׂרֵה
thirty .... שְׁלשִׁים
there (is) .... שָׁם
name .... שֵׁם
eight .... שְׁמוֹנֶה
eighteen .... שְׁמוֹנֶה עֶשְׂרֵה
eighty .... שְׁמוֹנִים
my name is .... שְׁמִי
left luggage office .... שְׁמִירַת חֲפָצִים
year .... שָׁנָה
Happy New Year! .... שָׁנָה טוֹבָה
seconds .... שְׁנִיּוֹת
hour .... שָׁעָה
clock .... שָׁעוֹן
alarm clock .... שָׁעוֹן מְעוֹרֵר
shekel .... שֶׁקֶל
shekels .... שְׁקָלִים
shared taxi, sherut .... שֵׁרוּת
lavatory .... שֵׁרוּתִים
six .... שֵׁשׁ
sixteen .... שֵׁשׁ עֶשְׂרֵה
sixty .... שִׁשִּׁים
two .... שְׁתַּיִם
twelve .... שְׁתֵּים עֶשְׂרֵה

שׂ

airport .... שְׂדֵה הַתְעוּפָה
call .... שִׂיחָה
emergency calls .... שִׂיחוֹת חֵרוּם
telephone call .... שִׂיחַת טֶלֶפוֹן
left .... שְׂמֹאל
to the left .... שְׂמֹאלָה
blanket .... שְׂמִיכָה
dress .... שִׂמְלָה

ת

have fun! .... תֵּבָלֶה יָפֶה
tea .... תֵּה
thank you .... תּוֹדָה
thank you very much .... תּוֹדָה רַבָּה
stop, station .... תַּחֲנָה
bus stop, station .... תַּחֲנַת אוֹטוֹבּוּס
gas station .... תַּחֲנַת דֶּלֶק
police station .... תַּחֲנַת הַמִּשְׁטָרָה
train station .... תַּחֲנַת רַכֶּבֶת
underpants .... תַּחְתּוֹנִים
slip .... תַּחְתּוֹנִית
purse .... תִּיק
tourist .... תַּיָּר
picture .... תְּמוּנָה
stove .... תַּנּוּר
oranges .... תַּפּוּזִים
apple .... תַּפּוּחַ
busy, occupied .... תָּפוּס
menu .... תַּפְרִיט
records .... תַּקְלִיטִים
ceiling .... תִּקְרָה
turkey .... תַּרְנְגוֹל הוֹדוּ
nine .... תֵּשַׁע
nineteen .... תְּשַׁע עֶשְׂרֵה
ninety .... תִּשְׁעִים
answers .... תְּשׁוּבוֹת

BEVERAGE GUIDE

This guide is intended to explain the variety of beverages available to you while in Israel. It is by no means complete. Some of the experimenting has been left up to you, but this should get you started. The asterisks (*) indicate brand names.

(hot beverages) מַשְׁקָאוֹת חַמִּים

coffee	קָפֶה
coffee with cream	קָפֶה הָפוּךְ
iced coffee	קָפֶה קַר
black coffee	קָפֶה שָׁחוֹר
Turkish coffee	קָפֶה טוּרְקִי
espresso	אֶסְפְּרֶסוֹ

The coffee house is an institution in Israel. Sit outside at one of the sidewalk cafes and sample one of the many varieties of coffee.

tea	תֵּה
tea with milk	תֵּה עִם חָלָב
tea with lemon	תֵּה עִם לִימוֹן
hot chocolate	קַקָאוֹ

(alcoholic beverages) מַשְׁקָאוֹת חֲרִיפִים

A variety of liqueurs and brandies is available in Israel, including local brands.

brandy, cognac	קוֹנְיָאק
Carmel Mizrahi 777	*שֶׁבַע-שֶׁבַע-שֶׁבַע

Israel produces a delicious orange and chocolate-flavored liqueur called סַבְּרָה . The name "sabra" also refers to a person born and raised in Israel.

gin	ג׳ין
gin and tonic	ג׳ין וְטוֹנִיק
whiskey	וִיסְקִי
whiskey soda	וִיסְקִי עִם סוֹדָה
vodka	ווֹדְקָה
neat	נָקִי
on the rocks	עִם קֶרַח
double	כָּפוּל

(beer) בִּירָה

beer	בִּירָה
malt beer	בִּירָה שְׁחוֹרָה

*אַבִּיר *נֶלְר

*מַכַּבִּי *סְטַאר

(cold beverages) מַשְׁקָאוֹת קָרִים

mineral water	מַיִם מִינֶרָלִיִּים
soda water	סוֹדָה
lemonade	לִימוֹנָדָה
orangeade	אוֹרַנְגָ'דָה
fruit syrup with soda water	גָזוֹז
sweet fruit syrup	גָזוֹז מָתוֹק
sour fruit syrup	גָזוֹז חָמוּץ
milk	חָלָב
milk shake	מִילְק שֵׁייק

(juice) מִיץ

Israel is famous for its oranges. You can buy a glass of freshly-squeezed orange juice from street vendors. It's delicious!

orange juice	מִיץ תַּפּוּזִים
pineapple juice	מִיץ אֲנָנָס
grapefruit juice	מִיץ אֶשְׁכּוֹלִיּוֹת
lemon juice	מִיץ לִימוֹן
apricot juice	מִיץ מִשְׁמְשִׁים
tomato juice	מִיץ עַגְבָנִיּוֹת

(wine) יַיִן

Israel has several wine-growing regions, which produce a variety of excellent white, rosé and red wines. The following wines can be either white or red.

* כַּרְמֶל * גַמְלָא גַלִיל

* עֲבְדָת * יֵין הַנָּשִׂיא

* שׁוֹשַׁנַּת הַכַּרְמֶל * מוֹנְפוֹרְט

* מָלוֹן מָתוֹק

red	אָדוֹם
white	לָבָן
rosé	רוֹזֶה
dry	יָבֵשׁ
sweet	מָתוֹק
sparkling	תּוֹסֵס

CUT ALONG DOTTED LINE, FOLD AND TAKE WITH YOU

תַּפְרִיט

שׁוֹנוֹת (general)

jam	רִיבָּה
jelly	גֶ'לִי
honey	דְּבַשׁ
salt	מֶלַח
pepper	פִּלְפֵּל
vinegar	חוֹמֶץ
mustard	חַרְדָּל
oil	שֶׁמֶן
ketchup	קֶטְשׁוֹפּ
cheese	גְּבִינָה
olives	זֵיתִים
olive oil	שֶׁמֶן זַיִת
sausage	נַקְנִיק
cake	עוּגָה
ice-cream	גְּלִידָה
whipped cream	קַצֶּפֶת
sandwiches	סֶנְדְוִויצִ'ים
pancakes	פַּנְקֵייקְס
hamburger	הַמְבּוּרְגֶר
french fries (chips)	צִ'יפְּס
popcorn	פּוֹפּ קוֹרְן
noodles	אִטְרִיּוֹת
rice	אֹרֶז

יְרָקוֹת (vegetables)

zucchini	קִשּׁוּאִים
cauliflower	כְּרוּבִית
cabbage	כְּרוּב
asparagus	אַסְפָּרָגוּס
kohlrabi	קוֹלְרַבִּי
cucumber	מְלָפְפוֹנִים
tomatoes	עַגְבָנִיּוֹת
eggplant	חֲצִילִים
beans	שְׁעוּעִית
spinach	תֶּרֶד
avocado	אָבוֹקָדוֹ

עוֹף (poultry)

chicken	עוֹף
stuffed chicken	עוֹף מְמוּלָּא
chicken liver	כָּבֵד עוֹף
turkey	תַּרְנְגוֹל הוֹדוּ
turkey schnitzel	שְׁנִיצֶל הוֹדוּ
goose	אַוָּז

Israeli/Middle Eastern specialties

humus	חוּמוּס
tehina	טְחִינָה
stuffed vine leaves	עֲלֵי גֶּפֶן
couscous	קוּסְקוּס
falafel	פַּלָפֶל
sour milk, assorted flavors	אֶשֶׁל
yoghurt	יוֹגוּרְט

FOLD HERE

בָּשָׂר (meat dishes)

veal schnitzel	שְׁנִיצֶל עֵגֶל
shashlik	שִׁישְׁלִיק
kebab	קַבָּאבּ
shawarmah	שָׁוַארְמָה
lamb ribs	צַלְעוֹת כֶּבֶשׂ
tongue	לָשׁוֹן
liver	כָּבֵד
goulash	גּוּלָשׁ
meatballs	כַּדּוּרֵי בָּשָׂר
sausages	נַקְנִיקִיּוֹת
steak	סְטֵייק

קִנּוּחִים (desserts)

strudel	שְׁטְרוּדֶל
ice-cream	גְּלִידָה
pudding	פּוּדִינְג
mocha mousse	מוּס מוֹקָה
chocolate mousse	מוּס שׁוֹקוֹלָד
Bavarian cream	קְצִיפָה בָּוָוארִית
crème caramel	קְרֶם קָארָמֶל
strawberries and cream	תּוּת שָׂדֶה בְּקַצֶּפֶת
torte	טוֹרְט
fruit cake	עוּגַת פֵּרוֹת
baklava	בַּקְלָוָוה
cookies	עוּגִיּוֹת

בְּתֵאָבוֹן!
(buh-tay-ah-von)
enjoy your meal

FOLD HERE

שִׁיטוֹת הֲכָנָה — methods of preparation

מְבוּשָּׁל	boiled, cooked
צָלוּי	roasted
מְטוּגָּן	fried
אָפוּי	baked
בַּגְּרִיל	grilled
מְבוּשָּׁל מְעַט מְאוֹד	rare
בֵּינוֹנִי	medium
מְבוּשָּׁל הֵיטֵב	well-done

מָנוֹת רִאשׁוֹנוֹת — (appetizers)

פִּטְרִיּוֹת בְּשַׁמֶּנֶת	mushrooms in sour cream
זֵיתִים	olives
עַגְבָנִיּוֹת מְמוּלָּאוֹת	stuffed tomatoes
בֵּיצִים בְּמָיוֹנֶז	eggs in mayonnaise
דָּג מָלוּחַ	herring
סַרְדִּינִים	sardines

דָּגִים — (fish dishes)

קַרְפִּיוֹן	carp
דָּג פּוֹרֶל	trout
בָּקָלָה	hake
פִילֶה	filet
דָּג מְמוּלָּא	gefilte fish
טוּנָה	tuna
סַרְדִּינִים	sardines

FOLD HERE

פֵּרוֹת — (fruit)

תַּפּוּחִים	apples
אֲגָסִים	pears
מִשְׁמְשִׁים	apricots
אֲפַרְסְקִים	peaches
בָּנָנוֹת	bananas
תּוּת שָׂדֶה	strawberries
שֶׁסֶק	kumquats
גוּיָאבוֹת	guavas
תְּאֵנִים	figs
רִמּוֹנִים	pomegranates
עֲנָבִים	grapes
שְׁזִיפִים	plums
תַּפּוּזִים	oranges
אֶשְׁכּוֹלִיּוֹת	grapefruit
מַנְדָּרִינוֹת	mandarin oranges
תְּמָרִים	dates
אֱגוֹזִים	nuts
מֵלוֹנִים	cantaloupe
אֲבַטִּיחִים	watermelon

סָלָטִים — (salads)

סָלָט מְלָפְפוֹנִים	cucumber salad
סָלָט חֲצִילִים	eggplant salad
סָלָט יְרָקוֹת	green salad
עַגְבָנִיּוֹת	tomato salad
סָלָט סֶלֶק	beetroot salad
סָלָט כְּרוּב	coleslaw
סָלָט גֶּזֶר	carrot salad
סָלָט תַּפּוּחֵי אֲדָמָה	potato salad

FOLD HERE

מְרָקִים — (soups)

מְרַק צַח	clear broth
מְרַק יְרָקוֹת	vegetable soup
מְרַק בָּצָל	onion soup
מְרַק בָּשָׂר	meat soup
מְרַק עוֹף	chicken soup
מְרַק עוֹף מוּקְרָם	cream of chicken soup
מְרַק עַגְבָנִיּוֹת	tomato soup
מְרַק שְׁעוּעִית	bean soup
מְרַק אֲפוּנָה	pea soup
מְרַק עֲדָשִׁים	lentil soup
מְרַק פִּטְרִיּוֹת	mushroom soup
חֲמִיצָה	borscht

לֶחֶם — (bread)

לֶחֶם לָבָן	white bread
לֶחֶם שִׁיפוֹן	rye bread
לֶחֶם חַי	grain bread
לֶחֶם שָׁחוֹר	black bread
בָּגֶט	baguette
לַחְמָנִיּוֹת	rolls
חַלָּה	challah (braided egg bread)
פִּיתָה	pita (flat pocket bread)

בֵּיצִים — (eggs)

בֵּיצָה רַכָּה	soft egg
בֵּיצָה קָשָׁה	hard egg
בֵּיצִיָּה	fried egg
חֲבִיתָה	omelette
בֵּיצָה מְקוּשְׁקֶשֶׁת	scrambled eggs

(ah-nee) אֲנִי — (roh-tseh) רוֹצֶה (♂) / (roh-tsah) רוֹצָה (♀)	(yesh) יֵשׁ (lee) לִי
(ah-nee) אֲנִי — (oh-mair) אוֹמֵר (♂) / (oh-mer-et) אוֹמֶרֶת (♀)	(ah-nee) אֲנִי — (muh-dah-bair) מְדַבֵּר (♂) / (muh-dah-ber-et) מְדַבֶּרֶת (♀)
(ah-nee) אֲנִי — (muh-vah-kesh) מְבַקֵּשׁ (♂) / (muh-vah-kesh-et) מְבַקֶּשֶׁת (♀)	(ah-nee) אֲנִי — (loh-med) לוֹמֵד (♂) / (loh-med-et) לוֹמֶדֶת (♀)
(ah-nee) אֲנִי — (roh-eh) רוֹאֶה (♂) / (roh-ah) רוֹאָה (♀)	(ah-nee) אֲנִי — (noh-seh-ah) נוֹסֵעַ (♂) / (noh-sah-aht) נוֹסַעַת (♀)
(ah-nee) אֲנִי — (muh-Hah-pes) מְחַפֵּשׂ (♂) / (muh-Hah-pes-et) מְחַפֶּשֶׂת (♀)	(ah-nee) אֲנִי — (bah) בָּא (♂) / (bah-ah) בָּאָה (♀)
(ah-nee) אֲנִי — (mah-gee-ah) מַגִּיעַ (♂) / (mah-gee-ah) מַגִּיעָה (♀)	(ah-nee) אֲנִי — (koh-neh) קוֹנֶה (♂) / (koh-nah) קוֹנָה (♀)

I want

I have

I say

I speak

I order/reserve

I learn

I see

I travel

I look for

I come

I arrive

I buy

אֲנִי (ah-nee) — מֵבִין (may-veen) / מְבִינָה (muh-vee-nah)

אֲנִי (ah-nee) — נִשְׁאָר (nish-ar) / נִשְׁאֶרֶת (nish-er-et)

אֲנִי (ah-nee) — צָרִיךְ (tsah-reeH) / צְרִיכָה (tsree-Hah)

אֲנִי (ah-nee) — גָּר (gar) / גָּרָה (gah-rah)

אֲנִי (ah-nee) — חוֹזֵר (Hoh-zair) / חוֹזֶרֶת (Hoh-zer-et)

אֲנִי (ah-nee) — אוֹכֵל (oh-Hel) / אוֹכֶלֶת (oh-Hel-et)

אֲנִי (ah-nee) — מְטַלְפֵּן (muh-tahl-fane) / מְטַלְפֶּנֶת (muh-tahl-fen-et)

אֲנִי (ah-nee) — שׁוֹתֶה (shoh-teh) / שׁוֹתָה (shoh-tah)

אֲנִי (ah-nee) — שׁוֹלֵחַ (shoh-lay-aH) / שׁוֹלַחַת (shoh-laH-aht)

שְׁמִי (shmee) . . .

אֲנִי (ah-nee) — יָשֵׁן (yah-shen) / יְשֵׁנָה (yuh-shen-ah)

אֲנִי (ah-nee) — מְחַכֶּה (muh-Hah-keh) / מְחַכָּה (muh-Hah-kah)

I understand	I stay
I need	I live/reside
I repeat	I eat
I phone	I drink
I send	my name is . . .
I sleep	I wait for

אֲנִי (ah-nee) — קוֹרֵא (koh-ray) / קוֹרֵאת (koh-ret)	אֲנִי — מוֹכֵר (moh-Hair) / מוֹכֶרֶת (moh-Her-et)
אֲנִי — יָכוֹל (yah-Hohl) / יְכוֹלָה (yuh-Hoh-lah)	תֵּן (ten) לִי (lee) . . .
אֲנִי — צָרִיךְ (tsah-reeH) / צְרִיכָה (tsree-Hah)	אֲנִי — כּוֹתֵב (koh-tev) / כּוֹתֶבֶת (koh-tev-et)
אֲנִי — טָס (tahs) / טָסָה (tah-sah)	יֵשׁ (yesh) לָנוּ (lah-noo)
אֲנִי — נוֹחֵת (noh-Het) / נוֹחֶתֶת (noh-Het-et)	אֲנִי — מְשַׁלֵּם (muh-shah-lem) / מְשַׁלֶּמֶת (muh-shah-lem-et)
אֲנִי — מַזְמִין (mahz-meen) / מַזְמִינָה (mahz-mee-nah)	אֲנִי — יוֹדֵעַ (yoh-day-ah) / יוֹדַעַת (yoh-dah-aht)

I read	I sell
I can	give me . . .
I must	I write
I fly	we have
I land	I pay (for)
I reserve	I know

אֲנִי יוֹצֵא *(yoh-tseh)* / יוֹצֵאת *(yoh-tset)*	זֶה *(zeh)* לוֹקֵחַ *(loh-kay-aH)* . . .
אֲנִי נוֹהֵג *(noh-heg)* / נוֹהֶגֶת *(noh-heg-et)*	הָאוֹטוֹבּוּס *(hah-oh-toh-boos)* יוֹצֵא *(yoh-tseh)* . . .
אֲנִי עוֹלֶה *(oh-leh)* / עוֹלָה *(oh-lah)*	הָאוֹטוֹבּוּס *(hah-oh-toh-boos)* מַגִּיעַ *(mah-gee-ah)* . . .
אֲנִי יוֹרֵד *(yoh-red)* / יוֹרֶדֶת *(yoh-red-et)*	בֹּקֶר *(boh-ker)* טוֹב *(tohv)*
אֲנִי אוֹרֵז *(oh-rez)* / אוֹרֶזֶת *(oh-rez-et)*	עֶרֶב *(eh-rev)* טוֹב *(tohv)*
אֲנִי מְכַבֵּס *(muh-Hah-bes)* / מְכַבֶּסֶת *(muh-Hah-bes-et)*	לַיְלָה *(lie-lah)* טוֹב *(tohv)*

it takes	I leave
the bus leaves . . .	I drive
the bus arrives . . .	I board
good morning	I get off/disembark
good evening	I pack
good night	I wash (clothes)

(oh-leh) (zeh) (kah-mah) כַּמָּה זֶה עוֹלֶה?	*(slee-Hah)* סְלִיחָה
(shlom-Hah) (mah) מָה שְׁלוֹמְךָ? ( ) *(shloh-mayH)* מָה שְׁלוֹמֵךְ? ( )	*(nah-im) (hah-yom)* הַיּוֹם נָעִים
(shah-lom) שָׁלוֹם	*(Hahm) (hah-yom)* הַיּוֹם חַם
(buh-vah-kah-shah) בְּבַקָּשָׁה	*(hah-yom)* הַיּוֹם
(toh-dah) תּוֹדָה	*(mah-Har)* מָחָר
(dah-var) (loh) (ahl) עַל לֹא דָבָר	*(et-mohl)* אֶתְמוֹל

excuse me	how much does this cost?
it is pleasant today	how are you?
it is hot today	hello/goodbye
today	please
tomorrow	thank you
yesterday	you're welcome

(Hoh-leh) (bah-ree) בָּרִיא - חוֹלֶה	(dahk) (ah-veh) עָבֶה - דָק
(rah) (tohv) טוֹב - רָע	(lah) (mee-tah-Haht) (lah) (may-ahl) מֵעַל לַ - מִתַּחַת לַ
(kar) (Hahm) חַם - קַר	(yah-meen) (smohl) שְׂמֹאל - יָמִין
(rahm) (buh-kohl) (buh-shek-et) בְּשֶׁקֶט - בְּקוֹל רָם	(mah-hair) (luh-aht) לְאַט - מַהֵר
(ah-rooH) (kah-tsar) קָצָר - אָרוּךְ	(nah-mooH) (gvoh-hah) גְבוֹהָה - נָמוּךְ
(kah-tahn) (gah-dohl) גָּדוֹל - קָטָן	(kah-tahn) (zah-ken) זָקֵן - קָטָן

thick - thin

healthy - sick

above - below

good - bad

left - right

hot - cold

slow - fast

softly - in a loud voice

high - low

short - long

old - young

big - small

(ah-nee) אֲנִי	(yah-kar) יָקָר - זוֹל (zohl)
(hoo) הוּא	(ah-sheer) עָשִׁיר - עָנִי (ah-nee)
(hee) הִיא	(har-bay) הַרְבֵּה - קְצָת (ktsaht)
(ah-naH-noo) אֲנַחְנוּ	(pah-too-aH) פָּתוּחַ - סָגוּר (sah-goor)
(ah-tah) אַתָּה (♂) (aht) אַתְּ (♀)	(ah-teek) עַתִּיק - חָדָשׁ (Hah-dash)
(hem) הֵם	(duh-Hohf) דְּחוֹף - מְשׁוֹךְ (muh-shoH)

I	expensive - cheap
he	rich - poor
she	a lot - a little
we	open - closed
you	old - new
they	push - pull